M BEAUTIFUL POPPY

A Story of Love in Chapters

By Mos Pracdel

Table of Contents

Dedication

I dedicate this book to the love of my life, my Poppy!

I miss you every day.

About the Author

Mos Pracdel was born in Barcelona, Spain, and has been living in the UK for over 30 years. He graduated in London with a First Class Honours Degree in Modern Languages. He currently divides his time between London and Spain.

Chapter 1

Years have gone by, and I can still vividly remember the look on her face on that fateful summer day…

It was a lovely afternoon at the end of August. The temperature was pleasant for the time of the year, the sun breaking through the clouds and winning the battle most of the time. A good omen, one may think.

We parked our car as close to the entrance as possible, as it was already very difficult for Poppy to walk more than a few steps. She had been given an appointment to see the consultant, get the results from the biopsy, and discuss a plan of action.

We arrived at the hospital with plenty of time. The appointment wasn't until 3:00 pm, so we went in and got ourselves some coffee, two cappuccinos, I seem to recall. Poppy loved her cappuccinos. We then approached the desk, she gave her name to the receptionist, and we were asked to wait in the waiting area to be called, a routine we were very used to by now.

While waiting, we were both excited, thinking about the prospect of Poppy finally having the right treatment so she could resume a normal life. A life in which she could do the normal things she had always done, things we had always taken for granted but slowly, little by little, were taken away from her. She could drive again, go and do her shopping, give a lift to our elderly neighbour to the doctor, walk up to the corner shop just 2 minutes away to buy the paper and milk or some biscuits, buy some plants and make the garden look beautiful again after the winter, or prepare delicious meals that required to be standing up for hours in the kitchen. The truth is that Poppy didn't enjoy cooking much, but she was a much better cook than she ever thought. Of course, I may be biased, but other people seemed to agree. Her Galician/Portuguese style of cod, Moules Frites, Steak with peppercorn sauce, or Sunday Roast dinner were all delicious, but her chocolate cake was to die for! She definitely had a good touch.

We were talking, excited, making plans for the future, and making lists of things we would like to do but hadn't been able to in the last few years due to Poppy's poor health. We were going to start travelling again – we loved Spain and the Mediterranean coast in particular, and it had been many years since we had not been able to go. Poppy loved the sea and sunbathing, and it was our dream one day to be able to retire in Spain, not in a big city, but in a smaller town by the sea or close to the beach, where we could go for walks holding hands. We thought of having a small apartment, perhaps, something that didn't require much maintenance, and we were talking of having a little coffee with a croissant in the bar in the morning and going out for tapas in the evening. We just loved that way of life.

We could go to the United States and visit her family there. I've been told it's a beautiful country. Having never been there, I was quite excited at the prospect. We could start going out again, to the restaurants, maybe the theatre and cinema as well. We never had much money, but Poppy was absolutely amazing at finding offers and deals, so when she was well at the beginning, we could do many things for very little money. I remember once she got some plane tickets to Barcelona for the tidy sum of £10.00 return for two people. Wow! It has been many years, and I don't quite remember how she managed to get those tickets, but she was truly a magician for these things.

Poppy always knew when our local Chinese take-away was doing half-price meals or 2 for 1, and she would sometimes surprise me when I got home after work with my favourite Chinese. She found a pizza restaurant not too far from where we lived that, on Wednesdays, would do a three-meal course for £9.99 per person and then a bottle of house wine for a pound. Needless to say, we were there every Wednesday until they closed down!

We kept talking until the nurse called her name and asked us to follow her to a room. She said that the doctor would come shortly to speak to us, left us there, and closed the door. There we were, finally, after all those years of trying everything, any possible treatment they could think of without results, just minutes away from what would change Poppy's life. We were so looking forward to good news and the right treatment...

The reason we were so optimistic is that a couple of weeks before, Poppy had been seen by a plastic surgeon specialist. They had discussed her case and the consultant, after having examined her leg and asked her many questions, concluded that they could certainly operate to remove the tumour growing under her knee, and then they would use a flap from her back to do a skin graft. The consultant was the head of the department, and he was one of those people who immediately inspire confidence, and his knowledge, experience, and skill emanated from him.

He explained to us that the operation in itself was not complicated from a surgical point of view, but the recovery would take some time. The operation entailed taking a large flap of skin and muscle from Poppy's back to reconstruct her leg after the removal of the tumour, which was now occupying a large area of her lower leg under the knee. She was told she would lose a bit of function on the arm on that side. However, with the rehabilitation, he was confident that Poppy would regain the use of that arm to a very good extent to enable her to lead a normal life. So after the consultation, we felt so much more positive and optimistic. That's why we were so excited about the future.

We didn't have to wait too long, perhaps 10-15 minutes, before there was a knock at the door and a doctor entered. We hadn't seen him before, but that's not uncommon, there are many doctors in the team, and you don't always get to see the same one. He introduced himself, asked Poppy how she was, and then sat at the desk in front of the computer, checking some notes. He was not from the plastic team but from the trauma/orthopaedic department.

He was a younger doctor. It has always amazed me how young people start to look when you reach a certain age, particularly medical professionals and policemen. To look at them, you would think they are still in medical school or in the police academy, but of course, we know that's not the case. He started asking Poppy a few questions about how she was doing, how she was coping in her daily life, and how her condition was limiting her life in general, particularly in terms of mobility. He also asked her about the pain and what she was taking to control it, the kind of questions we were so used to by now.

After these few minutes of breaking the ice, talking about things he probably already knew, surely having discussed Poppy's case in the multidisciplinary meeting in the morning, he turned to the computer, checking the report from the biopsy. He then, slowly, turned again to us and said something that would change our lives forever...

Chapter 2

His manner was impeccable. It was clear that he was used to conveying this kind of news. With a soft voice, looking gently and kindly at Poppy, the doctor then said, "As you know, we took some samples of your tumour last week, and now we have the results from the biopsies. I'm afraid I don't have very good news. It has come back cancerous."

On hearing these words, one's brain starts doing funny things. Suddenly the world seems to slow down around you. Everything appears in slow motion, time almost stops, the scene in front of you is almost frozen in time, and the last words resound in your head, over and over and over again, words that you know have been pronounced, and your hearing has registered perfectly well, but your brain seems to have difficulty assimilating and processing the information. It's just a few seconds, maybe not even that, but it seems like a very, very long time.

At the same time that my brain was dealing with what had just been said, my eyes were fixed on Poppy's face. Strangely, her expression did not change much. It was like she had been given some news, and she had been expecting this for quite some time, and therefore it did not take her by surprise. I must confess that, at the time, that reaction confused me. First of all, we were not expecting that kind of news, at least not myself. On the contrary, we felt very positive and optimistic after the last appointment with the plastic surgeon. Secondly, even if you don't feel that positive, after hearing the words that were pronounced, surely that would elicit the type of response that I was experiencing, or so I thought at the time.

The doctor then continued, "Unfortunately, the tumour has already infiltrated the bone around the knee. The bone structure is disintegrating, which is why you have so much pain and can hardly walk. The truth is that, as we've been discussing, you have lost the use of that leg." That was certainly true. By then, Poppy had lost the ability to use that leg. It was extremely sad, but it was the reality. And the pain was excruciating.

The doctor then continued, "What we would like to offer you is to eliminate the pain and give you a functional leg, which will allow you to have a better quality of life."

By then, my brain was in overdrive, with a thousand thoughts per second. I was thinking about the doctor's last words, asking myself, how do you eliminate the pain? What do you do to provide a functional leg? What exactly he meant by those words… At the same time that I was trying to make sense of the situation, of what was being said, I was looking at Poppy, trying hard to read the expression on her face, what was passing through her head at the time. I wish I could have read her mind and known what she was really thinking at that moment, her face almost expressionless.

The doctor, pausing at the right moments to give us enough time to digest the news, was waiting perhaps for Poppy to say something. Every so often, he would look at me, but mainly he was talking to Poppy, trying to have an expression of sympathy and empathy to accompany the news that had just been said.

Poppy didn't say anything, just kept looking at him, nodding as to acknowledge that she had understood everything and it was ok for him to continue.

He then continued with a more positive voice and said, "The good news is that the scan shows that the cancer has not spread to other parts of the body, and it remains localized." The voice a bit softer again, "What we propose is to amputate your leg so it can save your life."

I looked at Poppy in horror and could not believe her composure on hearing such news. As for me, I don't know what was more difficult at the time: to assimilate what had just been said or to try to make sense of Poppy's reaction which to me seemed nonchalant, almost indifferent, which I could not comprehend. Had she heard what was just said? Was she in shock? I just could not believe that she seemed so serene and composed after hearing such news. There again, Poppy was always the cool, calm, and collected of the two of us, and I was always the one rushing and panicking. Just one more reason why I loved her so much and why I needed her so much in my life, to bring that indispensable peace and tranquillity to my otherwise hectic, chaotic, and turbulent life of the past.

Naively, in the calmest possible way I could muster at the time and with the most forced smile ever in my life, I said to Poppy that perhaps we should get another opinion, that it was a big decision to make, and that she didn't have to rush into it. That was in no way a reflection of my trust, or rather lack, in the hospital and the medical team. We knew very well that it was a hospital of excellence, and that is why she had been referred there by the medical teams from other hospitals.

Poppy looked at me, but I think she didn't really pay much attention to my words. Later she told me that she knew, after all she had been through, that it was extremely unlikely that the outcome from further explorations in other hospitals would give a different result, she was really tired of so much pain, and she couldn't wait any longer. The truth is that Poppy's life had been extremely difficult the last couple of years, and she didn't want to delay any possible treatment that could improve her life.

With the bravery that characterized her in these situations, she turned to the doctor and asked where they would amputate. The doctor, with a strained smile of kindness on his face, said that they would have to amputate mid-thigh in order to leave a safe margin.

It was then, for the first time, on hearing these words, that I saw the reaction in Poppy, the tension in her body, and the expression of horror mixed with stoicism and acceptance on her face. Then she turned to me, and I saw in her beautiful eyes complete and utter fear, fear of the unknown, her whole face like a tight mask in which you could read the sheer sadness but also resignation on hearing those last words.

And then I understood Poppy's initial lack of response, no hesitation, and courage beyond words. She knew how bad her leg was. She probably had realised for a while, and knowing her, in all probability, she would have done her research, and therefore she knew that it could not be saved. In time I recognised that deep down, she knew she would lose her leg a while back. It was just a matter of time. The shocking news for her was the fact that the amputation would be so high up the leg.

And at that moment, that face could not be further from the beautiful face I had seen for the first time one night all those years back, face that belonged to Poppy, my beautiful Poppy, with whom I fell in love with that very first night.

Chapter 3

It was on a beautiful evening in May 1996 that my life would change forever.

I was at the dancing studio where I used to practise. I had been dancing for a while, something I had always wanted to do due to the fact that when I was in my teens, not even my girlfriends would dance with me, so clumsy I was. It was quite humiliating at the time and made me feel very self-conscious and a bit deficient, in all honesty. In my early twenties, I had come to terms with it and accepted it. I was quite good-looking at the time and never short of girls, so it didn't bother me that much anymore. However, I think that deep inside, that left a scar, and I promised myself that one day I would learn to dance, at least the very basics, so I would never have to experience that humiliating feeling again when on the dance floor with a woman.

Years went by. I was almost 30 and had broken up recently with my last girlfriend, one of many in the succession of disastrous relationships I had in the last few years of my chaotic life that seemed not to have a clear direction. I had passed many times by the door of a dance studio near where I lived but never had the courage to go in to enquire nor suggest it to my girlfriends of the past. So embarrassed and terrified I was just thinking of what could happen when I'd be on the dance floor with them.

One day, however, I decided it was time to face my demons, plucked the courage, and walked into the dance studio offering Ballroom and Latin American lessons for beginners. From day one, I just loved the music and the atmosphere of the place and got hooked very quickly. The fact that there were quite a few young and pretty women on their own made it all the most enticing but also very frightening at the beginning. I still remember how anxious and tense I was that first day, horrified, in fact, sweating profusely, so much that I had to go to the bathroom and dry myself with a towel. Interestingly, however, it turned out that once I learnt a few steps, I was actually quite good. My obsessive nature took over: I loved it so much that I was practising like mad, at home, at work in my breaks, and in the studio. Soon I was taking my medal exams, and I started competing. I got on very well with everybody. All so supportive, helpful, and patient with me. After a while, I was spending quite a bit of time at the school practising, had a few dancing partners, and soon was assisting the principal with the beginner's classes on Tuesdays and Thursdays.

And it was precisely on a Tuesday night that my life changed. On that particular Tuesday, just before the start of the beginner's class, a young woman attended for the first time. Her name was Poppy, and I thought she was utterly beautiful and looked so ladylike to me. Of course, the word lady can mean different things to different people, but for me, she fulfilled 'my' definition of a lady in the true sense of the word, the way she carried herself, her behaviour, her natural beauty, and elegance, the clothes she was wearing, not expensive brands but very well chosen, combined and worn. Her voice, so beautiful, softly spoken, and articulate. Truly classy in my eyes.

Truth be said, I was doing my best not to stare at her, and as we were changing partners, I was waiting with anticipation for my turn to dance with her. When my turn finally arrived, we stood in front of each other, smiling without saying anything, just looking at each other. That was one of the very few moments in my life when words didn't come to me easily with a girl, and normally I would have felt very awkward, but with Poppy, somehow, it just didn't seem to matter. It felt kind of natural. In any case, I asked her what her name was, to which she said Poppy in the most beautiful voice. Then, with a bigger smile, I held her right hand in my left hand and delicately placed my right hand round her waist while looking deeply into her eyes. She had the most beautiful blue eyes and a stunning smile, so naturally pure and simple, and the contact of her hand with mine felt, weirdly, as if they belonged together. If asked, I would say that I fell in love with her there and then, and ever since, my heart belonged to her. I just knew she was the one!

It may be difficult to understand that feeling if one has never experienced it, but I guess it's what they call love at first sight. And it was magical! When the lesson finished and she was just about to leave, I approached her and asked her how she had found the class and whether she had enjoyed it, and I praised her, saying that she had done very well. I also asked her with trepidation whether she would be back on Thursday, to which, to my delight, she replied yes, and that she had very much enjoyed the class and was looking forward to coming back.

The truth is that Poppy was a quiet person and didn't talk much. But that was ok for me. In fact, after my experiences with women over the past years, I definitely preferred the ones that talked less but said more to others that talked a lot but didn't really say much.

In addition, one may say after that first encounter on the dance floor that Poppy was not the most naturally gifted person as far as dancing was concerned. At least not at the beginning. But that didn't matter either, as I knew from my own experience how intimidating and terrifying it can be for someone not very good at dancing to get on a dance floor. Furthermore, she had come on her own, and I thought she had been very brave doing that. However, as I always say, life is full of surprises. Little did I know that in time the 'ugly duckling' would transform into this beautiful swan on the dance floor!

A couple of days passed, and Thursday came. I had been thinking about Poppy all the time since that first encounter, and I was very excited at the prospect of seeing her again. When I arrived at the dance studio, she was already there, waiting for the class to start. On seeing her, my heart jumped, and it must have been beating at 200 beats per minute with excitement. I said hello to her and asked her how she was, trying not to give much away as to the fireworks happening inside me. The class started, and we danced a few times briefly together as normal when changing partners. Then the class finished, and as she was leaving, I saw the opportunity to show her my gentlemanly side. I approached her with my very best manners and asked her whether she would allow me to accompany her to her car. When I was young, I could be a 'smooth operator' when I wanted, although of late, I was getting quite tired of that bullshitting. I just didn't have the patience anymore. However, with Poppy, it just felt different.

I knew she had come by car as in the few minutes we were dancing together I had already asked her whether she had travelled far to come to the studio to which she replied that she lived quite close by, less than 10 minutes by car. In any case, she said yes to me accompanying her to the car, and before we were going to say our goodbyes, I had to say it, I couldn't wait any longer. Something compelling inside of me was pressing me, and I didn't want to waste any more time!

Trying not to sound over-enthusiastic, I said to Poppy that I would like to invite her for dinner on Saturday, nothing fancy. I just wanted to make it sound casual, without pressure. She said that she would love to, but she was already going out with her friends on Saturday night. I asked her if it was an important get-together and she said no, just going out with friends. Then, I had one of those 'inspired' moments that came to me sometimes, and looking into Poppy's eyes, I said to her, "Poppy, let me tell you something. I truly believe in fate and that in life, there are moments that define our future, and the decisions we make in those situations will determine the course of our lives. I think this is one of those moments in life in which you have to make a decision between going with your friends as originally planned or accepting my invitation and coming with me."

Then, as honestly and profoundly as I could, and looking even more deeply into those beautiful blue eyes, I said to her, "In my humble opinion, to choose to come with me would be the best decision, and if you accept my invitation, I will do my very best so that you will never regret it."

One may think that I was being very pushy, selfish perhaps, and of course, no man likes having an invitation rejected, but the truth is that with Poppy, it was different. I really wanted to see her and be with her, and I didn't want to wait until the week after. It is difficult to explain, but being in her company felt just right, like when doing a puzzle and you keep trying different pieces, and suddenly one fits perfectly well, without forcing, just right. That's how it felt. She was the missing piece in my life!

I asked her to think about it and to please let me know the next day. When I think about it now, I guess it probably didn't sound too good at the time, but even then, soon after, we would laugh sometimes thinking about the episode, my choice of words, and my over-confidence, bordering on cockiness. But then, I was in my early 30s, and I had been around a fair bit and seen the good, the bad, and the ugly. At this time of my life, I had the confidence to say things like that to any woman and couldn't care less what they would think. However, with Poppy, it just felt completely different, I meant every word I said, and I definitely cared about what she thought.

Perhaps it was the power of those words coming from the heart or any mysterious reason which I will never know, but she called me in the morning and said that she had thought about my invitation and she would like to accept it. In my view, that was truly a momentous decision, as she chose to come with me instead of going with her friends, and I always thought it was very brave of her to make that choice, hardly knowing me at all. But there again, as I would find out, Poppy was a formidable woman, very independent and able to make her own decisions, regardless of what other people may think or say, provided she felt it was the right thing to do. That also was very appealing to me. I liked intelligent and independent women with strong minds but kind, gentle, and understanding at the same time, and in my experience, they were not that easy to find. The truth is that, from the very beginning, I saw in Poppy a very special person, quite unique and different from what I was used to. She was truly one of a kind, as time would tell. However, to my surprise and delight, soon it was apparent she also had some interest in me, and it was the beginning of the most wonderful time of my life!

Chapter 4

Our first years together were just amazing, although misfortune would creep in our way every so often, and not all was a bed of roses. When I met Poppy, and we got together, she had been off work for quite some time and didn't have much money. I didn't have much either, but I was working, and I had a few savings at the time. From day one, I felt that what I had, we had, and it was for the enjoyment of both. She was the woman in my life, for who I felt what I had never felt before, the person I loved more than anyone else, and what was mine was hers too. And with what we had, we certainly made the most of it.

After a few weeks of going out together, we decided to spend a weekend away in the Lake District and take our bicycles with us. It was a Friday afternoon at the beginning of July. I had arranged to finish earlier at work that day, got home, quickly packed Poppy's car with the bikes on the rack, and made our way to the Lakes. We had booked a room in a cosy Bed & Breakfast by one of the lakes, and of course, it was an excellent deal that Poppy had found online. I used to joke she was the best PA ever. Even our friends and neighbours would often use her incredible searching and organisational skills. In any case, the weather forecast for the weekend was pretty good, low to mid-twenties, and mostly sunny. It was our first weekend away, and we were very excited.

We had a wonderful journey and got to the hotel just as it was getting dark. Although it was a bit late, the hosts were very welcoming, and we had informed them in advance of our expected time of arrival. We were promptly shown to our room, and while Poppy unpacked, I took the bicycles to the hotel's garage. Then, a quick supper in the dining room, a little drink, and to our room. There, we looked at the route we had planned for the next day, chatted a little while having a drink, and went to bed in anticipation of the next day. It was our first weekend away together. Very special indeed.

The day dawned with a resplendent sun. We had our breakfast and soon were on our way to explore the area with the bikes. The lake district was as beautiful as I had been told, there was a little breeze coming from the lake, and we were just going around following our route. All very enjoyable so far. Then we came across a steep hill, which we took easy, as Poppy didn't like hills on the bike. I was helping Poppy in the climb, and we reached the top, but then, of course, the downhill on the other side was pronounced. I had been riding a bike since I was a kid and was used to going very fast when on my own. And it must be said, I loved speed and did not prioritise safety, either on a bicycle or in a car. However, not everybody liked speed as I did, so I said to Poppy to go ahead gently and carefully, and I would catch up with her. What a big mistake that was!

I didn't know the area. It was a bendy road. I underestimated the steepness of the descent, and if that wasn't enough, it was the first time I was riding with Poppy. Mix it all well together, and you have a recipe for disaster. Typical of the stupid things that I used to do when I was younger, although I was not that young anymore and should have known better!

Poppy had started the descent but felt uncomfortable with the steepness and, unknown to me, had stopped halfway down to wait for me. I started the descent and I was going quite fast, crazy fast, 55 mi/h according to the bike computer, and suddenly as I came out of a bend, there she was, Poppy, stopped on her bike on the side of the road. It was, of course, entirely my fault, I did not have the time to break, and I crashed onto Poppy. Badly. We both ended up on the ground by the side of the road, Poppy with a minor fracture to her knee and me with a broken hip! Totally reckless, but again typical of my behaviour in the last few years, of how I used to live for a long time, and it was difficult to suddenly change.

Needless to say, I felt awful. Our first weekend away together, and what could have been a beautiful day on the bike creating wonderful memories, sadly ended up with both of us in the hospital. And it was all my doing! I couldn't forgive myself for a while, but that taught me a very important lesson, and from that day, I realised that if I wanted to be with Poppy, make a success of our relationship together and have a proper future with her, I had to start changing things in my life. And fast! Perhaps it was time to start acting with the maturity that had eluded me all those years and was more suited to my age.

However, what was more amazing to me, and a bigger lesson, was how Poppy reacted to that. She had been knocked down by a 'missile' at over 50 miles/h in the form of her boyfriend, whom she had known only a few weeks, thrown in the middle of the road, sustained a fracture to her knee, and was lying there being assisted by a total stranger. And all thanks to me. Surely not the way that she would have wanted our first weekend together.

After the crash, the traffic stopped, and people came out of their cars very quickly to offer help. One of the ladies was a doctor. She was attending to Poppy and asking someone else to call for an ambulance. As for me, there I was, lying down, unable to move. All a bit surreal, in all honesty. When I fell, my hip had hit a rock and fractured the top of the femur, "a beautiful clean fracture," as doctors would tell me later when checking the X-rays. Luckily it was not my head that hit the rock, although, at the time, I felt I deserved it!

An ambulance soon came and, as the doctor had briefly examined Poppy and she was complaining of pain in the abdomen, she was rushed to hospital, sirens on, as the pain could have indicated something more sinister than a broken bone and in need of urgent attention. Luckily, and I thank God to this day, that was not to be the case. Once Poppy was examined by the doctors in the hospital, and all explorations and tests had been carried out, they ruled out any serious internal damage and that she had only sustained an injury to her knee and a cut in her upper lip. As for me, as I only had a broken hip and the rest of me seemed perfect, I waited for a second ambulance to come. When it arrived, the paramedics administered first aid and painkillers, lifted me on a stretcher as gently as they could into the ambulance, and then we made our way into the hospital. No rush, no sirens on this time.

On my way to the hospital, my mind was boiling, wondering how the hell our first weekend away together, which was supposed to be very enjoyable and cement our relationship, even more, had gone so badly wrong. I was lying in the back of an ambulance on my way to the hospital, Poppy already there, both injured after an accident that was clearly my fault. The answer was clear: again, as usual, I had fucked up big time!

Chapter 5

Whilst we were apart in A&E in the hospital, I had been thinking of what to say to Poppy, but nothing I could say would do anything to change what had already happened, or rather what I had caused to happen on our first weekend away together. I truly did not find any words that could mitigate the situation. What would she be thinking of me? Would she still want to continue a relationship with someone like me, so careless, so reckless, so… stupid?

Eventually, when I was reunited with my beautiful Poppy and had sheepishly asked her how she was, I apologised to her profusely. I think I have never felt so ashamed of myself in my life than there and then in front of her at that precise moment. But then came the second lesson, which was hugely bigger for me than the first. She wasn't angry, while I would've been furious, I didn't understand. On hearing my words, Poppy was truly gracious about it. She didn't complain to me, didn't shout at me, didn't pull a face, didn't blame me for the accident. In fact, she never blamed me for the accident, not even once. She just looked at me with her beautiful blue eyes, asking me how I was, whether I was ok, and then she said that if we were going to have a future together, I would have to do things better. She said it calmly, with her beautiful and gentle voice, almost drawing a smile, but I knew she was being dead serious. It was her way of saying I love you very much, and I want to be with you, but start getting your act together, or I'm gone.

On hearing those words, but even more in the way they were pronounced, my heart melted, tears came to my eyes, and my love for her grew even more. I promised myself that it would be the last time that, through my reckless actions,

I would put Poppy at risk. I loved her so much, and it could easily have gone so wrong. I would never have forgiven myself if something had happened to Poppy that day. It was definitely time to change things in my life, and so changes I made!

I think Poppy, in the few weeks we had been together, had already seen the kind of person I was inside, and she knew me quite well. She knew of my problems in the past, that the last few years had been difficult, that I had made many mistakes, and I was paying the price. I wasn't very good with money. In fact, I could be totally reckless at times. I wasn't a bad person, but I had hurt a lot of people in the past. I had a terrible temper, and I was living my life without much purpose or direction, and that had been the case for quite a while. But with her, I was different, I was trying to do it better, and I was trying to do it right. I think she saw some potential in me, the person I could be, much better than what I was. Someone whom I, myself, could be proud of and start conquering the demons of the past and make something of myself. Poppy was patient, kind, supportive, and loving with me. She was an inspiration, and being with someone like her made me want to change, to be better as a person, and to improve. I didn't mind what I had to do because no sacrifice was too much, and no price was too high. I just wanted to be with her.

That day there in the hospital with Poppy, it was clear to me how exceptional a person she was. How she behaved that day made me love her even more, but most importantly, my respect and admiration for her as a person was growing exponentially. When I was younger, I was very fiery, and even by the time I met Poppy, I could still have a short fuse and a really bad temper, although by then, I had learnt to control it most of the time. In time I would realize that it was all due to not knowing how to deal with my internal frustrations and personal dissatisfaction of many years. However, in reality, I was more like a pussycat that only wanted to have an easy life and not to be disturbed too much. It was more like the roar of the lion, meaning don't bother me now. Leave me alone. Give me a few minutes, and I'll calm down. But many women I had met before didn't realise that, even if I almost begged them to stop, and at the moment that the fire was blazing, they would add more fuel and then it would become ferocious. Physically, I had never touched a woman in my life, but I had a venomous tongue, sharp and nasty, and I could easily make extremely hurtful comments to that person. If I became really angry, I could also occasionally hit anything that was around me very easily and then completely disregard that person as if she had never existed in my life. I just couldn't care less at that moment about anyone or what they thought, and I would never go back to that person and try to sort things out. For me, it was over completely. She no longer existed. Time to move on and get someone else. That was my behaviour for many years. Not something to be proud of.

But Poppy was different. She understood my character and personality and knew she could never fight me with fire but with water. She would tell me things in a gentle way and at the right time, and I would listen to her. After all, my bark was much worse than my bite, and 99% of the time, she was right! I always knew she was much better than me, and I perhaps never deserved her, really, but she gave me another chance, and I certainly took it.

While in the hospital, they fitted Poppy with an external and removable frame to support her leg as they were afraid to operate in the area where she had had the operations and skin grafts in the past. The doctors felt that it was an unnecessary risk and that the fracture would heal on its own by immobilising her knee. It would just take longer. As for me, they operated and put four pins and a plate to stabilise the fracture, and they did a fantastic job, as, apart from some discomfort every so often, I could soon lead a normal life and do everything I was doing before. The rehabilitation people taught us how to use crutches, and Poppy having had them before, was whizzing up and down the corridor in no time while I was still taking very tentative steps. After a few days in the hospital, we were discharged, and some friends came to pick us up and brought us home. They also drove our car down for us, as neither Poppy nor I could drive at the time.

As soon as we had recovered enough and the medical appointments had been sorted out, we decided that having a few weeks on our hands, we were going to take advantage of it. And so, it was decided to pack Poppy's car and tour a bit around Europe. It was one of the most fantastic experiences of my life. We were together all day, every day, without a care in the world, without almost knowing where we would end up, let alone sleep, from one day to the other. We were just going where we fancied, within our limited budget, of course, and with our phrase book, but positively enjoying our freedom and each other's company. It was truly amazing, and as unfortunate as the accident was, we certainly did make the most of the circumstances!

Also, strange as it may seem, the accident united us, like creating a bond which could not be broken. And so it was that we went to France, Belgium, Germany, Switzerland, Italy, and then to Spain, which Poppy loved, having spent many summers with her family there in various parts when she was young. Also, when she was younger, being so naturally beautiful, she had been a model and, not surprisingly, had a boyfriend from an extremely wealthy family. They owned an apartment in Marbella and had a yacht moored in the harbour. I used to ask her, jokingly, what she saw in me. The truth is that Poppy was not that kind of person and never fitted in that world. Neither did I. Perhaps she was a bit odd in certain ways, but so was I, and much more than her, I would say. However, what Poppy had were some amazing internal qualities, values and principles which I would find out in time and which would change and enrich my life beyond words.

In any case, we had a fantastic time. I still remember the day we stopped for lunch in a motel restaurant by the side of the road in Switzerland. We arrived and parked the car just outside the terrace area, where some locals were dining. Of course, pulling out with a car with an unfamiliar number plate always attracts attention. It happened to us many times, people just turning their heads, unconsciously and without any malice, just curiosity. Poppy came out of the car, on the left side, with her big black leg frame, almost from a horror movie, and then got her crutches out. People looked at her in disbelief, but then they realised that it was an English car and you could almost see the relief on their faces: she was not the driver! Then, it was my turn to step out of the car. It was only a few weeks since the operation, and it was all still quite sore, particularly after driving a few hours. It wasn't very graceful, one could say, but I stepped out of the car, got my crutches, opened the life-saving phrase book, and said, "Guten Tag. Sprechen Sie English?" Until this day, I remember the faces of the people there. They must have thought the circus was in town! Poppy and I laughed so many times when thinking about it. We had many funny episodes like that, so many things done together that made us laugh. So, so, so many…

However, as money was running low, we made our way to Spain. I was born in Barcelona and still had many friends and family in the area. Our plan was to spend a couple of weeks there before coming back. I was so proud of being with Poppy and couldn't wait to introduce her to my people. I wanted to take her to the many significant places and areas of my youth. Then, after we returned, I would resume work in the hotel, and Poppy would start looking for a job and carry on with our happy lives. However, as usual with Poppy, and as I would learn the hard way, things were never so straightforward. After a few days, the nightmarish situation started, a big struggle in our lives ahead due to just sheer bad luck. Typical of my beautiful Poppy.

Chapter 6

The first few days in Spain were fantastic. We went out on our own to see places or visit friends and family. I have a large family, many uncles, and aunties, and even more cousins. When I was in Spain, I was always going out and meeting with them, even with my girlfriends at the time. This time was different, though. I hadn't seen them in years, and I had an English girlfriend with me!

Everybody wanted to meet Poppy, and I wanted everybody to meet her. They were inviting us to their houses and restaurants, taking us to places and never letting us pay a penny, always invited, and almost taking offence if I offered to contribute. All very Spanish. However, at the time, it was a bit difficult and uncomfortable for Poppy as she was quite shy and not used to that way of life, constantly meeting new people and not even speaking the lingo, just a few words she had learnt with me. I was never very good at noticing these kinds of things, and in the past, I didn't care, but with Poppy, it was different. This was one of the many things that I would learn being with her, and after that first time, I did it better.

One day while we were walking in the park, Poppy tripped, fell, and hit her injured leg against one of the benches. By then, her knee felt much better from the accident, and she had stopped using the frame, but her leg gave way. She got a cut in the area where she had had the skin grafts previously, and being a bit concerned, we went to a clinic. There she was treated topically, but no stitches were applied, as the doctors didn't want to take the risk in such a badly affected area, with the skin already in a very poor condition. Sadly, the wound got infected and started spreading through the skin, and she ended up in a hospital in Barcelona, having another skin graft!

We just couldn't believe it, such bad luck. What was supposed to be a couple of weeks in Spain enjoying ourselves became a few weeks until we could come back. By then, we had gone through all our savings, and our finances were in dire straits.

When we came back, to begin with, we had very little money, and for months and months really struggled to make ends meet. I remember our first month back. We had only £11 left in our pockets to get us through the last week of the month. We were really desperate, so desperate that we decided to spend £1 on the lotto. Unbelievably, we won £72, and we felt truly like millionaires that day. Beginner's luck, one would say, and, of course, it never happened again!

Fortunately for us at the time, banks were handing out credit cards as if there was no tomorrow. As I have already mentioned, Poppy was incredible at researching and finding deals and offers, and although our finances were pretty dire, she managed it somehow, and soon we found ourselves with three credit cards thanks to her. We used them to our advantage and borrowed from one to repay the other. I also took a part-time job as security at the weekends in addition to my job in the hotel, and after a few months, we started seeing the light at the end of the tunnel.

I will not say that those times were easy, but we were truly happy as, no matter how hard the times were, the important thing is that we had each other! Nothing else seemed to matter much at the time, just being together, and we were spending as much time as we could in each other's company. We had also decided that, as we were both previously living in separate rented accommodations, it made sense to live together and pay just one rent. After all, we had been living together for the last few weeks. And the most wonderful thing for me was that I was going to bed every night with the person I loved, her face the last thing my eyes were seeing before falling asleep; and I was waking up the next day with that person by my side, her beautiful face greeting me in the morning as I first opened my eyes. Priceless!

I find something truly fulfilling in going to bed every night with the person you love and waking up in the morning with that person by your side. The presence of that person next to you, the warmth and the smell of her body, hearing her breathe deeply as she sleeps, her beautiful face relaxed, her movements next to you, the gentle touch of her bum as she turns round, all that is very special to me because it only happens with a special person. In any case, we were spending more and more time together, and soon we were to be married.

We married not by the Church, as neither Poppy nor I were deeply religious, and furthermore, she was Church of England, and I was Catholic. The truth is that neither Poppy nor myself believed much in marriage in the sense of the grand ceremony that seems to be nowadays more for the benefit of the guests than for the bride and groom, which was utterly ridiculous in our view. As for signing the paper, we both believed that you marry a person in your heart, you make the decision in your heart and your mind to love that person, in good times and in bad times, until death do us part, as they say. The bond that one creates in one's heart is much stronger and more precious than any signature on any official document, or at least that's how we felt.

Nevertheless, following our adventurous spirit at the time, we discussed it and decided that an escapade to Gretna

Green would be wonderful and quite funny, in all honesty, and that's what we did. Besides, I had never been to Scotland, and it seemed like too good an opportunity to miss. We packed our bags in our old car and made our way up to the border; therefore, not even six months into our relationship, we had been living together for a couple of months and were already married. We definitely didn't like to waste our time!

Some of her friends would comment on how quickly our relationship was progressing. I suppose that would be right for many couples, but our relationship was very different from the very beginning, and we spent a lot of time together. I used to say, half-jokingly, that we had spent more time together in three months than many couples would spend in three years. The truth is that we had already gone through a lot in such a short period of time, and we grew stronger for it. In a way, that was our answer to anyone that would question it. In addition, we were living together. It wasn't like one of those relationships where the couple sees each other at the weekends, all dressed up and going to nice restaurants, cinemas, and theatres, and then on beautiful holidays. Of course, those relationships are always wonderful until you start living together, when sometimes cracks may appear very quickly.

I think that Poppy and I had a kind of tacit understanding from the very beginning of what we wanted in our relationship and, most importantly, in life in general. She hadn't had an easy life before meeting me, and I had had my fair share of bad things happening. We both knew from our experiences in the past how precious and fragile life is and how it can be taken from you so easily and quickly, with a devastating effect on the ones left behind. Providence had brought us together, I always thought, at a much-needed time for both of us. In the journey of my life, by serendipity, I had found Poppy at a time when I was quite lost and without clear direction, and that had been the case for very many years. At the same time, just by walking that day into the dance studio, Poppy had found me. We both felt fortunate that life had put us on each other's path, and we were grateful for the opportunity that life had offered us of true happiness, something so elusive nowadays. We were not going to waste that opportunity and were determined to make the most of it!

Life is so short when one thinks about it, too short in reality and in an untold way, 'carpe diem' became our motto, in a good sense, without doing stupid things but without wasting time and opportunities to enjoy. It is undeniable that from the moment we are born, we are destined to die. That's not being pessimistic. It's just being realistic. What we don't know is when and how. Therefore, we may be here today, but there is no guarantee that we will be here tomorrow. That is why we just wanted to be together, enjoy each other's company and share experiences as much as possible. We always felt that money, or sometimes the lack of it, would not stand in our way of enjoying ourselves and being happy together. And the little spare we had at the beginning was always spent together, shared for the enjoyment of both.

And that was always the way we liked to live, living life to the full within our very limited possibilities, enjoying every day as much as we could, treasuring the wonderful times together, and sharing experiences that were making our relationship stronger day by day. I've always said that you don't have to worry about the future of a relationship if you do your best every day. You plan for the future, but you don't worry about the future. By doing your best every day, that takes care of the future: days become weeks, that become months, and then, without realising, you look back, and you've been together, with the person you love so much, for years.

We both understood that it is what you do every day in a relationship which makes the difference in the long term, and therefore we invested 100% in our relationship to make it work. However, that commitment to each other never felt like a chore or hardship and was neither ever asked by the other person. We just gave ourselves to each other gladly in our entirety because of how much we loved each other and because it just felt right and wonderful.

The little details we had with each other were important to us. As money was tight for many years, I couldn't buy Poppy expensive things. Although she was not a materialistic person in the slightest, it nevertheless would have given me much pleasure to be able to buy her the expensive things that women usually like. However, it would be a few years until I could buy her a little diamond ring that I had seen and knew she liked and for which I had been saving for quite a while. For a long time, it was quite different, and even the cheapest bunch of flowers that I would sometimes buy for Poppy would be received with such appreciation and happiness that it truly made our day. And it would not need to be any special occasion, as every day being together, enjoying each other's company, was indeed a special occasion. That's why I would always rush home after work, turn up every so often with some flowers or a small box of chocolates or a cuddly toy or a silly little thing! No matter what it was, as simple or inexpensive as it could be, I could always see the joy in Poppy's eyes when she would receive it, and that would make my heart explode with happiness. She was definitely very different from many women I had met in the past who only wanted expensive things and could hardly bring themselves to utter thank you when being given to them!

Yes, I have always said I was truly fortunate that destiny put Poppy on my path and that her beautiful face would accompany me every night and every morning for many, many years. That is, apart from the unfortunately numerous occasions she would be in hospital over the years. At the time, of course, that was unknown to us, but doctors and hospitals sadly would become a fixture in our lives.

Chapter 7

It had all started for Poppy in her early twenties. She had just finished her studies as a midwife and graduated first in her class. I was always amazed at how intelligent Poppy was, but what was truly exceptional was her photographic memory. I have never been very intelligent nor clever. All my academic achievements are due to much hard work. Neither do I have a good memory and for this reason, having someone like Poppy by my side made me feel very proud. That someone like her would even consider being with someone like me, let alone marry me. Wow! Yes, I always felt truly fortunate to have met Poppy and that she was my wife. My 'wife,' what a beautiful word!

As soon as Poppy graduated, she started working in a hospital. I could really see Poppy as a nurse, as she was the kindest and least selfish person I had ever met. I could also see her very easily as a midwife, as she loved kids, and her patience, kindness, love, and understanding would make her a great mum. Sadly, life had other plans for her, and her career as a midwife was short-lived.

Working in a hospital as a junior doctor or recently graduated nurse or midwife surely must put a lot of stress on someone's life, the physical and mental pressure and demands of the work itself, working days and nights terribly long shifts. Poppy was no exception and had a bit of a hard time initially trying to adjust to the pressure of a new job with such responsibility. After all, she was delivering babies and responsible for both the baby and the mum. But her impressive academic knowledge, kind and loving personality, and gentleness with the patients soon saw her being promoted, and she started working less night shifts and having a bit more of a social life. Furthermore, as she was truly stunning, she was not short of admirers and soon met a doctor, and they started going out together. Everything seemed to be going very well for Poppy, and after the difficulties she went through in her youth, she was finally reaching a phase in her life where she could have some stability, support, and love.

Poppy's life didn't have a great start. She was abandoned by her dad, who left her with her mum to fend for herself when she was only a few weeks old. Although soon after, her mum would meet someone else and marry him in due course, Poppy always felt inadequate and unloved, and through her teenage years, she was quite rebellious and caused quite a bit of trouble to the family. Her biological dad had all but disappeared completely from her life, and she never had any contact with him, despite Poppy's several attempts to find him and get in touch with him. Her stepdad, however, was a wonderful man and clearly, by all accounts, became her real dad. Nevertheless, Poppy always felt that, in a way, she was responsible for her biological dad leaving her and her mum, and she blamed herself.

Interestingly, I have met a few women in my life that seemed to have had a similar negative experience with their dads, and that has marked them enormously. For many, it has taken them a long time to overcome the feeling of inadequacy, very low self-esteem, and lack of confidence in themselves. The vulnerability and feeling of needing someone made them easy targets and prompted bad and sometimes abusive relationships with their partners, which in turn aggravated the initial problem. It appears that the relationship between a daughter and her dad is very complex, and it is essential for the right kind of relationship through infancy and adolescence for the healthy psychological development of the girl. I'm not a psychologist, though, it is just what people have told me, but my experience seems to corroborate that.

Soon after I met Poppy, I realised there were some issues and that she may have had bad experiences in the past, particularly with men who I felt had a negative impact on her life. But we all have our past, and mine was nothing to be proud of. I had learnt not to jump to conclusions very quickly, neither to judge nor criticise based just on first impressions. However, with Poppy, I always thought that she was too kind and sometimes a bit naïve and didn't see that people can be not very nice at times. She was just too good, I felt, always thinking the best of everyone and trying to help everybody and therefore, it was quite easy to take advantage of her. And I'm sure some people did and must have caused her a few bad experiences and rough times in the past.

In the hospital, however, at the time, things were looking up for Poppy in all areas of her life. A promotion in a job she adored, she was making new friends and had just started a relationship with someone that could provide her with a stable future. All was going well after all those years, and Poppy was starting to feel a bit happier within herself and in her life.

Life, however, has a habit of throwing nasty surprises when one expects them the least. In Poppy's case, on this occasion, an initial sporadic pain in her left lower leg soon developed into something else, and after initial explorations, she was referred to a skin clinic. There the specialist sent her to have some tests done, and before she knew it, Poppy had been diagnosed with skin cancer! She was just in her mid-twenties, with a promising future, and the world must have been crumbling down. Furthermore, her mum had already passed away after contracting skin cancer in her late 30s, so one can only imagine the kind of thoughts that must have been crossing Poppy's mind at the time.

Unfortunately, Poppy's cancer proved to be more aggressive than initially thought, and the surgical team had to do a larger resection of skin and muscle in her lower leg, with an extensive skin graft, and amputate the small toe. Needless to say, the look of that leg would never be the same again. Pity, because Poppy had such beautiful legs, svelte but firm. In addition, Poppy also needed a course of chemotherapy and radiotherapy to ensure the best chance of survival, and the side effects didn't make her feel very well. Furthermore, at the time, she had no relatives or close friends living nearby, so she had no alternative but to go through it all pretty much on her own. If things weren't bad enough, the doctor she was going out with reacted unexpectedly. As soon as Poppy told him she had been diagnosed with skin cancer, that it was quite aggressive, and explained the treatment involved, he decided that he no longer wanted to be part of her life and ended their relationship. When she told me one day, once we were together, how she had been treated by that person, I felt sick and furious, and thankfully, he was not in front of me at the time. In fact, I had never met him, and I'm glad to say this. Otherwise, I think I would have hit him as hard as I could. Having said that, until I met Poppy, that's how I was and how I would have behaved. Interesting how your outlook on certain things changes in life when you are with the right person.

Unfortunately, things deteriorated, and Poppy soon needed another operation. Then her leg got infected, and it took quite a long time to heal. By then, she had been on and off work for over a year, and it soon became quite clear to her that it was going to be a bit difficult to go back to her job in the hospital, and she was considering other options. She was very intelligent, and she could have done anything she wanted.

By then, she had lost quite a bit of muscle mass and strength in that leg, and the physio had recommended taking up some physical activity to start recuperating what she had lost. Among the activities suggested by the physio was swimming, which Poppy loved. In fact, she was a very good swimmer, having even competed in her school days. She loved the water and sunbathing, be it in a swimming pool or, of course, on the beach. However, she had an open wound at times and was advised against going in the swimming pool as she could easily get an infection. Poppy didn't like running, and it would have been difficult for her in any case. She liked gentle cycling, and she had a cheap and heavy bike at the time, but living in a flat on the first floor wasn't easy to get it in and out.

One day, when talking to one of her friends, she was told that dancing is also a very good exercise as it strengthens your legs and helps with balance and coordination, and perhaps she should give it a go. Furthermore, as Poppy had moved recently to a new area in London, her friend suggested that perhaps going to a dance school would help Poppy physically with the recovery of her leg and also socially as she could make new friends easily and have fun. And that is how one day, on a beautiful evening on a Tuesday in May 1996, Poppy decided to go to a particular dance studio, and her life would also change forever.

Chapter 8

Poppy was incredibly photogenic. After all, in her late teens, she had been a model, and even after I met her, for a while, she would still receive, every so often, complementary products from the company. She was very beautiful but naturally beautiful, elegant without having to try, and her smile was absolutely stunning. Everybody would always mention how beautiful her smile was, and it truly was. That, coupled with such amazing blue eyes, pure and kind looking, made her a real beauty, but not in a sexual kind of way, and anywhere we went, I always felt incredibly proud of having her by my side.

In our early days together, I used to take lots and lots of photos of Poppy, and she could always strike a pose for me. Photography had been one of my obsessions when I was much younger, and I had spent a lot of time, and money, taking photos. My girlfriends at the time could attest to that, but as we were going out to different places every weekend for me to take photos, they never complained. Now, however, instead of taking photos of the natural world or working on my chiaroscuro or superposition technique, I would take lots of photos of, and with, Poppy. Even if she wore a pair of jeans with a T-shirt, she would still look amazing. On the other hand, I never liked very much photos of myself, I don't think I look particularly good, but I don't mind if I am with someone else, friends, family, or of course, Poppy. She also liked taking photos, and she was much better than me at taking selfies, but not the kind of selfies, or rather selfie in the singular that you see so often nowadays. Our selfies were mostly together. I think it is very sad nowadays when you see so many couples where the woman is constantly taking selfies of herself with a fake and forced smile to the camera, without her partner, who is usually standing just a metre away from her holding her handbag! I really don't understand why they don't have the photo together.

For us, taking photos together was a way of reinforcing our relationship. It was as much the enjoyment of the moment and the place where the photo was taken as well as being able to talk about it afterwards. My arm around her shoulders or her waist, our heads leaning together, a little kiss on the cheek, a gentle touch with our fingers, and her smile, that incredible smile, Poppy's smile that would brighten any photo like the rays of the sun. Every photo we could share, look at it and talk about it after was connecting us more and more, bringing wonderful memories of the hundreds and thousands of very special and unique moments that we spent together. For us, a photo together was a shared experience that united us even more. She would make albums, and once at home, we would look at the photos and make comments, laugh, and reminisce about the myriad of magic moments spent together. But of course, every couple has their own way of making their relationship work. There is no right or wrong. For us, our way worked.

In a way, it is the same with mobile phones nowadays. I have been going on my own to restaurants many times lately, and it never ceases to amaze me. You can be in a restaurant, and you see a lovely, young, good-looking couple, and of course, that immediately reminds you of what your life once was. Suddenly, they get their mobile phones out of their pockets or handbag, and the enchanted moment is gone. They immerse themselves in whatever it is on their phones that is so mesmerising and completely ignore each other! I find it extremely sad that two people who should be enjoying a wonderful sharing experience of a meal together cannot put their phones away for a little while and just enjoy the moment and the company. After all, the rest of the day, we are just bombarded with phone calls, texts, and emails. Of course, in my youth, we didn't have mobile phones, so perhaps that explains it.

I am 'old school', probably prehistoric by now. I have always been like that though, and for me, the little details are very important. Taking the time to think of the other person and make her feel all right, special, like nobody else exists in your life. Every day, not only at the weekend or on holidays. A gentle touch, a kind comment, a sweet word, a flower or a chocolate, even a little piece of poetry, it all happens because that person is on your mind. That's the beautiful thing about it. And that's how it was with Poppy. She was always on my mind. At the same time, she knew how to make me feel like the most important man in the world, wherever we were and no matter who we were with. She didn't have to say anything. It was clear from her body language that I was her man, and she was my woman and that, to me, was priceless. 'Old school' indeed!

I remember once a Spanish friend of mine came to visit us with his new partner. They spent a few days at home, and one evening, we stayed in and had a barbecue on the terrace. It was clear from their body language that they hadn't been going together very long and that their relationship was also very physical. Nothing strange there, knowing my friend. I have nothing against it. On the contrary, my relationships have always been very physical, and in my view, that is an essential pillar for a long and healthy relationship. Furthermore, with my friend, we had numerous 'adventures' together when we were young, so I knew very well what he was like. However, what I don't like, and in fact never did, is the showing off and too much touching in front of the others. It wasn't done on purpose, I know, but after a few drinks, that was happening a bit that night, and Poppy clearly noticed. She didn't say anything, though.

We had finished our dinner and very much enjoyed the food and the wine. I helped Poppy to clear the table, left her in the kitchen preparing the coffee, and I was chatting with my friend and her partner, who were sitting across me on the other side of the table, both very touchy. I still remember it as if it was yesterday. Poppy came out holding a tray with the coffees, placed the tray on the table, and distributed the coffees around with a smile and a nice word, as the perfect hostess that she always was. Then, without saying a word, she came round to me, sat on my knees, passed her beautiful long arm around my shoulder, up to the side of my neck, and gently caressed the back of my head with her fingers, smiled at me and gave me a kiss on the cheek. All so casually done, like nothing was happening, but at the same time, so much was being said.

For many people, that may not mean much, but for me, I knew exactly what it meant, and so did my friend, and that was one of the reasons why I loved Poppy so much and why she was so special to me. So classy and elegant, always knowing what to do, how to behave, and what to say, regardless of the context or situation. There and then, without saying anything, she left my friend and partner with no doubt that she was my woman and I was her man. She was mine, for me to do as I pleased, when I pleased, how I pleased, but not there and then, it was not appropriate, not the right place or time. That was Poppy, my beautiful Poppy, always surprising me to make me feel unique, like one in a million. She belonged to me, and I, completely, utterly, and entirely belonged to her.

Chapter 9

After the first few months of really struggling to make ends meet, things slowly started to get a bit better. I was doing as much overtime as I could in my main job, had taken a second job at the weekends as night security in a yard, and we were saving for a deposit to buy a flat. Poppy had decided she didn't want to retrain and go back to the pressure of being a midwife. She loved the job but not the bureaucracy and politics that seemed to go with it. As she was very good with new technologies, she took a part-time job working with computers and mobile phones, sometimes assisting elderly people with no previous knowledge. Poppy actually loved it, as she was helping people to use something frankly quite alien to many of them at the time. Soon she would have the computers set up for them, and they would be sending emails and using social platforms to chat with their families across the world. It gave Poppy a great sense of personal satisfaction, and we would sit on the sofa at home, and she would tell me all about it. She would say what she had done that day and the pleasure that her job had given to someone else, and how a particular person had been able to have a conference call and see their loved ones on the screen for the first time. Poppy was that kind of person, always happy when helping someone.

By then, her leg was much recovered, and we were dancing more and more, to the point that, being something we both enjoyed, we decided to train seriously and compete together. Dancing competitively is expensive, no doubt about that, and we had to make many sacrifices, but we discussed it and thought it could provide us with a better future. If we reached a certain level, then from a successful amateur career, we could turn into professionals. It truly was an expensive business, travelling to competitions all over the country, entry fees, expenses, hotels, shoes, dresses, you name it. Just in shoes, as we were dancing both Ballroom & Latin American disciplines, Poppy could go through 8-10 pairs of dancing shoes a year.

Fortunately for us, we met some wonderful people along the way that would help us at the beginning and who gave us very good advice. Also, one of the dancers we met was a seamstress doing ballroom dresses, and she made a couple for Poppy at a fraction of the cost of the ones in the shops. The expensive ladies' ballroom dresses could easily cost well over £1.000, nearing £2.000 for the best quality ones, and we could have never been able to afford that, especially as Poppy needed a few. Luckily for us, one of our best friends, who was very wealthy and also a dancer, would lend Poppy those incredibly beautiful but very expensive dresses for the big competitions. It is true we were very fortunate. We made lots of friends, and they gave us an awful lot of help.

For a few years, we trained a minimum of four to five nights a week, even six before big competitions, and we had private lessons with some of the best professional dancers in the country, including former Ballroom and Latin American world champions. We worked very hard and trained even harder, and soon the results were speaking for themselves. We moved from beginners to amateurs in barely a couple of years, and then the big fight started. It is a 'dog-eats-dog' business, and we were dancing against people usually much younger than us and that had been dancing much longer than us.

Needless to say that our meteoric ascent was not welcomed by everybody, although thankfully by a minority. Poppy had a bit of a rough time in the beginning, as girls could be a bit unpleasant to her, bitchy, in fact. She was a tough cookie though and braved it the best she could, but I knew that was affecting her because she was not that kind of person and didn't like the atmosphere. I must confess there were times, in the beginning, I thought that if it hadn't been for the fact that I loved dancing so much and I saw a good future for us, she would probably have given it up. She did it for me mainly, I suppose, and also for our future.

As for me, with all my respect for anyone, I couldn't care less what the other guys thought. I wasn't there to socialise. From day one, I meant business, and if they didn't like it, tough. This is not to say that I was rude or unpleasant to anyone, but I knew what I wanted and what I had to do. If they had something to prove, they could prove it to me on the dance floor. In any case, I was bigger and stronger than most of them, so nobody ever said a bad word to my face. However, it was clear that not everybody wanted us in their world, and one day, during a competition, I got a nasty surprise. Once the Ballroom section had finished, as usual, I left my dancing suit in the changing room and changed into my Latin outfit. When the competition finished and I returned to the changing rooms, I saw that my Ballroom suit had been taken out of the suit carrier and someone had drawn across the back some lines with permanent fluorescent blue ink, very striking against the black, of course, and impossible to remove. I never found out who did it, and in reality, it didn't matter, but if they thought that it would act as a deterrent, they were completely mistaken.

We reported it to the organisers, and the Dancing Board and security measures were put into place for future events. Furthermore, as I had insurance against damage, the suit was replaced with another one, made to measure, of course, and from one of the best Ballroom tailors in the country. We were starting to get noticed by then. Therefore, whoever soiled my suit, in reality, did us a favour, as I ended up with a better Ballroom suit and we got better known among dancers and judges. Poetic justice, I thought!

As we were determined to make it to the top, we followed the advice of our teachers. Many couples we were dancing against were doing many fancy steps and combinations on the dance floor, but we were told to keep it simple and concentrate on the quality of the basics. One of our best teachers once said to us at the beginning of our career, it is not what you do, but how you do it. That became our motto. Our forte was a very strong basic technique, elegantly performed, and that saw us coming up through the ranks pretty quickly, reaching the top 12 in the country. We thought we would continue dancing at the amateur level for two to three more years, acquire more knowledge and experience, get into the top six in the country and then turn professional. That was our plan for the future. Everything seemed to be going according to plan at the time, and then once we turned pros, we could start having a bit more of a life

That is not to say we didn't do anything else. On the contrary, after every big competition, we would take a few days off and travel somewhere. The wizard that Poppy was on the internet got us some amazing deals and saw us travelling to many places, in the UK and Europe mainly. We also had many friends, and we were going out with them as often as we could. The truth is that we really enjoyed those first years, spending all that time together creating our future, travelling around and going out with friends. But mostly, we were really grateful to have each other. However, the investment had been exceptional, and the cost was very high, financially as well as socially, in our lives. Therefore, we thought we would do it a bit longer and start teaching. Our credit cards were always 'maxed up', and practically all the money we had in the last few years had been dedicated to dancing. But I loved it so much. And we were doing it together for our future!

Being together on the dance floor was wonderful! Not the training itself. That was blood, sweat and tears, literally. I remember once I broke Poppy's toe practising, and on another occasion, I also broke my big toe a few days before a big competition. It was an important competition for us, so I rested a couple of days, wrapped it well, loaded myself with painkillers the day of the competition, and we got on the floor. I managed to do the Ballroom in the morning, and we even got second place, but then it became sheer agony, hardly able to walk, let alone dance, and I had to retire for the Latin in the afternoon.

That was our life at the time, and the truth is that we put ourselves through a lot, physically and mentally, but surely was it for a better future together? However, looking back, I think it would have been totally impossible for me to do it without Poppy. Her unconditional love, sheer commitment and unbelievable support made it all possible. The achievements and the feeling of accomplishment were undeniably important. Every trophy we held in our hands was another milestone. However, mostly for me, it was the fact of being able to dance together, with Poppy, and at a fairly high level by then, when neither Poppy nor I were naturally gifted, and both had found it difficult in our youths. Soon we could reap the rewards of all those years of hard work and sacrifices.

Chapter 10

We had just won our biggest competition to date, and we were over the moon. There is something magical about dancing in the Winter Gardens - such a wonderful venue! We were starting to be recognised, and everything seemed to be heading in the right direction. On our way down from Blackpool, the day after the competition, we felt really positive about our future and were discussing options. I was dreaming of teaching dancing full-time, and by then, I had not only the passion but also the skill. Poppy would teach part-time, and then we would also do our dancing demonstrations. We had done a few already, and we loved it. We also had lots of contacts by then, and everything looked very promising. Wonderful plans that we had for our future indeed.

However, once again, life seemed to have other plans, and soon after, Poppy started having problems with her leg again. We decided initially to have a break of a few weeks, but it soon became apparent she would not be able to continue with the training regime we had been following the last few years. The stress of those years of training at that level had taken its toll on Poppy's leg. The problem was that we were not at the level we wanted to be to turn into professionals and make a fair living of it. At least I did not feel that way at the time. In hindsight, perhaps we should have taken our dancing teacher examinations then and just start teaching dancing socially. But I had dreamt of so much more and of doing it together with Poppy, and at the time, it did not appeal to me.

It was a very difficult time for both of us. I had left the job at the hotel a couple of years before for another job far less rewarding but with better working hours to be able to concentrate on dancing. I didn't enjoy my current job, and I had seen it as something temporary, just to keep us going while we were pursuing our dancing career. As for Poppy, she had dedicated so much to her dancing and become so good at it that it felt truly unfair. To make matters worse, we had put all our eggs in one basket, and dancing was our ticket out of our present life and into a better future. I had declined better jobs that I had been offered in the past, some of them significantly better paid and with very good prospects, to be able to pursue my dream with Poppy, a dancing career together and a better future for us.

Also, there was another consideration. I had done a few courses during my stay in the hotel but had no higher education to degree level, and neither had I any skill in any trade. At the time, I felt I was only good at dancing. That brought the question of which direction to follow as there were two options: I could continue my dancing career with another partner, which would not have been difficult. At the beginning of my dancing with Poppy, there were a few people that had advised me to have a stronger partner because, clearly, Poppy was not at the same level initially. But I didn't mind because I wanted to dance with Poppy and what we would achieve, we would achieve it together.

Then, when we informed our dancing friends that we had to have a break because Poppy's leg was deteriorating, I was contacted by a few dancers offering to become my partner. It was a difficult time, yes, but it was never a difficult decision. My decision was already very clear in my mind, and I never had a shred of doubt: I would dance with Poppy or give up my dancing career. I loved dancing enormously, and it had given me a lot in just a few years: physically, I was very fit, and mentally, I was in a much better place than a few years back. It had also given me a focus and hope for the future. However, my love and passion for dancing was nothing compared to my love and passion, if one may come to that, for Poppy. I loved Poppy so much more, and she would always come first. For me, the rest was secondary. Dancing without her would have never been the same, and it was not the feeling of betrayal that stopped me from doing it, but the feeling of love for Poppy, whose future was shared and interlinked with mine, and whatever was the fate of one, it would be the fate of the other. Easy decision: we would be together, do things together and move on together.

We would reconsider our life and our plans for the future and see which options we may have available, but together. After all, we had been through much worse in the past, and we had survived. I always thought that we had this symbiotic relationship. We both benefited from having the other person in our life. We enriched each other, were much stronger together, and our lives would have been lacking and much poorer without the other person. However, I always felt that Poppy's contribution to mine was so much more significant than mine in hers by a mile. Therefore, in a way, I didn't only love Poppy and wanted to be with her, but I also needed her in my life. Badly. She had been my salvation.

Chapter 11

I was now in my mid-thirties, and after a long time in my life, I seemed to be more at peace with myself. It may be difficult for people to fully understand how important and crucial Poppy had been in my life. My friends and family knew as they could see the changes in me. Poppy had given my life stability, a stability which had eluded me for very many years and that I desperately needed. I had started to accept myself as I was, with all the mistakes I had made in the past, and had stopped blaming others for my mistakes, my inadequacies, and my inability to do things right.

It had all started going wrong for me many years back when also, after a phase in my teenage years of being a bit lost, I had finally decided what I wanted to do, and I was following my dream.

I had never been academically brilliant, but until I reached my teenage years, I always managed to do very well at school by pushing just before exams. I was very active, never at home, always out with friends. It was a different time, of course. Society, in general, was a safer place than today, and our parents didn't worry that much if we spent all day out, just going home to eat, or to refuel, as we used to say. In fact, it was pretty much the norm. We didn't have computers, video games, or social media. It was all playing outdoors, being on the bike, and running around pretty much non-stop. I didn't much enjoy studying and doing all that homework when one could be playing with friends, although I still did it most of the time. However, I loved reading, and my parents were always buying me books.

Suddenly I reached my teenage years, I must have been 12 or 13 at the time, and everything changed. Girls became much more interesting and fun to be with than books, and for a few years, I didn't do very well academically. I kept passing most of the exams, though, and suddenly there I was, a 17-year-old boy in his last year of Baccalaureate and not having done very well at school lately. However, by then, my silly phase had passed. I had matured quite a bit and decided that I would do what I had always wanted to do. I was fascinated by the human body, in particular the heart, that amazing organ inside our body that will keep working tirelessly, pumping blood around our bodies, oxygenating our cells millions and millions of times in our lives. Yes, I was truly fascinated by the human body and the heart in particular. I thought it was the most amazing piece of engineering. In my last year, before university, we had done a lot of work on the human body, and I loved it. Therefore, I decided to become a doctor.

In reality, I had always wanted to be a doctor. I never knew why, as there was nobody in my family remotely close to that profession. Furthermore, I wasn't from a wealthy background but from a working family, and I would be the first one going to university in all my family. However, since I was a child, when asked, as adults do, what we would like to be when we grow up, I used to say, "Surgeon of the heart and lung." A crazy thing for a kid to say, surely, I must have heard something on the television.

In my teenage years, as we all do, I lost interest in it. I think mainly due to the fact that I didn't particularly want to spend my time studying, but also, it was clear from my academic behaviour and results that I was not medical school material. The truth is that I was going out with friends and girls all the time, far too much, I guess, although, at the time, I definitely thought it never is too much when you have fun. Those few years were absolutely fantastic, I don't think I could have enjoyed myself more than I did, but also, they saw me going through less pleasant experiences. The unexpected death of two close family friends, and mostly the illness, pain, and suffering of my granddad.

I had always had an amazing relationship with my grandparents, and it did hit me very hard. We used to spend many weekends and holidays with them in my childhood and, to this day, I still have the fondest and most wonderful memories of my Christmas holidays in my grandparent's flat. I will never forget that. However, I will not forget either when my grandad past away. I was 16 at the time and started to see things in a different way. I was still going out a lot and enjoying myself, but my mentality was starting to shift. I was thinking how wonderful it would be to be able to help those suffering, to cure someone with a disease, like, for instance, my grandad. With maturity came thinking about the future, and my decision was made. I would become a doctor. There was only a 'minor' obstacle on my way: I first had to get into medical school!

That was never going to be an easy feat. That year there were 260 places, and there were well over 1000 students applying for it. There was an exam in September based on the eight chosen subjects which had been studied in the last year before university. The average of those eight exams would count as 50% of the overall mark, whereas the other 50% would come from the average of the four years of Baccalaureate. That clearly was of no help to me, as I hadn't done very well during the four years, and my average was well below that of my fellow students applying to medical school. Nevertheless, I was determined to give it my all and get into medical school, even if it was the last thing I did. I could be very stubborn and determined when I got something in my head, and the two weeks before the exam in September, I studied as I had never studied before in my whole life. I truly didn't know that one person could spend so many hours enclosed in the same small space, with their head immersed in the books. And worse of all, without seeing and going out with their friends! I was just being fed and watered by my mum, it seemed to me at the time, but something inside me found it strangely enjoyable, almost in a masochistic way. That was a revelation to me.

The days of the exam came. Each day, two subjects in the morning and two in the afternoon, one day after the other, eight exams in all. Once the last exam was over, on my way home that day, I surprised myself by thinking that I had enjoyed the experience overall, and almost relished, in fact, the long hours of study at home, the pressure of those exams. It was a totally new experience for me.

I knew the odds were not in my favour. After all, the students that had a much better average to start with had a head start, but also, clearly, they had been studying for four years, whereas I had been doing anything but. Therefore, my preparation for the exam in September was savage, as I had a lot of catching-up to do and very little time in which to do it. But I always say that miracles do sometimes happen. When I got my results, the envelope in my shaking hands, my mum and my dad by my side, that day, and at that time, I was praying for a miracle.

There and then, I opened the envelope and I took out the paper with the result. I looked at it and then at my parents, who, without a doubt, were more nervous than me but they didn't let it show. Then I said to them, with a shaky voice, "236, I did it!" That's all I could say, tears coming to my eyes, a huge lump in my throat, the tension, stress, and pressure of the last few weeks bursting at that precise moment, under the kisses and hugs of my parents, that must have been the proudest parents at that moment in the whole world.

Chapter 12

I must say it here for the record, my parents were absolutely amazing, not that I realised this in my teenage years, and I know I gave them many headaches when I was growing up, which they never deserved. I had a strong and difficult personality when a teenager, and my dad also had a very strong character, so we clashed every so often. But that day, in a way, I felt that I had repaid them a bit for all their love, support, and sacrifices they had made for me and my brother over the years. I felt very proud that I could make them proud of me. Not that they weren't, they loved us very much, and I never felt pushed to do anything we didn't want to. In reality, they probably just wanted me to have a bit of common sense and be safe and happy.

Soon I started medical school. Students, we are all very excited in the first year, but we do not always do as we are supposed to, that is, to study. Again, I met new people, it was exciting, new friends and new girls from different backgrounds, and it is true that I did not apply myself as much as I should have. Nevertheless, I still don't know how I managed it, but then I was in my second year. The subjects then are much more interesting and appealing, and one tends to study more, which I did, and suddenly again without realising I was in my third year through medical school. Not the best by any stretch of the imagination, but neither was I the worst, and I was sort of managing to pass the exams somehow. And then it all changed...

It was a lovely summer day in August. Hot as usual, I decided to go to the beach with my girlfriend at the time, a lovely girl that I had met at university. We had been going out for quite a few months, a record for me, my family loved her, and her family really liked me as well. We were spending a lot of time together, and it seemed we could have a very good future. She was studious, very mature for her age without being boring and really knew what she wanted. And she was beautiful, with a great body as well. She had it all. We spent the day there on the beach. I drove her to her parents in the evening, and then I went home.

It was a bit late, and my parents weren't at home, but I didn't think much of it as they had gone to my uncle's summerhouse in the mountains to spend the weekend with them and my grandparents. They probably hit some traffic on their way back, that was all, I thought.

Then the phone rang. It was a nurse from a hospital. My first thought was, why would a nurse from a hospital be calling home at this time? Alarm bells started ringing in my head. She said that my parents had been involved in an accident on their way back from the mountains, and they were in the hospital. Unexpected terrible news, your brain starts thinking the worse, and the first words that come out of your mouth are, "Are they okay?" She said she only had that information and had been asked to contact the family. I didn't like the reply, I didn't believe her, in fact, but as a medical student, I knew the protocol. Therefore I didn't waste my time asking her for more information, as I knew very well she would not give me any more information over the phone

At the time, we didn't have mobile phones, and the previous attempts from the hospital to contact a next of kin had been futile. I was, therefore, the first one that had been informed, and there was nobody else at the time I could speak to gain more information.

The hospital was an hour away from home, so I got in the car and drove as quickly as possible. While I was

55

driving, I was thinking of my parents, what had happened, how they were, and praying they were ok. In particular, I was thinking of my mum, how she had come to my room on Saturday morning to say that they were leaving, and I almost didn't open my eyes, just a kind of guttural prehistoric sound coming out of my throat to acknowledge her comment. I had got home quite late the night before and couldn't be bothered to make an effort to open my eyes and wish them a safe journey and a good weekend.

I drove fast but not crazy, as I didn't want to risk being stopped by the police. When I arrived at the hospital, I introduced myself, explained what the situation was, and asked for my parents. I was then informed that my dad had sustained a few injuries, including broken ribs, shoulder dislocation, and concussion. They were not life-threatening, and he was being looked after in a ward. "What about my mum? Where is she? Can I see her?" I asked with tension and impatience that were already bursting inside me.

I was told, "I'm really sorry, but your mum was pronounced dead at the scene."

And that was it. In a split fraction of a second, a car crash and a beautiful life gone, my mum's. Her life ended. So was my medical career.

Chapter 13

After my mum died, our household collapsed. My dad was a great man, but my mum was the glue that held the house together. We tried to move on, to carry on with our lives the best we could, but it didn't work out very well for any of us. At the time, I felt very angry with my life. I unconsciously blamed my dad for my mum's death, as he was driving that day. We started going out drinking and smoking, and more drinking and more smoking, and then more drinking again. I was initially doing low-paid jobs here and there, factory work and night security, as a temporary measure, as I always thought it was a matter of time before I would get back into a studying routine. After a while, it became quite clear to me that I wouldn't be able to resume my studies, at least for a while, and I started looking for better jobs. Better jobs I did get, in the sales industry, mostly, and I ended up doing some courses for an insurance company. With better jobs came better salaries, but the more I earned, the more I spent. I was out four to five nights a week, not always with the best company. It did spiral a bit out of control at times. I treated my lovely, kind, and caring girlfriend appallingly, and to this day, I feel ashamed of what I did to her and many others during that time. They certainly didn't deserve it. In my defence, I could say that half the time, I didn't even know what I was doing. So drunk and angry inside I was at times, but still, it's no excuse. I always wondered how I could be out so much, drink and smoke so much, go home to have a quick shower and a change of clothes, and go to work and perform! I never understood how I managed, but it certainly took its toll physically and mentally.

Five years went by, wasted, one may think, and I would certainly agree in my case. The promising life that I had dreamt of was all but gone. In those five years, I saw lots of things which I didn't need, nor want, to see, and I did lots of things that I shouldn't have done. But by then, it was done. I couldn't change it. The lovely person that five years back wanted to become a doctor and save lives was doing the opposite and ruining the lives of anyone that would get too close. It was very toxic, and the more I was doing it, the deeper I was getting into the hole, the darker my world, and the more I hated myself. I hated the person I had become, and I blamed everybody for my failures and inadequacies. It took a long time for me to realise that my dad was not responsible for my failures, particularly not for me dropping out of medical school, but rather my lack of maturity in dealing with the inevitably difficult circumstances following my mum's death. It wasn't my dad's or anybody's fault, for that matter, but mine. Sadly, I never got to say to him how much I loved him and that I was not blaming him for my life. It would have been nice to say that to him in person, but the opportunity didn't present itself, perhaps, and also, I have always had difficulty expressing my most intimate feelings. It doesn't come naturally to me. I know, however, that my dad knew that meeting Poppy had changed my life. She had saved me. He saw the transformation in me. With my beautiful Poppy, I eventually found my peace, and I know how big a weight off his shoulders that was. I know he knew.

However, one day I woke up, and something happened inside me. It was as if my mum was telling me off, which she very rarely did when alive as she was too good, saying that it was time for me to change things. Enough damage was already done. I had my bit of fun, but at what cost? I had sold my soul to the devil and paid too high a price. That was not the person I was supposed to be, the person they, my mum and my dad, had brought into the world with so much love, kindness, and support in my upbringing. Wasn't

I ashamed of what I had become? The time had come. I had to stop being this horrible person wasting his life and hurting everybody along the way. I had to go back to the person I was before, even starting a new life, if necessary.

That is one of the weirdest experiences I have had in my life. I knew it could not be real. My mum could not be physically speaking to me. After all, she had been dead for many years. Yet, it felt so real, she was talking to me from high up, on the left, at the corner, and it was clearly her voice that I could hear pronouncing those words. I don't believe in the supernatural, neither am I very religious, and I do not know whether there is life after death. However, I believe in God as that All-Powerful Entity, and although I lost my way for a while, He, our Lord Almighty, gave me another opportunity, for which I will always be grateful. The way it was going, I could have easily ended up one day in a hospital, in prison, or worse, like some of the people I knew at the time.

I also believe that our loved ones, truly loved and special ones, they never leave us. Although they're physically gone from this world, they will always be with us, in our hearts and our minds. Our memories of the wonderful times together keep them alive, and they'll never truly leave us. Therefore, I believe that, borrowing a bit from Paul McCartney's amazing song 'Let it be', when I find myself in times of trouble, my loved ones come to me, speaking words of wisdom... and so I think it happened with my mum that day and it has happened a few times since, when things have been really bad, and I have felt utterly lost, very lonely and desperate, in complete darkness. Somehow, help and guidance seem to have been given to me at very difficult times.

In any case, that morning after the supposed words from my mum, I just suddenly realised what I had been doing those last few years. I felt very angry inside with myself for having allowed my life to become that way. It was the wake-up call I needed to change things. However, I didn't feel I could do it there, living at home: too many bad memories, tensions, arguments, and bad companies. I thought about it and made up my mind. The decision was made, and I gave up my job. And that is how one day I said my goodbyes to my dad and brother at a Barcelona station, got on a coach with an open ticket destination to London, a bag packed with two pairs of jeans, a jumper and a few T-shirts, a few pounds in my pocket, and left in search of a much-needed break and a new life.

Chapter 14

Meeting Poppy was the best thing in my life. I clearly felt very attracted to her physically, which has always been very important for me, but it was Poppy's personality that seduced me and made me fall in love with her. She was unique, the missing piece in my life. She 'completed me' and made me feel like I had never felt before. I am not special by any stretch of the imagination, but she was so special that just being with her made me feel special too. In reality, and this came to me as a huge surprise, being with her was all I needed to make me feel good, to be happy.

It may be difficult for people to understand, and before I met Poppy, I don't think I would have understood it either, but anyone that has ever been so fortunate to meet that special person in their life will know. You love that person so much, with a love you never thought yourself capable of, and you would give your life for that person, literally. Nothing makes much sense without that person, and you can't conceive your life without them. In years to come, I would ask God many times to take me instead of her, as she was so much better and deserving than me, but, as we all know, things don't work that way.

However, you can only have true happiness in a relationship with the right person by your side. Otherwise, any attempt is futile. And in my case, that happened with Poppy. I have always said that for me, there are two types of happiness: external happiness and internal happiness. The external one, as important as it is, is what I had the last ten years of my life. I would have it with more material things or experiences, going out with friends, having a good time with girls, going on holidays or to a restaurant, for example, but for me, it is fleeting. Difficult to explain, but the more you have it, the more you need it, and it becomes like an addiction. In a way, I was living my life like a drug addict looking for the next fix. The true happiness, however, the one that eluded me all those years, the one that made me feel at peace with myself, the people around me, and the world, is the one that brings a sense of calmness, inner tranquillity, and stability to my life. It gives me internal peace. That, for me, was far more difficult, and it was only through meeting Poppy that many things started changing in my life and inside me, and in time I would find that internal happiness. Poppy was the catalyst in my life that started the process of internal healing, and thanks to her unconditional love, support, and kindness, I would finally be at peace with myself and accomplish many things in my life.

That is the main reason why when Poppy's leg started deteriorating, and a decision had to be made about our dancing career and our future direction in our lives, there was no hesitation. Furthermore, I had seen first-hand the effect that dancing with another partner may have on one's relationship. All the hours I had spent training with Poppy, I would have to spend now with someone else, travelling to the competitions with that person, etc. I had seen many broken marriages or relationships due to that, and we all knew how easily that could happen in that world. I had no interest whatsoever in putting myself in that situation and even less when that would mean not being able to spend time with Poppy. That is how after all those years of hard work, sheer commitment and dedication, and huge sacrifices, our dancing career would come to an end. Poppy was my life. Dancing was secondary. Therefore, no regrets.

However, it would still be years from the moment I arrived until I met Poppy. Little did I know at the time that one day our paths would cross and I would meet this most extraordinary person, this amazing human being, the person that would become my wife and true companion in life, my beautiful Poppy.

Chapter 15

Arriving at Victoria coach station after a 24-hour journey, with just a written address in one's pocket and without speaking the lingo, won't be the ideal scenario for many people to start a new life. Neither was mine, but here I was. However, before coming to London, I had spoken with some people that had been here before, and they had given me some tips on what to do once I arrived.

Also, a friend of mine knew someone here, and they arranged for me to spend the first night in their flat. I had studied a bit the map of the tube, and therefore I knew exactly which line to take and which station to go to. I made my way to Elephant and Castle, and at the station, I was given directions more by hand signals than anything else as I couldn't understand what they were saying, but I somehow found the house. I knocked at the door. A young English girl opened, the flatmate of my friend's friend. They were very kind, and after the introductions, they took me to a pub. After a while, suddenly, I heard this bell ringing inside the pub. They explained to me that it indicated it was time to place the last orders. I looked at my watch, and it was 10:30 pm. I almost fainted when they told me they close at 11:00 pm. In Spain, I would be getting ready to go out. That was my introduction to English life!

I slept very well, got up in the morning, and thanked them for their hospitality. I needed to look for accommodation, and they explained to me then where there would be many ads to start looking for. There were some in Spanish, I tried a few, and one had a room available to share. It was in Willesden Green, and so I made my way there. It turned out that I was sharing the room with a boy from Madrid, similar age as me, and we got on very well. Don't believe what they say about people from Barcelona not liking the ones from Madrid and vice versa. When we get together, we have fun!

After a few days of sightseeing with a phrase book as my best companion, as I didn't speak English at the time, I had to make a decision. I had money to last me for a couple of weeks at most, therefore either I found a job or I had to go back home, as I had an open return ticket. That night I decided that I would get up early the day after, be in Oxford Street by 9:00 o'clock in the morning and start looking for a job. It was not easy. My very few words in English totally insufficient, but I was always told that a please, a thank you, and good manners will get you far. On this particular occasion, it got me as far as having been offered four jobs by 3:00 pm. All of course, in restaurants or hotels as washing-up or similar. Hard work and lowly paid, but it was a start. I chose the one in a hotel because of the working hours, Monday to Friday, 7:00 am to 3:00 pm. That would leave me the afternoons free, and I could study English. I had decided that I would stay for a year, learn the language and then decide what to do. Slowly, my English improved, I got a better job in another hotel, I did some courses, and got a few promotions.

A few years went by, and slowly I felt I was in a better place. I had lots of friends, and I was going out a lot, but still, there was an area of my life that didn't go very well: relationships. Being in London, young, single, and with a bit of money in your pocket, it is a paradise for meeting women. I met some younger, older, in between, blonde and brunette, of many nationalities, and it was always the same. Not only did I not find myself attracted to any of them, apart from a couple that lasted two to three months, but I also had great difficulty in trusting a woman, based on my experiences in the past. Furthermore, as soon as they started getting serious, I was gone. I had this enormous fear of losing my freedom, of not being able to do what I wanted, when I wanted, how I wanted, and the thought of being controlled horrified me. However, at the same time, there was a gap that was growing inside me. Something was telling me that there was something missing in my life, and I didn't feel happy inside. I knew I hadn't been happy for a long time, but there was something different this time. I needed my external fix more often, and it had less effect every time. And it was at this particular time in my life that I met Poppy, my beautiful Poppy, and, as they say, the rest is history.

Chapter 16

We had stopped dancing, but Poppy's leg would never be the same, although, for many years, she could still lead a more or less normal life. However, they say that bad things come in threes, and that was certainly the case. Poppy's leg was the first.

At the same time, our very old and high mileage car had a problem with the gears, and it would also need a new clutch, full service, and brakes replaced. We loved that car, as we had been to many places with it and had fantastic memories. It was Poppy's car when I met her, a red Peugeot 309, but it was only a 1.3-litre petrol and already almost a quarter of a million miles on the clock. It was time to say goodbye, and we took it to the scrapyard. We used to laugh about our car, saying that it was always one of the oldest cars on the ferry or the Eurotunnel train in our many crossings to the continent. On our last holiday, we were in France crossing the Massif Central, fully loaded, including bikes, and clearly struggling on the uphill. We pushed the car as much as we could but still in the slow lane, being overtaken by all kinds of vehicles. Very embarrassing for someone that loves speed! In any case, I had given up a long time ago on my racing habits. I was also very conscious of having other people in the car with me and being responsible for their lives. However, I would have certainly liked a more powerful engine at the time. In any case, there we were, plodding along in the slow lane, being overtaken by everybody, and I started laughing, unable to stop.

Poppy looked at me and said, "What's happening?" I looked at her, still laughing, and I said, "You see, Poppy, we always say our car is almost the oldest car in our crossings. Well, now we might not only have the oldest car but also the slowest car!" With that, we continued our journey laughing and talking and making jokes, and needless to say, we had a fantastic holiday.

The problem with the car was easily solved. One of our dancing friends was a motor dealer, and he got a nice sports car for us at a very good price. Sorted.

The third issue was not so easily solved, sadly. A year after we stopped dancing, Poppy noticed something in her left breast that she had not noticed before. She made an appointment with her GP, was referred to a clinic, did some explorations, tests, and biopsies, and before we knew, she had been diagnosed with a type of borderline breast cancer! She was then sent for more explorations, and by then, they had discovered she had a few nodules in her right breast. More biopsies, sent to different centres for examination, and still, the histology was not conclusive.

At the time, double mastectomy was put on the table as a possible treatment, followed by chemotherapy, but Poppy declined as the biopsies had not been conclusive. We talked about it, and as usual, I was in agreement with her decision. I also felt that to undergo such radical treatment without total certainty on the diagnosis was not the right path to follow. She also had her previous experience with chemo and radiotherapy, and she didn't fancy it in the slightest.

Furthermore, Poppy had these most beautiful breasts, and I knew how important that part of her body was to her. How feminine it made her feel when she was wearing the sexy lingerie I would buy for her and how much she liked the contact of my hands caressing and my lips kissing that area. However, would she had decided to have the operation, I would have also supported her 100%, as we had discussed. With or without breasts, she would have always been my beautiful Poppy.

Eventually, the medical team, together with the oncologist, decided that the best course of action was localized radiotherapy. They could then target the affected areas, and the side effects were not that pronounced. It was just before Christmas, and they agreed to start treatment on the Monday first week of January after the celebrations. That Christmas may not have been the best, but for us, it was still wonderful. We were together in our flat, and we put up our little Christmas Tree with the decorations (every year, we bought one or two special ones for us, and we were starting to have a few by then).

Life was still wonderful, and my strong, brave and beautiful Poppy would not be defeated by a few little nodules in her breast!

Chapter 17

When we stopped dancing, we bought some nice bicycles, as cycling was not load-bearing, and that allowed Poppy to be active and mobile. We would go locally or ride on the canal, and she tried to keep as fit as possible and use that leg as much as she could, so she was always on her bike. In fact, she was well known in the area as the lady with the red bike. We got some panniers, and often she would go, do her shopping and come back with full panniers! And that would be many years that we could still have a pretty normal life, like going on holidays or out with friends.

However, as years went by, Poppy's leg was progressively deteriorating, the skin breaking more often, the ulcers more extensive, and taking longer and longer to heal. It got to the point that she had her leg bandaged most of the time. Eventually, she was referred to a specialist wound clinic, and for 2 years, every night after coming back from work, I would clean the wound in Poppy's leg and change her dressing. We tried everything we were told: standard dressing, multilayer dressing, charcoal dressing, maximum strength Hanuka honey dressing, and anything that was mentioned to her that may heal the wound. In reality, she had become a bit of a guinea pig for them. I don't blame anyone; they were just experimenting on her new treatments as nothing seemed to be working, and her leg was getting worse.

The constant infections in the wounds and the progressively larger areas affected made her leg quite smelly, and Poppy became very self-conscious, which, coupled with the increasing pain, started reducing her mobility and made her a bit of a recluse. By then, we were hardly going out or socializing, and we were seeing very little of our friends. I felt almost embarrassed at our friend's and her family's invitations and our constant declining, but Poppy was already struggling a lot by then. Although on the few occasions that we went out, we really enjoyed it, that enjoyment was cut short by the pain Poppy was experiencing, even with the ever-increasing doses of painkillers, already morphine-based, that she was being prescribed. She always put on a brave face when we were out, not letting anyone be aware of how difficult it was for her until it just became almost impossible for Poppy to walk.

The truth is that life was being very difficult for Poppy, but somehow I never seemed to realize how bad the situation had become until the moment she just couldn't stand on that leg. I have always blamed myself for not having been more assertive and forceful all those years, and the many times I asked Poppy to get a referral or see someone else and accepted her evasive answers. I was trying not to get cross with her as I know that I have a strong character, but I always trusted her in everything. She was much more sensible and clever than me, and we both knew that. That is why I always respected her opinion and decision not to seek further assistance and medical treatment then. Somehow I thought she was right, but in hindsight, I think I was just being blind, and possibly it was easier for me at the time to accept her decision not to seek further treatment than to get further explorations and tests that may result in a more sinister diagnosis than an ulcer that was just not healing because of the condition of her skin. Naturally, after three skin grafts, the skin in that area was so poor that the minimum injury would trigger the huge problems she had been having the last few years.

Almost two years had passed, trying all kinds of dressings, and Poppy's leg had been getting worse, much worse. It was around July time, and we were in the garden. By then, she couldn't really do much but still always wanted to be there with me, to support and help when I was doing some work. And it was then, when trying to help me a bit, moving things around, that suddenly her leg gave way. She fell on the floor, crying with pain, and told me she felt that something had happened inside her leg. I didn't know what she meant by that, but I obviously didn't like the sound of it. It was a Sunday afternoon, and we should have gone to A&E immediately, but Poppy said she would rather wait until Monday and speak to the GP as he knew all her medical history and would be able to advise the best course of action. Again, I gave in, not wanting to have an argument with Poppy which, ultimately, I would not win. And up to a certain extent, I could understand her position.

The truth is that over the years, Poppy had been so many times in so many hospitals, seen by so many doctors, and had so many procedures, tests, explorations, and operations done to her, that she was very reluctant to get near a white coat unless totally desperate. She was very independent, strong, and brave, but it is also true that my beautiful Poppy could be quite stubborn sometimes. However, as I could also be very stubborn, I tended not to say anything.

In any case, that day we didn't go to A&E. I helped her to get inside the flat and onto the sofa. Then I lifted her leg into a more comfortable position as she couldn't move it, put a pillow under it, and went to get the painkillers that were in the bedroom. She took as much as she safely could, and after a while, the pain started settling a bit. The day after, she phoned the surgery first thing in the morning to get an appointment with the GP, which she was given for that same afternoon. However, her GP being a wonderful man, always very kind and supportive, and fully aware of Poppy's condition, phoned her after the morning session and spoke to her. After that telephone conversation, it was clear that Poppy needed some help, serious and urgent help, and the doctor told her not to come to the surgery. Instead, he would do an urgent referral to a trauma unit so she could be seen and assessed by a specialist. She would receive a letter in the post over the next few days with a date for an appointment at the hospital, and they would take it from there. In the meantime, as the pain was getting worse, he was going to prescribe a stronger painkiller. What that meant was a stronger dose of the same drug, as she was already taking morphine-based medicines.

Over the next few days, Poppy was hardly able to move at all, the constant pain in her leg almost completely incapacitating her. However, I look back, and I cannot believe I didn't realise how bad the situation was. I was still working full time, doing overtime when required and when I was at home, Poppy never complained. She always had her beautiful smile ready for me, playing everything down. She was just sitting most of the time on the sofa, reading her books or with the kindle. She was the most avid reader I have ever seen. She truly loved reading and had always done so. Therefore for me, to see her sitting on the sofa with a book was something normal. It didn't make me think that there was something more wrong than usual.

I will never forgive myself for not having been at home more at the time and perhaps noticing earlier the gravity of the situation, how bad Poppy's leg was, how much pain she had been under all that time, trying to hide it from me so as not to worry me. Perhaps I could have seen a much clearer picture of what was happening just under my nose. But she hid it so well from me! That was my beautiful Poppy, suffering unbearable pain and still trying for me not to worry so I could carry on with my normal everyday life, my routine of going to work and training on Saturdays.

Chapter 18

The truth is that somehow I always knew that Poppy's leg would give her trouble later on in life. I didn't know, of course, how bad it would get, and neither did I think it would be so soon. When I met Poppy for the first time, she had already had the operations, and I saw the state of her leg. Perhaps someone else may have looked at it in disgust, as many people did over the years when her leg was bad, but for me, I truly didn't care. To me, she was always beautiful, and, to be honest, she still had a great body, but it was her personality that was unique. There was no other Poppy. I loved her crazy with every cell of my body, although I know I didn't do it very well at the beginning. I was very opinionated, impatient, and stubborn, and I guess not an easy person to live with. But she was patient, loving, and caring with me, and in time, I mellowed. I became more patient, more loving and more caring, and most of all, more understanding. I was starting to see the world more from Poppy's perspective, through Poppy's eyes, and things that I initially didn't understand when we started our relationship were making more and more sense. We were coming from very different backgrounds, and it took me a bit of time to grasp certain things and fine-tune the relationship. It didn't happen overnight. But from the very beginning, I loved her very much, like I had never loved anyone, I just wanted to be with her, and I would have given my life for her, literally, with no hesitation. Poppy was worth a thousand of me.

Poppy was everything in my life and meant everything to me. She was the person I was getting up for in the morning, the person for whom I was working so hard all day, and the person I was rushing home to after a long day at work. She was the person that had given stability to my life but also made me feel alive, be it going for a walk holding hands, sitting in a restaurant sharing a meal, travelling together, or in our intimacy. There was nobody else I would rather be with. Poppy was that special person who was everything to me, and she wasn't only my wife, she was my best friend, my confidant, and my lover.

For me, a relationship is like a stool with 3 legs: communication, trust, and intimacy. If one of the 'legs' is missing or is too short in relation to the others, the stool will fall, and the relationship will collapse. Communication in a relationship is essential, to be able to talk about anything and everything openly and without fear and to respect the other person's point of view. However, that is not to say that one should say anything at any time, which is what I used to do, usually very badly and at the wrong time: with Poppy, I learnt that things can be said, but in a better way, trying not to hurt the other person's feelings, and at the right time, otherwise it is detrimental. Trust is also essential for me, and that has always been a great problem, as I have found it quite difficult to trust women in general in a relationship because of what I saw and did. Many I met in the past were married, engaged, or in a relationship, so it didn't fill me with great confidence for the future. But I could trust Poppy implicitly, and that, for me, was priceless. The third leg is also fundamental for me, and all my relationships have been quite physically intense. Otherwise, it didn't work. Here again, I could never complain about Poppy: I know it was not easy for her at the beginning, but I tried to be more patient and understanding than in the past and gave her more time. She truly was my Anastasia Steele. That's why Poppy was the only woman I was faithful to, and for 23 wonderful years, she gave me all I needed: communication, trust, and my fifty shades of grey. Once I met Poppy, the grass was never greener on the other side. That's how special Poppy was to me. I had it all!

Apart from being the only person I could talk to about anything and everything and share my inner feelings with, she also was the only person that truly understood my slightly troubled and bipolar personality and the only person that knew how to treat me and deal with me. She knew that I had an excess of energy, that I could be very obsessive about things, and that I would work tirelessly towards achieving my goals. But she accepted me for what I was and knew how to work around it and find solutions to my problems.

Also, I am an old romantic, probably set too much on the ways of the past. It is true that I don't even have much interest in modern ways, but Poppy's presence somehow protected me from a world which does not always make sense to me. It may be difficult to understand, but being with her, I felt shielded from the worse of myself. In all aspects and at all levels, my life without Poppy would have been much worse.

When our dancing career came to an end, I went through a bit of a low patch, uncertain of what to do next. I definitely didn't want to continue working where I was for too long, and the lack of activity and excitement of our dancing life over the last few years had left a void, and I felt a bit lost. Poppy, again, was my salvation. She knew that the inactivity and uncertainty of the near future was affecting me, she would probably say that it was driving me mad, and in the process, I was driving her mad as well. She knew me very well, and she knew that I needed to have a goal, a purpose, a project, something to keep me busy, occupied, and entertained, my mind and body always racing at 100 m/h otherwise in all directions. Her solution? She bought me a guitar, a cheap one, a book for absolute beginners, and a 5-lesson pack with a guitar teacher. Suddenly I had my hands occupied, my brain engaged, and life was wonderful again. At least for a while! In any case, I started playing the guitar, very badly at the beginning, but that didn't matter, it was the most wonderful present for me, and I enjoyed it very much.

Interestingly, the first song I learnt to play with the guitar was 'Let it Be', and somehow it has since always had a special meaning to me. Furthermore, completely unknown to me at the time, destiny would make me have a special connexion to Liverpool through a very special person that I would meet later in my life, but that would happen many, many years after.

In any case, I loved playing the guitar, and with practise, I started getting a bit better. I could even play a few songs, so much so that I even wrote a song to Poppy, chords, and lyrics included, to which I gave the title 'Till the end of time'. Problem solved. That was my beautiful Poppy. She always knew what to do, what I needed, and when, and she would do it for me. And I was determined to do everything I could for her. After all, I owed everything to her, and without her, I was nothing.

Interestingly, the guitar would become something very important in my life, cathartic at times, and for a couple of years, I played a lot, as normal with my obsessive nature. I wanted to sing as well. Sadly, the beautiful and angelic voice that I remembered of my performances at school when I was 12 years old was no longer there. Instead, there was this raspy voice, not able to hit the high notes or be in tune. At least I wasn't deluded, and any thought I may have harboured of a singing career was quickly dispelled. Poppy, however, had to endure every so often my poor attempts at singing, whichever was the last song I had found. We used to laugh, saying that before I start singing, I should ensure all windows and doors were properly closed so the sound wouldn't escape so as not to annoy the neighbours. And Poppy with her earplugs well in! In any case, that was my beautiful Poppy, always putting up with whatever it was my latest crazy idea or obsession. But she meant the world to me, and I still remember a little episode many, many years ago that made me work as hard as I could to provide Poppy with a better future.

It happened on one of our first holidays abroad together when I said something to her that would drive me for years. She had found, again, an incredible deal. Return flights to la Costa del Sol and accommodation in an apartment near the beach for £99 per person for a week. The complex was modern, with a lovely pool, and our apartment was very comfortable. There was an avenue just outside the complex leading to the beach with plenty of restaurants, and every night we would dine in a different one. It was very cheap, as it was when Spain was still using the old currency, the peseta, and we felt like millionaires.

The beach was only ten minutes away, so most days, we would get up, have our breakfast and then head to the beach. One day, we were lying down on the sand, Poppy was sunbathing, and I was applying sun cream to her back. She had the softest skin and a divine back. It was late morning, starting to get quite hot but still very pleasant as it was September. I lifted my eyes, and suddenly I saw something that I had seen hundreds of times probably but had never had such an impact on me until that moment, there, with Poppy. I said to her, unable to hide my excitement,

"Poppy, Poppy, look, look there!" Used as she was at my unexpected and uncontained bursts of excitement and my silly comments, Poppy lifted her head without rushing and looked in the direction I was discretely pointing at. She looked and looked again, and then she said, "What am I looking at?!" And then I said, "Look at that couple. Can you see them?"

There, walking on the beach holding hands in their swimming outfits and a lovely tan, there was this couple in their 60s, both very fit, stylish and elegant for their ages. Poppy looked again, and turning to me, she said, "Yes, I can see them, so?" I looked at them again and then at Poppy, and I said to her, "You see that, Poppy? That is my dream! That's my dream for us, to grow old together, retire in a lovely place like this and go for walks holding hands. That's what I want our life to be in the future." Poppy looked at me with those wonderful, pure, blue eyes, even more now contrasting with her tanned skin, and she gave me her beautiful smile. That was all I needed.

With that, I gave her a gentle kiss, but I didn't say I love you. Even after a few years together and still those words didn't come easily to me. Not even with Poppy!

That image and those words would drive me tirelessly for years as I always feared that Poppy's life wouldn't be too long. I always thought that leg would trouble her, perhaps in her 60s, and I was working as hard as I could to provide Poppy with an early retirement and a happy and enjoyable last few years of her life. Nothing else mattered to me, just Poppy and our future together.

We all have dreams, and we must have them to keep us going, particularly at difficult times in our lives. They don't always materialise, though. Life will throw a spanner in the works every so often, and sadly with Poppy, more often and savagely than with anyone else I have ever known. Looking back from that day on the beach, with a dancing career on the up and a dream for the future, so much had happened. So many incredible experiences shared together, and a fair share of bad ones, too many, one may say, so harsh and unfair. Suddenly there we were, after all those years gone by, after so much pain and suffering, after so many dreams shuttered, on our way to the hospital on a beautiful Sunday afternoon in September for Poppy, my beautiful Poppy, to have her leg amputated.

Chapter 19

The day of the operation was arranged for Monday. The medical team had been superb and rushed the operation to take place as soon as possible. We arrived on a Sunday afternoon for pre-ops, signing of consent forms, and other formalities as the operation was going to be the next day. We spent the afternoon together chatting and, in a way, although the operation in itself would be clearly mutilating, at the same time, for Poppy, it was a chance to improve her quality of life that so dramatically had deteriorated in the last couple of years.

It is difficult to express in words and perhaps to understand, but at the time, I think we were both relieved, and even pleased, that she would have the amputation. As horrific as it may seem, for Poppy, it was a chance to have a life again without the constant pain. I personally just wanted her to be happy again, as I had seen how devastating and traumatising physically and mentally the last years had been for her. I wanted Poppy to go back to being the happy, strong, and independent Poppy I had always known, and not the one of late, hardly able to move, go places and do things without unbearable pain. Of course, I won't deny that there was a consideration of the physical aspect as a result of the operation. Nobody ever wants to lose a limb, I guess even less a leg, but clearly, that leg was of no use to Poppy anymore, and we were thinking of the positive. Still thinking of our future ahead. We kept talking until it was time for me to leave, and as usual, as many times before, I gave her a kiss and said I would text her once I got home. I always did, and then we would text for a while or chat on the phone until she was tired and wanted to sleep.

It is true, many times before I had gone home, leaving Poppy in a hospital bed at night, so many, in fact, I think I had become immune to it. However, this time was different. I was leaving Poppy there, on her own, when tomorrow she was going to have an operation that was very mutilating and would have clear implications on her mobility and independence in the future. I was also worried about the psychological effect that the operation could have on her. We hadn't talked about it yet, but surely she would see herself differently. At least so I guessed, although, with Poppy, you never knew! In any case, I felt very uneasy leaving her in the hospital that night, knowing that the day after, they would amputate the leg of my beautiful Poppy.

On my way home, my mind was in turmoil. A roller-coaster of thoughts, feelings, and emotions: worry, elation, fear, hope, acceptance but most of all, sheer admiration for Poppy. Even after so many years and so many incidents, it would still take me sometimes as a surprise how strong, brave, and determined Poppy was. She truly was one of a kind.

It is interesting how unconnected events can trigger a memory. That's what happened that day when I was driving home, and I thought of another occasion where I could have lost Poppy. It was a few years back, at least 5 or 6, when I had already finished my degree, and having more time, I was going to the gym a couple of times a week after work. That day I had finished work and made my way to the gym, but somehow, something inside me felt uneasy.

I always texted Poppy when I was finishing work to let her know whether I was coming straight home or I was going to the gym. We were always texting a few times a day, here and there, a quick text if busy. This day, it took me almost an hour to get to the gym, I checked my phone, and she hadn't replied to my text yet. Then I realised that I hadn't heard from her since lunchtime, so I texted again just to check that everything was ok. As there was no reply, I phoned, but there was no answer. I thought she may be busy, and she'll text back soon. Another half hour passed and still no reply, so I phoned again, and again no answer. My uneasy feeling growing inside. I called a couple of friends and neighbours as she may be at one of them and had forgotten her phone at home. Nobody had heard from Poppy, and nobody had seen Poppy. One of our neighbours went to our flat and knocked on the door, but nobody opened it. By now, I was really worried, that was definitely not Poppy's normal behaviour, so I decided to leave the gym and drive home. On my way, I tried to call a couple of times again but still no reply.

When I got home, I couldn't open the door as it was bolted on the inside. I knocked at the door but no answer. I knocked harder and again even harder, and still no answer. I was awfully worried by now. I went round the back calling Poppy, and when I looked over the garden fence, I saw Poppy lying on the grass, unconscious. I shouted her name, stupidly as she clearly couldn't hear me, threw my bag on the floor, jumped over the fence, and rushed to Poppy. I tried to wake her up, but she was greyish in appearance, totally unconscious, and I couldn't. I checked she was still breathing and called an ambulance.

I was given instructions over the phone on what to do and how to manoeuvre Poppy and place her in the right position, just in case she was sick, so it would not go in her airways. Trying to keep as calm as possible, as in reality there wasn't anything else I could do at the time, I waited for the paramedics that were on their way. I had learnt to keep quite calm in these situations as it wasn't the first time that Poppy had given me a scare. 10 minutes after, there was a knock at the door, the paramedics came in, and I showed them the way to the garden. They attended to Poppy, and they saw that the oxygenation in her blood was already very low, under 70%. They asked me if she was on any medication, and of course, by then, Poppy was on very strong painkillers. In fact, she had almost a pharmacy at home! I brought them the bag with all the meds. Their first thought is that Poppy had overdosed, although it was expressed by asking me whether I thought she could accidentally have taken more (significantly more and orally, that is) painkillers than prescribed. Knowing Poppy, to me, that was nonsense, but how it could have happened, I could not explain.

The mystery was solved when we realised she had accidentally stepped on one of the morphine patches that she was using that must have felt from her arm, and it was still stuck to the sole of her foot. She probably hadn't realised and stuck another one on her arm. I loved my beautiful Poppy with all my heart, but she was a little disaster for these things, always looking after everything and everybody else but not paying enough attention to herself. It was not the first of the many scares she gave me over the years. There had already been others, and there would be more.

In any case, that night, on my way home from the hospital, I thought of how easily I could have lost Poppy that day, and I shivered at the thought of it. I was told that if I had carried on training in the gym and returned home at the usual time, it probably would have been too late. Why I thought of that incident at that time, I can't explain, but it had not been her time again. Therefore, in my mind, as long as we were together, we could overcome anything, including amputation and cancer.

Chapter 20

The last few years have been immensely important in my life. I had, after struggling with myself for many years, found that inner peace that had been so elusive. I could say that I had everything I needed, and I was happy in general with my life. All thanks to Poppy, though.

I had learnt to discern between *I want* and *I need*. For many years I had always been more *I want*, but with Poppy, I learnt what was really important in my life, what I really *needed* that made me happy, and that was Poppy and my life with her. The rest was secondary.

When we stopped dancing, she had bought me the guitar to keep me busy or, most likely, not to drive her mad. I loved it, but it was just a bit of fun and certainly wouldn't give us a future. The interesting and promising prospects that we had of a better future, more stable and financially secure with our dancing career had all vanished. We needed a plan B. The problem is that we had never considered plan A not working. Therefore there was no plan B.

I have always thought that if from something negative, one can get something positive, as minimal as it may be, then you start transforming the bad into good, and the negativity starts shifting into a more positive state. Transmutation at its best. It may be psychological, but it seems to work for me. Furthermore, being with Poppy, I also learnt not to dwell too much on the past and look forward to the future no matter what. With that in mind, we talked about our options, and I decided to study for a degree. From the unfortunate circumstances that prompted us to give up our dancing career, we would make something positive for our future.

Working full time one is a bit limited, but we looked at the options available, and I decided to study with the Open University as it offered the flexibility I needed. I could attend lectures and study after work. In times of assignments and exams, I would shut myself in the room for hours after work and at the weekends a minimum of 10-12 hours a day. Poppy would every so often open the door to check whether I wanted a coffee or needed anything. She would also ask what time I was planning to eat, and she would have the food ready for me, always something light but nutritious. As I was studying part-time, it took me five years to complete my degree, but all the sacrifices were worth it, and I finished my university studies with a First Class Honours degree in modern languages; French and Spanish. Miracles indeed do happen sometimes!

Although it wasn't easy at the time, the simple truth is that it would have never been possible without the amazing support I had from Poppy. My degree allowed me to become a Spanish teacher, which I loved, as not only did I get on extremely well with my students, but they would also get very good results, and the parents were delighted. It was also significantly better paid than my previous job, and we had long holidays in the summer where we would disappear to the continent for weeks. I considered myself very fortunate, and certainly, I was feeling much better about myself and my life.

However, it almost did not happen due to a coincidence of some tragic events. Not only Poppy provided that support all those years, but she was also instrumental in me continuing my studies. That is because one day the phone rang and Poppy answered: it was my brother and he wanted to speak to me. I took the phone, and my brother, without a preamble and with a shaky voice, said, "Dad is dead!"

Chapter 21

It was the time when we were waiting for Poppy to have the radiotherapy to treat the nodules that had been found in her breasts. As always, we did our best to have fantastic Christmas festivities regardless of the looming prospect of radiotherapy treatment in the New Year. And we did!

It was Saturday, and I had just returned from a guitar lesson. I was now going only from time to time. I had a very good relationship with my teacher, who was extremely patient with me, and we always had a good time together. The following Monday, Poppy was starting her treatment every day for 5 days to start with. Our plan for the weekend was to take it easy and possibly have a takeaway and a nice bottle of wine. We would enjoy, as always, each other's company and get ready for her treatment on Monday.

After the phone call from my brother, on hearing those 3 words, 'dad is dead!', I slammed the phone down. To this day, I still don't know why. I took a deep breath, looked at Poppy, who was standing by my side, clearly alarmed by my reaction, and I repeated to her my brother's words. I was a bit in shock, I think, not sure I had heard properly. In any case, I called my brother back straight away, and then he explained. After breakfast, my dad said he wasn't feeling very well and had gone to the bedroom to lie down for a while. When, after a while, my brother checked on him, he was dead. The doctor said it appeared he had a stroke in his sleep. That was it. With that, our plans for the weekend clearly changed.

The burial was on Sunday, the day after, and I had to take the first plane down to Spain. However, being the weekend after New Year's Day, travelling arrangements weren't easy at such short notice. By now my brother was no longer living in Barcelona, but two hours south of Madrid, so my beautiful Poppy, brilliant as she was on the internet, found a ticket available to Madrid airport returning the week after, which we immediately booked and also a hire-car to be ready on my arrival. Always my perfect PA.

There was something else that concerned me: clearly, I had to go to bury my dad and sort out whichever paperwork we had to, but that meant that I could not accompany Poppy to the radio treatment starting on Monday. It was the first time that I would not be with her for any serious treatment, and I felt very uneasy about it. Although she hadn't mentioned anything, I knew how worried she was, and I was leaving her on her own. But I had no choice.

I buried my dad, and I know how bad Poppy felt she could not accompany me and be there with me. She had no choice either. Her treatment came first. That was the priority. I spent the week with my brother, did the necessary formalities, and then I came back. Poppy came to pick me up at the airport, and it was difficult to explain the happiness I felt inside me when I saw her. It had only been a week, but it was the first time we had been apart for such a long period of time since we got together, apart from when she was in the hospital. The circumstances also were conducive to raw emotions and feelings, and that night was wild!

We had talked on the phone every day while I was away, several times a day, in fact, so I knew about the treatment. Everything had gone according to plan, and it was one less thing to worry about. I'm a bit of a worrier if I have no control over things, and clearly, the week away while Poppy was having treatment here was totally out of my control. The truth is, those days, I felt I was almost letting her down, not being by her side at that difficult time for her. She had already done so much for me in those few years. Thankfully, one of our friends could take some time off and accompanied Poppy a couple of times and was checking on her.

When I came back, I felt a bit down. My dad had just died, again suddenly, just like my mum, and I couldn't say my goodbyes. Déjà vu! Now I could never tell him how much I loved him, how much I owed him. How great a dad he had been and how much I had missed him the last few years. Mostly, however, I could now never tell him that I didn't blame him for my life. My shortcomings and mistakes of the past were all mine. However, thanks to the strong principles they had brought me up with, both my dad and my mum, I had eventually managed to turn my life around, find a wonderful woman and settle in my life. No, I could never say that to him now.

Again, and as always, Poppy was there saying the right words at the right time. She said that my dad knew all that, even if I didn't say it to him. She had seen how much my dad loved me every time we visited him, and she also knew I loved him very much, although unable to show it. But with Poppy, it was always more the way she would say it to me, kind, gentle, and loving, with her hand casually resting on my arm or shoulder.

My head was not in the right place to study, and I was considering deferring and continuing the next year. Poppy, with her wisdom and kindness, told me to speak to my tutor and ask for an extension for my next assignment, and I was granted a 2-week compassionate extension. Had it not been for the wonderful presence of Poppy in my life at the time, I would probably not have continued. But with her, I just felt I could conquer the world. I was going to study as hard as I could and get my degree in memory of my parents, to honour them for all they did for me while alive, as much as for a better future together with Poppy, without whom I would not have achieved what I did. The day of the graduation, when up on the stage receiving my degree, I kissed it, briefly looked up, thinking of my parents, and silently said this one is for you. Then, I looked at Poppy, who was sitting among the audience with our friends. I smiled at her and, engaging our eyes, I also said silently, "thank you," as I knew very well that graduation day would not have been possible without my beautiful Poppy.

Chapter 22

The day of the operation came. I had arrived at the hospital in the morning, although Poppy was most likely to be taken to the theatre early afternoon. Unfortunately, there were some complications with one of the operations in the morning list, and also, the surgical team had to deal with some emergencies, which resulted in Poppy still being in the room by 6:00 pm. Already a very long day, she had been 'nil by mouth' since midnight the day before, but Poppy never complained. Our only fear was that it became too late and the operation would be cancelled that day, although the nurses kept reassuring us that she would still have the operation today.

During the years, Poppy had the misfortune of going into theatre many, far too many times. But it always amazed me how strong and brave she always was, never complaining about anything, just accepting her fate and the circumstances. That day, typical Poppy was like any other day. Although she clearly wanted the operation done and over with, there she was, in the hospital room waiting, just waiting with the stoicism I had become accustomed to seeing in her. There was, however, a bit of anticipation, mixed with some nervousness and fear, when just after 7:00 pm, the nurse came to say that she was next, and they were just waiting for the porter to take her down to the theatre. Before we knew it, we were outside the theatre waiting for the anaesthetist. Soon they were ready for her, and it was time for me to go, as on many other occasions. I leaned over, gave her a big kiss, and said that I loved her very, very much, that everything would be ok, and I would see her soon. By then, I could certainly say those 3 magic words: I love you. With that, I looked into Poppy's eyes, always and still so beautiful after all she had gone through. She smiled at me, saying I love you too and she was taken into the theatre.

As years went by, I was able to express my feelings better. I am very glad of that as I know how much Poppy appreciated it and I suppose also needed to hear it. Another important lesson I learned from Poppy is. I was brought up in a macho society where men are strong, don't expose their feelings, and don't cry. Poppy made me realise that I can be as strong while opening my feelings to her, saying how much I love her, and crying my eyes out. In fact, she made me realise that it was positive to express your feelings, talk about one's problems and worries, and there was nothing wrong with crying. That is not to say Poppy was a softy. On the contrary, she was the toughest woman I have ever met. Interestingly, she didn't open up much either and hardly ever cried. But she made me understand that it can be done, if necessary, with the right person. Yes, I was very glad that day when I could look into Poppy's beautiful blue eyes as she was taken to the theatre to have her leg amputated, and tell her, deeply, truly, from the bottom of my heart, how much I loved her.

I left, knowing it would be at least three to four hours before I heard anything. It certainly was going to be a long wait. As I was walking along the corridor, I couldn't help but think of the beautiful Poppy I had met that evening in May 20 years back. How her beautiful blue eyes and amazing smile had captivated me and stole my heart that very same day. How she had saved me, transformed and enriched my life beyond words. How we had danced at the top all those years back. How the Latin dresses she wore on the dance floor would reveal her legs in all their glory. How those calves and thighs were the envy of many, so magnificently sculpted and firm her long legs were. And how the irony of destiny had decided to slowly take all that away from her, the look, the mobility, the independence, the cancer insidiously making its way through that leg.

All those thoughts were flashing through my head like a series of images, some still, some moving, and I couldn't fight the tears that came to my eyes when I thought that when I next saw Poppy, my beautiful Poppy, she would have only one leg...

Chapter 23

I tried to kill time the best I could, trying not to think too much. Easier said than done, though. Time is the most interesting thing I have always thought, because of its relativity. Our perception of it is always dependent on the circumstances. When we are having fun, it goes so quickly that we even say time flies to indicate how fast it goes. One is having that fantastic time, and suddenly it is gone. It just went so quickly, we say. Sadly, the opposite is also true. In less propitious circumstances, time seems to go so slowly, eternally dragging, almost never-ending. The hands of the watch lackadaisically making their way around the sphere and, with total disregard for how often one looks at it, they don't move any faster.

On that occasion, it was clearly the latter. I made my way to the restaurant as it would be hours until the nurses would come to the room in the ward with some news, and I couldn't face the thought of being all that time in there on my own. I didn't mind being on my own - I usually was - as Poppy didn't have any family close by, and one doesn't want to bother one's friends constantly, as wonderful as they have always been to us. People have their lives.

I looked at the menu in the restaurant. I'm always hungry. That day, however, although I hadn't eaten much the whole day, I had no appetite either. I forced myself to have half a sandwich, as I needed to keep my sugar levels up. Otherwise, I get easily irritable, to put it mildly. I also had a coke. I never had a coke. Only when we were travelling or on rare occasions when we would go to McDonald's or Burger King. That day I had three.

Sitting there in the hospital restaurant sipping my coke, I was pondering the different scenarios when I saw Poppy next. What could I say to her? What should I say to her? In all honesty, I didn't know, but it didn't matter that much at that moment: I would know what to say when the time came. However, I did know very well what I would do, and that was to hold her right hand on my left, gently place my right hand on her left cheek, and as I would be leaning over, looking into her beautiful eyes, I would say how much I loved her and give her the biggest kiss ever. That I would do!

I knew I would do that because I had already done it before. Well, almost. The memories came to me at that precise moment. I don't know why. It had been very many years, and I had hardly ever thought of it afterwards.

We had been together a couple of years, and we were now in our one-bedroom flat. We always said that we preferred to be living together without sharing accommodation and with less disposable income than to share and save money that way. We loved our independence and being together on our own. Also, to have a bit of extra space, so a studio flat was a no-no. The flat also had a garden, and Poppy loved her gardening. One day on her way to the garden, she tripped and hit her head against a rusty nail that was sticking outside the door. The nail luckily missed her left eye by a fraction and went in just over her eyebrow. However, with Poppy, nothing was ever simple and straightforward. She got an infection and ended up in the hospital for weeks! Unfortunately, the initial antibiotics she was treated with didn't have the desired effect, there were complications, and she ended up with meningitis that seemed to be getting out of control. One day I received a phone call from one of the nurses saying she was very poorly and I'd better go. When I arrived at the hospital,

Poppy was in bed, unconscious. It was the first of a few scares she gave me over the years.

It wasn't her time, though. Although it may seem difficult to believe, Poppy was very strong and healthy, apart from her leg, of course. They administered every possible antibiotic they could think of, and although it had been touch and go, the day after, she regained consciousness. However, when I saw her, she looked poorly, very poorly, thin and pale. Her eyes sunk in the orbits, but she certainly recognized me. Those were the memories that came to me that day when I visited her in the hospital: as soon as I stepped through the door, I saw her face radiating, her eyes looking at me open, bright, loving, her beautiful smile again on her face. That melted my heart, the vision of me arriving to see her would cheer her up so much and give her that happiness. I was so proud I could have that effect on her. That day, I held her hand, leaned over, and kissed her. However, I didn't say I loved her. Those words were always so difficult for me to pronounce at the beginning. But I did love her very much, and I wanted her to love me that much as well. In our early days together, I used to think that she didn't love me as much as I did, but as time went by, I understood that her way of showing love was just different from mine. I was very physical and tactile, and she was less. As it was difficult for me at the beginning to pronounce those magical 3 words, 'I love you', it was difficult for Poppy initially to show that affection in the physical way I was more used to. However, in time I realised that she loved me so much more than I ever could.

Chapter 24

After a couple of hours, I made my way to the ward. I asked the nurses at the station if they had had any news, to which they replied that they hadn't heard anything yet, but they would inform me as soon as they knew. They told me that being that sort of operation, which is very traumatic and stressful on the body, Poppy would be taken to intensive care to be in observation overnight.

Another interminable hour went by, and it was well past 11:00 pm by now, and still no news. Of course, experience had taught me there was no point in keep asking the nurses, and they would let me know as soon as they knew. Furthermore, I have the utmost respect for the incredible work they do, particularly the first few hours of their night shifts, when they always seem to be so busy. I wasn't going to keep pestering them. They already had enough on their plates. Around 11:30 pm, one of the nurses came to the room to tell me that they had phoned from the theatre saying that Poppy was already out. Everything had gone well, she was being taken to the intensive care unit, and I could make my way there. The nurses explained to me how to get there, as intensive care was in a different part of the hospital. I made my way to the unit with mixed feelings: on one hand, my heart was pushing my legs quickly forward in anticipation of seeing Poppy, and I couldn't wait to be reunited with her. On the other, my head was slowing them down, the uncertainty and anxiety of not knowing what I would find, what to say when I saw Poppy. I would find out very soon.

I got to the intensive care unit, rang the bell outside the door, and a nurse came. I said I was coming to see Poppy and that she had just been brought up from the theatre. She confirmed that and said they were going to get her ready, and then I could come in. More waiting outside as customary. One gets used to it, but on that occasion, I was really anxious and nervous.

It was almost midnight, the nurse came to get me, and I followed her. I asked her how Poppy was, and she said that she was doing very well, but she was very sedated and wouldn't be able to talk much. Also, I could see her briefly, but then I would have to go as they didn't allow visitors to the unit. But they understood I wanted to see her, and they would give me a few minutes, for which I was extremely grateful.

She stopped by one of the beds, said she would come and get me in a few minutes, and with that, she let me there with Poppy.

Chapter 25

There she was, my beautiful Poppy, lying in bed, very pale indeed, with the drips and drainage bags connected, looking all the worse for it. Yet, looking at her, to me always so beautiful. She was indeed very sedated and was not aware of my presence.

Even to this day, I ask myself what I was expecting. It is clear what it was going to be. Yet, somehow my brain had not envisaged the image that would meet my eyes when I looked at Poppy from the waist down. To this day, I haven't forgotten the harrowing vision that assaulted my eyes. Under the sheets, on the right side, there was the contour of Poppy's right leg all the way down. On the left side, however, under the same hospital sheets, immaculately white, without a crease, reflecting the light, which was so bright as to attract one's attention, there was… nothing!

My eyes were glued to that area, my brain processing the unfamiliar and totally but naively unexpected vision, like trying to make sense of it, trying to get used to the flatness of it. I felt bitter inside. I thought how cruel life had been to Poppy so far, how undeserving she was of all that misfortune. At the same time, I was glad the worse was over, or so I thought at the time. Little did I know!

In any case, after all that Poppy had gone through the last few years, I was glad the operation was over. Perhaps now she would have the chance to have a life again, without all the pain and suffering. And I was determined to do all I could to ensure that would be the case and we would still have a future, slightly different, of course, as adaptations inevitably would need to be made, at all levels, physically and mentally. But there was something very clear in my mind, Poppy was still here, alive, with me, and I loved her more than ever. I would fight even harder for us.

I was on the right side of the bed. I held her right hand with my left, at the same time caressing her face with my right hand, the light touch of my fingers on her cheek as if with that gentle touch I could say how much I loved her, give her all the strength in the world, and suddenly heal her.

With the biggest lump in my throat and fighting the tears wanting to burst, I leaned over and said in a low voice, "Hi Poppy, I love you so, so, so much. We're going to do it together, and we'll be all right."

Surely not the most inspiring words. Those lines wouldn't get me an Oscar. She tried to respond to me, half opening her eyes and trying to say something. I asked her how she was feeling, but there was not much response. She was far too sedated. I just stayed there, by the side of the bed, looking at Poppy and holding her hand for a few minutes until the nurse came. She said what I had already been told: it was a very traumatic operation that put a lot of stress on the body. I should now let her rest, and she would feel better in the morning. With that, I kissed Poppy goodnight, saying again how much I loved her, and to get some rest, and I would see her in the morning. Almost no response from Poppy. I made my way out of the ward, and when out of the building, I called her dad, our best friends, and my brother to let them know the operation had gone well and Poppy was now in intensive care for the night. I would call them again in the morning once we had spoken with the doctors.

It was almost 1:00 am, and I very much welcomed the cool night air of September, a thousand thoughts per minute racing through my head as I was making my way to the car park. I had forgotten where I had left the car in the morning, but I found it easily, being very few cars in there at that time. I opened the door, sat in the car, and cried as hard and loud as I could, the pain I felt inside me so raw, bitterly oppressive, tearing through me. I sat in the car for a few minutes, and then I made my way home. I opened the door, our 2 cats welcoming me home with their meows. After I fed them, changed the water, and cleaned the litter trays as customary, I made myself a coffee and sat on the sofa.

Our cats had been a lifesaver for Poppy, keeping her company the many days she was unwell and I would be working long hours. One in particular always seemed to know when something was wrong with Poppy and would hardly leave her side. The other would give her cuddles and purr as if there was no tomorrow.

Anyone that has had pets will know that the bond between a human and an animal is something very special. They're your best friends because they give you unconditional love and companionship, particularly with people on their own, even when things are not well with them when they're sick or in pain. You see them as one of your children. They are a massive part of your life, and you would do anything for them. And if you don't have children, as was our case, they perhaps are even more important and special, almost a substitute for the children one couldn't have.

Poppy and I had always wanted to have children once we were more settled and our future more financially secured, which was supposed to be once we started teaching dancing. That, however, never materialised, so once we stopped dancing, we tried. I would have loved to have children, and so would have Poppy. I knew she always wanted to be a mother, and I have no doubt she would have been the most wonderful mum, always so caring, loving, and supporting, and I would have tried to be a good dad. We tried a lot but to no avail. Poppy's radio and chemo in the past had taken their toll, and she had also had some cysts in her ovaries in the past that had required surgery: unfortunately, to our despair at the time, she could not conceive naturally. We spoke about it and tried IVF. We did 3 cycles, but they were all lost at some point in the implantation period in the uterus. I know that affected Poppy very much, not only because she could now not have the children that she so wanted but also because she felt she was letting me down. However, to me, it was very clear that I would rather be with her without children than with anyone else, even if they could give me a child. I made that very clear to Poppy as well, and hopefully, it made her feel a bit better. The truth is that I couldn't think of my life without Poppy: even after just a few years, she had done so much for me already.

I was sitting on the sofa, thinking about Poppy. Just sitting on the sofa, unconsciously sipping the liquid from the cup held in my hands, my sight lost on the wall, utterly sad inside me, and Poppy's image lying in bed with a leg amputated engraved on my mind. But I had made my decision: Poppy needed me more than ever, I would do all the crying tonight, and from tomorrow, we would take the bull by the horns. I knew I wouldn't sleep much that night, but I was used to it. I would get up in the morning, have a shower and go to the hospital to see Poppy. Tonight was for crying, tomorrow for fighting, and I had to be strong for Poppy. I would work even harder and do my very best to ensure that Poppy was ok and we could have the best possible future together. After all, I couldn't conceive my life without my beautiful Poppy.

Chapter 26

I have said it before, and I will say it again. I have never met anyone like Poppy. The day after the operation, the surgeon came to visit her and asked her how she was feeling. He explained that the operation had gone very well from a surgical point of view. They had removed all the area affected by cancer and a margin that would ensure that cancer would not affect any other areas. After the initial visit from the surgeon, a team from the physio/rehabilitation department came and started explaining what would happen next, how they would get her out of bed as soon as possible, start the physio, and in a few weeks, with the swelling reduced, arrange an appointment to do a cast in plaster so a prosthetic leg could be made.

The day after, the physio team got her out of bed in a wheelchair in the morning, and in the afternoon, Poppy was already moving about on crutches. There she was, having had an amputation less than 48 hours ago and already mobile. Crazy as we both were, she was doing so well that we made our way to the hospital's cafeteria and had a drink. Poppy wanted a nice drink from the cafeteria, and who was I to deny her that?! She trusted me that much, I suppose, she said I could hold her if she stumbled, and at the time, I was fairly strong, and I could have held her easily. However, that probably wasn't the wisest thing to do, and when we returned to the ward, the nurses were horrified. In any case, as Poppy didn't want to waste any time on her recovery, the day after, we were at the hospital's rehabilitation unit, and she was already starting the physio-rehabilitation exercises.

If I said that I couldn't believe my eyes, I would actually be lying. I knew Poppy very well, how strong and determined she was, physically and, most important, mentally. She was always an inspiration to me.

That is not to say that it was easy at the beginning. On the contrary, to say that, at the time, it was difficult is an understatement. The process was slow and painful. The inflammation on the area of the amputation had to reduce, the scar had to heal, and she had to deal with phantom pain. She would tell me many times how she could feel the pain like a vice gripping her leg, that is to say, her left leg, the one she didn't have as it had been amputated!

Every night after dinner, we would sit on the sofa, I would apply a special cream to the scar to aid healing, and I would massage her stump with a product we had been given to reduce inflammation and swelling. We were doing everything we could to speed up the healing process. At the same time, we were going to the physio unit as often as they could get an appointment for her, and she was doing amazingly well in the use of her stump with her practice leg. The therapist was commenting on how fast she was progressing, as an amputee needs to learn to use different muscles in order to effectively use the prosthetic leg.

It appears that in a lower leg amputation, as the knee is preserved, it is comparatively easier for the amputee to learn to walk with a prosthesis. However, in a high leg amputation, for instance, mid-thigh, as Poppy had, the absence of the knee requires the use of muscles that we are not accustomed to using to propel the leg and therefore makes it much more difficult.

I took a few weeks off but then when I returned to work, we requested the latest appointments on the day that, luckily, was the least busy, as then I could drive Poppy to the hospital. I saw the frustration when she did not get the practice leg moving, but also the determination to keep going, and she never complained. I cannot even begin to comprehend how difficult it must be for someone who used to live all their lives on two legs suddenly to be on one and have to learn to use a mechanical leg. Really having to learn to walk again, I suppose, but on one leg.

However, what always broke our hearts was seeing the little kids with their prostheses, some of them no more than five or six years old. We could see the happiness on their faces, radiating emotion, when they were fitted with their colourful 'little legs' and, in seconds, were buzzing around the corridor. Some of them hadn't known any better in their lives. We used to say with Poppy how unfair life is sometimes, and we were not referring to ourselves: I could not put into words the admiration we felt for the kids and their parents, a very humbling experience indeed.

Poppy wasn't a kid, but she was very motivated and kept trying. At home, we cleared an area in the flat so she could lie down and do all the exercises she had been recommended by the physiotherapist, a young Irish woman. She would explain everything to Poppy, would take her time, and was very supportive. She was superb. At the same time, they were amazed at how well Poppy was doing, apparently due to the many years of dancing training, using different muscles, the core muscles in particular, much more than in normal life. Although it had been many years, Poppy still had it!

The truth is that, difficult as it was, Poppy was doing extremely well. After a few weeks, a cast was made, and we were hoping that the prosthesis would be ready before Christmas. We had decided to go on holiday to France for two weeks, and we thought it would be a great opportunity for Poppy to start getting used to wearing it. A seminal moment indeed. Our first holiday away with Poppy as an amputee.

Everything seemed to be going in the right direction. Poppy was much stronger, and the prosthesis would be ready soon, which would enable her to be much more mobile and hopefully give her practically 100% of her independence back. We had decided to buy an automatic car that would allow Poppy to drive and go places on her own as before, and we would start looking as soon as the prosthesis was ready. Our project for the coming year.

The next follow-up appointment was at the end of November in the trauma department. Although they had surgically removed the tumour and got rid of cancer, they had to check that the wound was healing well. However, two weeks before, Poppy had felt a lymph node enlarged in her groin area. I thought this cancer doesn't spread, right? So, it's possibly just due to the inflammation and swelling she would sometimes get in her stump. Surely there wasn't anything sinister? Or was it? That would soon become the beginning of another nightmare.

Chapter 27

The day of the appointment came. I knew Poppy was a bit worried about the enlarged lymph nodes in her left groin, although she wouldn't say much, typical Poppy, just making the odd comment. I was just convinced that it was nothing serious, and I was telling her not to worry. After all, I was the one usually doing all the worrying!

We arrived at the hospital with plenty of time, and as usual, we were asked to wait in the reception area. When Poppy's turn arrived, we were directed towards a room by the nurse, who said that the doctor would see us shortly. Again, a new doctor we had not seen before, very pleasant, as they all were. He looked at his notes and asked Poppy how she was doing. Poppy said she was doing well but had noticed something in her groin that wasn't there before. The doctor then examined her and concluded that yes, in fact, there were some enlarged nodules, but not to worry about. It was probably nothing. In any case, he would arrange for an MRI of the area and some biopsies.

An appointment was given to Poppy two weeks after to discuss the results. The same doctor this time, gladly for us, explained the results of the explorations. The MRI had shown some reactive tissue in the lymph nodes, and the biopsies had shown cellular anomalies: in other words, cancer. Poppy was not cancer free as we had thought after the operation: the cancer had already made its way up from the lower leg to the left groin area.

The truth is that looking back, I realise how many times I wasn't perhaps as supportive of Poppy as I could have been, and my comments reflected that. That was one of many instances in which I should have listened to Poppy more and better. After all, it was her body, and she knew it and understood it very well. Again, I had been a bit dismissive of her comments, as I could not contemplate a more sinister explanation for her enlarged groin nodules than just a bit of inflammation. And again, as usual, I should have listened to her as, sadly, she was right.

I remember feeling very sad and heartbroken after that visit. I had seen the suffering and excruciating pain Poppy had endured over the years, how cancer had been insidiously taking everything away from her, and how that most traumatic but totally necessary treatment, the amputation of her leg, had offered her hope of an independent and decent quality life again.

Poppy was doing very well, and it hit us hard. We had already been discussing our plans for the future; the early retirement in Spain was now more critical, imperative almost. I was determined to work even harder to make it happen as soon as possible. We had been talking about going for walks by the beach, holding hands as we had dreamt of all those years back. There was no reason why Poppy could not do it with her prosthesis. We were totally certain. Yes, it did hit us quite hard. From being full of hope a few weeks after the amputation to realising that it was transitory, and we had a big fight ahead of us. From a prosthesis soon to be ready to allow Poppy to be much more independent to an uncertain future, the only certainty at present was more treatment - aggressive and incapacitating. From our plans to start looking for an automatic car for Poppy in the new year to start looking for a wheelchair.

It may be difficult to understand from the way we lived our lives, but we really valued our independence. We were together as much as possible, and we would always make significant decisions together. We always went on holidays together and out with our friends as well. Rarely we would go out without the other socially, but that was because it was more enjoyable together, sharing that with our friends, and our friends were mostly couples. We always included the other in pretty much everything we did, but at the same time, we enjoyed the fact that one person did not depend on the other. Poppy ran the house completely and efficiently, but I appreciated she would tell me what she had found or bought: then I could say that was great, what a good buy! I trusted her completely and implicitly, as I knew she would always do the best for us. But we loved our independence. We were each our own human beings with very different interests, pastimes, and personalities. Clearly, we shared the fundamental values and principles that solidified our relationship, but perhaps it was the fact that we were quite different in certain aspects and really valued what the other person brought to the table that one lacked: it was being together that made us complete and stronger. In any case, it was important for us that Poppy could go and do her shopping or go to Brent Cross with a friend to do window shopping and have a drink or some lunch somewhere. For many years I worked very hard and long hours to try to ensure an early retirement and a better future for Poppy, and it was important she could go out and do her things. That Poppy could be again mobile and independent was crucial to us, hence the importance of the prosthesis and our intention to get an automatic car for her. Then she could go back as much as possible to the life we had known before.

Needless to say, after that last appointment with the doctor, our world changed again, suddenly and unexpectedly, and Poppy would be thrown into one of the most difficult times of her life.

Chapter 28

Following the last visit, Poppy was referred to the oncology department of another hospital, and due to the proximity of the Christmas period, she was given an appointment to see the consultant in January.

That Christmas, we did as we had planned, regardless of the looming prospect of cancer progressing. As usual, I had checked the water and oil levels and tyre pressure, washed the car, cleaned it inside, and filled up the tank. We were ready! We loaded the car, put our cats in the carriers, and made our way to France to spend Christmas and New Year. Again, as usual, Poppy had managed to get an incredible deal with the crossing. Of late, we were favouring the Eurotunnel as it was significantly quicker and it seemed to have less queues. Poppy's cancer wasn't going to stop us!

The truth is that from the very beginning, we had always tried to enjoy life to the full within our capabilities. Perhaps, as I said, because of our experiences in the past, we both knew very well that life is fleeting, and we felt very fortunate to have found one another. When we didn't have money, we would buy a frozen pizza and a cheap bottle of wine and do a 'big' celebration with a romantic candlelight dinner. We could always afford a candle! And the 'dessert' was left to our imagination!! When we had to stop dancing, we adapted and overcame and always tried to enjoy our new experiences. We travelled more and did different things. Every time Poppy had a big operation or a mishap, once recovered, we would celebrate as if it was our first night together. When she had the amputation, we were continuing as much as possible with our lives as before, and when she had this last bad news, we were not going to sit at home as if it was all lost.

However, like it may have happened to many other people, Poppy had started doing her research. She wanted to have all the information. She wanted to know everything, and the internet nowadays provides access to all kinds of information. It probably is an instinctive reaction, but one also has to be cautious as not all the information provided may be accurate. But Poppy always knew where to look and what to look for. Therefore, even before seeing the consultant, she had a pretty good idea of what was going to happen.

During those holidays, we almost didn't talk about it. In reality, there was nothing we could do until our next appointment, so we didn't want to spoil that time. We just wanted to enjoy it, and we would worry about treatments and side effects once we were back. Now, it was time for celebration and enjoyment, and that's what we did.

January came, and we went to the appointment with the oncologist. The consultant was a lovely man in his mid-forties and always gave the impression that he really cared about the patient.

As it had been quite a few weeks since the last MRI, another one was arranged for Poppy, as well as more biopsies. Another appointment and another anxious wait to be given the results. The MRI didn't lie: unfortunately, it showed that the cancer was progressing, a larger area affected in comparison with the last scan just a few weeks back. Definitely not the news we wanted to hear.

On hearing that news, we looked at each other, both trying not to show disappointment to the other. However, we thought it may be the case as Poppy had told me she felt the nodes were larger, and we were ready for it. It was time for facts and figures, not for bemoaning. Bring it on!

The consultant explained to us that Poppy's cancer was a type of cancer that very rarely would present in the location where Poppy had it, and usually, it was significantly much smaller and fairly contained. However, in 1% of cases, it would behave in a much more aggressive fashion, and that was Poppy's case. The luck of the draw, one may say, and that one had to be my beautiful Poppy!

As the cancer was quite aggressive, the treatment would have to be quite radical. Therefore she would need chemo-rad, which the consultant said would offer the best chance of survival. He explained that the chemo-rad consisted of three courses of chemotherapy, once every three weeks, followed by localized radiotherapy for ten days targeting the affected area. But first, we had to deal with the chemo. When I say 'we', I am under no delusion that I cannot even begin to comprehend what Poppy went through and had to deal with. I was just a passenger. She had to do all the driving.

We were also given some statistics as per our request: the life expectancy of someone with the type of cancer that Poppy had and as aggressive as it was manifesting, was 13% at 3 years from the moment of diagnosis. Only 13% at 3 years! And it had already been almost half a year. It certainly wasn't great. Those figures make your world crumble around you, believe me. However, from the beginning, the consultant was very clear about something: statistics are there for research purposes and to aid in making some decisions, but ultimately it is the individual we must consider and forget the statistics. Every person is different, and we all have minute differences from each other that make us unique. Therefore, the same treatment may well have a different response in different people. The message was: every individual is unique, and we should not worry about the statistics. But one does worry inevitably, even more, when those figures are so hopelessly low!

The next few months would be some of the most difficult of Poppy's life, and her physical and mental strength and resilience would be truly tested. Chemo has dramatic implications, and it is very tough at many levels, but the most important thing is emotional stability, and Poppy was amazingly strong in that department. Thankfully, one would say, as that chemo-rad treatment was so hard on Poppy.

Chapter 29

February arrived, and the chemotherapy treatment commenced. It is difficult to express with words what someone undergoing the treatment experiences: at the very best, a physical and emotional roller-coaster, I would guess. I can only describe a bit of what Poppy went through, as many others do.

The day of the week allocated to Poppy was Tuesday. We would arrive early, usually around 8:00 am, as they would need to do the blood tests and paperwork before she could be administered the chemotherapy drugs. If everything was ok, she would start the treatment around 10:00-11:00 am, and we would be out by 4:00-5:00 pm. If there were issues, like, for instance, a delay in the preparation of the drugs in the hospital's pharmacy, a vein blockage, or an adverse reaction to the drugs, we could be in the hospital until 6:00-7:00 pm or even later.

The following days Poppy would feel pretty rough, very nauseous, and with aches and high temperature. She was also extremely tired, but then she would start recovering. As the treatment was every three weeks, usually the first week she would feel awful, the second week a bit better, and the third week almost normal, unless there were complications, which unfortunately happened every so often.

All chemo patients are given a card with an emergency number because chemotherapy lowers the immune system, and the body is not able to fight infection. As soon as they get a high temperature, they must call the emergency number or go to A&E, and we had to do so on many occasions. In addition, as we all know, there are many side effects. Therefore Poppy, like all chemo patients, would end up with so much medication that we could have opened a pharmacy! The nausea, vomiting, constipation, blood clots, nose bleeds, extreme tiredness, aches, and pains are sometimes very severe, and of course, some chemo will cause hair loss. However, she was told that the drugs 'cocktail', as we would call it, given to her would not usually cause much hair loss.

They had put a line to administer all the drugs, and she would keep it in her arm for as long as possible. Unfortunately, it would get blocked sometimes, a common recurrence that happened to Poppy a few times. Her arm would get inflamed and blueish, but the worse is the risk of thromboembolism, which can go to the lungs and can be fatal. Therefore, we had to call the emergency number and go to the hospital. There she was prescribed heparin injections that must be administered daily for 6 months. Yes, every day for six months! Already hard in itself, as anyone that has had to do it would tell you.

The chemo treatment is not easy, and one must be mentally very strong and have all the support possible to overcome it. If there is something I would have really liked all those times when Poppy was unwell in hospital, undergoing operations, or even feeling so rough at home, it is for Poppy to have had someone close, a family member of the fairer sex to help her, to support her, to assist her. Someone to just be with her and keep her company. I would say to her sometimes, I wish your mum or my mum were here with you, but of course, they were both gone a long time ago. Someone like a close auntie, a sister. I felt utterly inadequate sometimes, so frustrated with myself that I could not do more for Poppy. Yet, she never complained to me, not even once, of not having someone else apart from me, and she never let it show, in all those years, that I wasn't enough. That is one more reason why I loved, respected, and admired my beautiful Poppy beyond words. She was truly exceptional.

Our friends and family were superb as well, always very supportive, trying to help as much as they could, and always asking how Poppy was doing. My brother, in particular, I think, felt that being abroad and I here on my own, he was not able to help how he would have liked. It is one of the problems of living abroad and without family, he was just too far, and Poppy's dad also lived a few hours away, so we had to do everything pretty much on our own. Thankfully we had some great friends that could sometimes help, in particular, an older neighbour and good friend very close to Poppy.

As I mentioned, the next few months would be very hard. I can't recall all that happened, but I remember we talked about it and said we would take it one day at a time. We loved each other very much, and we could overcome anything. On the bad days, we would just do the best we could, and on the good days, we would try to enjoy them. She had to go through the chemo and then the radio, but after, she would be able to go back to physio. A new prosthesis could be made for her, and then we were definitely going to get the automatic car for Poppy to go anywhere she wanted on her own. To regain that independence was so important to us. We really tried to keep as positive as we could. Not an easy task for Poppy with all she had to endure, nor for me seeing my loved one going through it all. But we would do it and then go on holiday in the summer with Poppy's new car!

Conversations with my brother would be almost daily, be it on the phone or by text. Looking back is a glimpse onto a six months period, and as usual, I never realized how much happened to Poppy and how hard it was on her. I think one focuses so hard on being strong to fight every day that one almost forgets what happened the day before.

Chapter 30

A lot happened in six months, some bad but also some good. It was undeniably difficult, but we always tried to enjoy ourselves when we could. After the first chemo session, Poppy felt very grotty. Also, she had a pump that would slowly administer the drug, so we had to go every week for check-ups between the treatment day.

The second week the line got blocked, her arm inflamed, and we ended up in A&E, where they prescribed a daily heparin injection for 6 months. The line would be placed in the other arm, and the week after, she would have the next session. I remember texting my brother to explain and saying to him at the end, "But we are ok. Keep positive and look forward to the summer." Tempting fate? The day after, Poppy had a very high temperature. We called the emergency number, spoke to the oncologist, and were asked to rush to A&E. They ran all the tests and concluded that it was probably the clot. In any case, Poppy was given intravenous antibiotics and was discharged. We got home at 3:00 am. One of many, sadly.

Better or worse, and with a few more minor incidents, Poppy managed to go through the three sessions of chemo. Now it was time for the radio. An appointment was given to Poppy in the radiotherapy department for the technician to mark with millimetric precision the area where they would apply the radio.

It was the second half of April when Poppy had the treatment and to say that she struggled is an understatement. Every day for two weeks, I would rush home after work, pick Poppy up and take her to the hospital. I could see the devastating effect that the chemo-rad treatment was having on her. There were two days when I almost had to drag her out of the house and lift her into the car, so weak and unwell she was. And I remember on one particular occasion, she wasn't even pale. She was grey, so much so that even the receptionist made a comment!

I had never seen anyone looking like that. I know that day Poppy would have stayed at home if it wasn't for me, for how much she loved me. I know she did it for me more than for her. She also had some side effects common to the radiotherapy treatment: redness of the skin in the area treated that started ulcerating, breaking, and peeling off. Poppy had as well some abdominal problems, mainly nausea and vomits, but also abdominal blotting and some bleeding when going to the toilet. That lasted a few weeks, but after 5-6 weeks, she felt much better. We kept at it, and she managed to get through it. It was time to go back to physio and get that prosthesis. What a remarkable woman Poppy was.

She made an appointment for the week after. We felt very positive. Poppy had gone through the chemo-rad, and as hard as it had been, it was now behind us, and we could look again to our future ahead. It was June now, and we were already talking about getting the car and having our holiday in the summer.

Unfortunately, a few days after, Poppy started feeling unwell again, complaining of pain in the stomach and in her back, but I remember saying to her that it probably wouldn't be anything serious. Sadly, I was wrong, and the day after, we were in A&E. They found a problem with her gall bladder, possibly related to the chemo-rad treatment. They administered some medicine that seemed to work, and she had a good night's sleep. She was also given an ultrasound appointment to further investigate. The day after, I went to

119

the hospital at the time when the pharmacy was open to collect the prescribed medicine, and I was glad also to see that Poppy was able to eat a bit better, without all the pain and discomfort. It was the first time in days.

Chapter 31

Poppy felt better after a few days, and another appointment was given to her in the physio department. Unfortunately, in the few months that she had been undergoing the treatment, her leg changed shape, and her prosthesis didn't fit. It was a bit of a blow for Poppy as another full prosthesis would need to be made, with the inevitable delays.

It was now the 14th of July, and I recall perfectly well as it was Bastille Day, and I was talking to one of our best friends who is French. That day they commemorate the storming of the Bastille in the French Revolution and is the French National Day. We were chatting at night, I was asking them about the celebrations, and then they were asking me about Poppy. And they were talking to me instead of Poppy as she was in bed, again quite unwell. I said to our friends that she was having a really bad couple of days with severe abdominal pain and if it continued, we would have to go to A&E. Indeed, a while after, the pain became so severe that we had to go to A&E. Again a drip, again wait for the specialist who concluded that it was most probably a stone in Poppy's gall bladder, again more antibiotics and medicines, again another appointment for an ultrasound, again another five hours in A&E, again arriving home at 3.30. It was starting to become the story of our life, but Poppy never complained.

Poppy was this extraordinary human being, she never complained, and I wasn't complaining either. I still had Poppy, and we were together. That was all I needed. I won't deny it was difficult at times, but God or someone up there kept giving me health and strength to go to work and, most importantly, to help and support Poppy in all she was going through. And she had gone through so much already!

It was coming to a year since she had been diagnosed with cancer, so aggressive and advanced that the medical team had not been able to save her leg. An amputation was the only available treatment to save her life. Then we had realised that, contrary to what we thought, the cancer had already made its way up into her body, and radical chemo-rad treatment, very aggressive and debilitating, had been necessary. Then she had to suffer and endure all the side effects. The truth is that when one is diagnosed with cancer, you just want to get rid of it, and you would probably pay any price. One has the treatment, suffers the consequences, and hopes for the best.

We certainly were hoping for the best, still with our big plans for the future. A few days after, Poppy felt better, and we didn't hesitate: the car that we had ordered had been ready for a few days. A few weeks back, we had been going to the showrooms for Poppy to see the cars and, more importantly, sit in them. It had to be comfortable for her and easy to get in and out with the crutches and/or the prosthesis. After all, she would be driving it most of the time. It would be our first new car together, brand new, with that amazing smell.

We had always had second-hand cars, some of them very old, and we were really looking forward to Poppy driving her new car. But as she had been under the weather the last few days, we had to wait until she felt better. Today was the day! I remember Poppy was so excited about it, and so was I! However, regardless of whether the car was new or not, the important thing is that it would allow Poppy to drive again and go places as she did before. I was so happy for her. She now had a car she could drive.

The day after, we went to her appointment with the physio for the new prosthesis in the new car. She was in there for almost 3 hours, so many adjustments had to be made that day. However, I could see the hope in Poppy's beautiful eyes. A prosthesis to walk without crutches and a car she could drive and go places. That was it. She would regain her independence.

Unfortunately, the new prosthesis kept giving her problems, it was rubbing too much in certain areas, irritating the skin, and being painful, and she couldn't wear it as much as she would have liked. In any case, most importantly, we were now waiting for the next appointment with the oncologist, the first week of August, when we would find out how successful the treatment had been. They had done a full body scan the week before, and we were praying that Poppy, my beautiful Poppy, was now cancer- free.

Chapter 32

The day of the appointment came, and sadly, that visit did not give us the news we were hoping for. The scan showed that there was still some activity in the groin area, so the cancer was still active. In addition, they had detected 'something' in Poppy's breast, and she would have to have a mammography to further investigate, as well as a gastroscopy due to the abdominal problems she had been experiencing of late. Never-ending, it seemed… On the other hand, the good news is that the scan had not shown at present any metastasis in the organs. Another scan would be arranged for the end of September, and then a visit in October to get the results.

With this news, we made our way home. Not the best news, but not the worst either. With Poppy, we always tried to have a pragmatic approach to her cancer, and at this moment in time, there was absolutely nothing we could do for the next few weeks. Therefore, as usual, we tried not to think too much and carry on with our lives. The physical limitations imposed by Poppy's condition had to be taken into consideration, but in our minds, we were still the two young people that had met over 20 years ago, fallen madly in love with each other, and decided to live their lives together to the full. There was still so much we wanted to do, and we were not going to waste any opportunity. Poppy was still well enough to travel, so we decided to go on holiday and enjoy ourselves as much as we could while we still could. And so we did. A few days after, we packed our new car and went off to the border to cross to France.

Although Poppy could travel, by now, she could not be in a sitting position for long periods, so every so often, we would need to stop and have a break. That was no problem, though. We never tried to break any records, not that we could have even attempted it with our cars before. This car also wasn't too fast either, but it was comfortable enough for Poppy to make relatively long journeys without too much pain and discomfort, and that was all that mattered. We could no longer drive around Europe as before, but we could still cross to France and spend some time there.

For us, it was very important to go on holiday. For me, it was the opportunity to break with the everyday routine and to spend more time with Poppy. Most important, however, was the opportunity for Poppy to have a change of scenery. She could disconnect from her life of the hospital, clinic, and GP appointments, of treatments, operations, and procedures, almost non-stop for a very long time now. Having said that, during our visits to France, we ended up in the local hospital a few times, usually due to Poppy's medications running out, her leg getting infected, or being unwell and with a high temperature. As the drugs she was taking were control prescription drugs, we always carried with us a letter from our doctor with Poppy's clinical history and treatment, including the prescribed drugs, professionally translated into French. After all, she was taking morphine, and our car looked like a pharmacy, so many medicines we were taking with us!

Regardless of the few times we had to go to the hospital, it did Poppy a lot of good to be away from here, not only physically but also mentally. She could switch off from the reality of her life here and enjoy the pleasure of the countryside, a much quieter and more peaceful life in any case, and just read, rest, and do her things. We could still go out to the supermarket together. She loved looking at different products, the quirky markets on the main square of the little towns, or the department stores in the bigger cities. By now, she could not really be out on her leg for long periods of time, but enough to see different things and still enjoy being together and sharing those experiences. We would always buy something to bring with us, practical things mostly that she would use, or whatever she liked.

As for me, it may sound silly, but I would derive enormous pleasure from being able to wake Poppy up in the morning, prepare her medication and take her a cup of tea to bed. I'm an early bird, always been, and I never slept much anyway. I would get up earlier, read for a while, feed the cats, clean the litter trays, sweep the patio area, and in the winter, clean the glass in the wood stove so it would be nice and clean when Poppy would get up to start the fire. Then, at the right time, wake Poppy up with her medication and the first cup of tea. I would leave her to doze on and off for a while, and then I would open the shutters, letting the rays of the sun greet Poppy the new day while she was still laying down in bed, half asleep.

It is difficult to explain, but when you see your loved one going through all what Poppy went through, you feel absolutely useless, hugely inadequate, and utterly desperate at times. But you cannot let that feeling overpower you. One must fight it and overcome it. You do it not as much for yourself, as important as it is not to allow yourself to fall deep in a well of desperation and depression, from which it is very difficult to escape. It must be done more for your loved one, as you must constantly put a brave face so as not to show what is going on inside, so it won't have any detrimental effect on them. They certainly already have more than enough on their plate with their cancer and treatment to not have to worry about the effect their condition or disease is having on their loved ones, families, and friends.

That is not to say it is not on their minds. I know it is. But that is also why, at least in my case, just being able to give Poppy her medication and make her a cup of tea or a hot chocolate would be so extremely important. It made me feel useful somehow, and she knew how important that was to me. Every cup of tea I made her, every painkiller I gave her, and every dose of liquid morphine I prepared for her meant hope, and that not all was lost. We were still strong and ready for anything.

As always, we made the most of it and enjoyed as much as we could with our barbecues and with our friends there. By now, it was much more difficult for Poppy to socialize, and we would have to leave early on many occasions, or if she was unwell, we couldn't go. I loved the atmosphere in the little village fete. I find it very interesting to listen to the stories that other people have to tell about their everyday lives, in different countries, with different cultures and mentalities, and from different walks of life. I remember at one of the fetes, we were sitting at one of these long tables, and we had the mayor on one side and the dustman of the village on the other side. Everybody sat at the same table, eating the same food and drinking the same wine. I loved those kinds of experiences, but it is fair to say that Poppy wasn't that keen. Therefore when she wasn't that well, I feel it would have been too much to ask of her to attend. If she wasn't too bad, I would go on my own for a while, mostly just to say hello to people I may not have seen in a year! Say hi to everybody, have a couple of drinks with them, and then go home with Poppy. But if Poppy was in bed or wasn't great, I would present my excuses and stay at home with her. Everybody loved Poppy, and they understood. They also knew me very well by then. Therefore it was of no surprise to them as they knew that for me, Poppy always came first. There would always be another time, another fete, another occasion to socialize and meet up with friends.

I must say, however, that, at the time, even I was enjoying less the parties and socializing. The truth is that it wasn't the same without my beautiful Poppy.

Chapter 33

All good things come to an end sooner than we would usually like, and before we knew it, our holidays were over. Poppy always felt better after some time away without doctors and hospitals. It was time now to come back and tackle everything head-on: the gastroscopy, the mammography, the appointments with the physio for her prosthesis, the scan at the end of September, and the appointment first week of October that would be so crucial for Poppy.

It won't be difficult to imagine that September was a hard month for Poppy, with so many appointments, so many tests and procedures, and, of course, she continued wearing the prosthesis that didn't fit very well. She had the scan at the end of September, as arranged by the oncologist, and we were now waiting in the room to get the results. I was saying to Poppy not to worry and that everything would be fine, but I knew her, and I knew she was worried. The reason I knew that is not because she had said it directly but because she had felt the groin area getting worse, the lymph nodes getting larger, and she was experiencing more pain. I knew what that meant, but still, I would arrogantly dispel the idea that the cancer was progressing. Something inside me couldn't accept that thought.

Regardless of whether my being able to accept the reality or not, the visit left us in no doubt: the treatment, unfortunately, had not had the desired effect. The affected area was larger, and the cancer was still active. The chemo-rad treatment had worked, but not 100%, and some lymph nodes were still active. However, as the scan did not show signs of metastasis, the oncologist said that they would speak to the surgeons to see whether they could remove the lymph nodes that had not responded to the treatment.

We were told that it was a difficult operation: the surgeons would remove superficial lymph nodes and attempt to remove all the iliac ones as well, which were very deep, and they didn't know whether they could all be surgically removed. However, the operation itself was not the most concerning, as long and difficult as it may be. The post-operatory and recovery would be much more challenging. As always, we discussed it, and I would have supported whichever decision Poppy would make. But she felt in a way that she had no choice and agreed to the operation: if there was a chance she could get rid of the cancer, she was going to take it. And I would be by her side all the way to help, albeit minimally, in any way I could.

I remember explaining to family and friends about the operation, the challenge of it, and the difficulty of recovery. But I also remember saying to them that, although it was not the best news, we would continue fighting, and we remained hopeful.

Poppy's operation was arranged for the 1st of November. She had the pre-ops the days before, and everything was ready: the operation was scheduled first thing in the morning. I drove Poppy to the hospital and waited with her until she was taken to the operating theatre. As always, I would give her a kiss, say I love her very much, and see you soon. She would say, "I love you more," our little game. I guess it was our way of downplaying the gravity of the situation, making it as casual as possible, like if we were going to buy some milk at the corner shop. "Poppy, we've run out of milk. I'm going to get some from the corner shop. See you soon." Obviously, it's not quite the same, but after so many times, so many operations, and so many procedures, it was our way of dealing with it.

Knowing that it would be many hours and the hospital wasn't far from work, I decided that it was better to be at work with one's mind occupied than to be waiting in the hospital, doing nothing, as the hours would feel never-ending. We had arranged with the nurse she would call me once Poppy was out of the theatre, and I would make my way back to the hospital.

People would ask me many times over the years whether I didn't feel nervous when Poppy was having an operation. I used to say that all stress and nerves would disappear once she was taken into theatre as then, whatever happened, there was absolutely nothing I could do. It was completely out of my hands and in the hands of the surgeons and the One up there that so far was working little miracles to keep my beautiful Poppy here with us.

The operation lasted six hours, after which the nurse called me at work as agreed, and I made my way to the hospital to see Poppy. As usual, she was fast asleep.

I remember looking at Poppy lying down in bed, with the three drainage tubes from her tummy draining blood and discharging onto the containers and the two drips onto her arms. And I remember thinking how amazingly strong she was, physically and mentally. What a remarkable woman. And I also remember thinking, "Please, God, let this be the end of her suffering and cure her now. She has already suffered more than enough. Just please get rid of this cancer and give Poppy a chance. She deserves it so much!" And again, as on many occasions, I would kindly ask God, if He had to take someone, to take me instead, as she was worth 1.000 of me. But He didn't…

Three hours later, Poppy was much more awake but felt very sick and nauseous and with a lot of pain, which was normal after such invasive and traumatic surgery. After a while, the doctors came to check on Poppy and said that the operation had gone well. They had managed to resect/remove all the inguinal nodes and, as much as possible, of the pelvic lymph nodes and then used a muscle to cover and protect the blood vessels. The problem was that Poppy had had radiotherapy in the area, which we were told may reduce the healing process, and it was more prone to complications.

Poppy had a really bad 24 hours after the operation, but by mid-afternoon the day after, she started feeling a bit better. The nurses had tried to get her up that day, but she was too sick, so they decided to wait until the next day. The day after, Poppy felt a bit better in the morning, and they got her out of bed, briefly though, as nausea returned and she had to be taken back to bed. She had a rough afternoon, but in the evening, she felt better, and they removed the drip, and the day after, they removed the urine catheter. She was getting better, but five days after the operation, she still had two drainage tubes attached, so much it was being discharged, and the nausea was still quite persistent. It wasn't until a week after the operation that she was discharged, and we went home.

I took a week off to stay at home with Poppy and help her the first few days. In any case, now was the beginning of a long road ahead, as we were told it would take months for Poppy to get back to normal. We knew it would be a difficult first few weeks, such a long and arduous recovery process, but we were mentally ready. We were saying that we just had to go through the next few months, and then it would start getting easier. As always, we would take it a day at a time, and next summer, Poppy would feel like new, and with a new prosthesis for her to wear again, as she would sadly not be able to use it now for a while.

Day by day, the days became weeks, and soon it was mid-December. Poppy felt better and stronger, and Christmas was round the corner. We talked it over, checked with the doctors, and the decision was made. She was well enough to travel, and we would go on holiday for a couple of weeks over Christmas. We loaded the car, and on the 21st of December, we crossed to France. We had booked a little hotel an hour from the border to spend the night. Poppy couldn't do many hours at one time in the car anymore, and I had worked that day. I had started at 7:00 am to finish early: went home, loaded the car, and drove to Dover to catch our late crossing. By the time we got to the hotel in France, it was well past midnight: most welcomed to rest and spend the night in the little hotel, which we had already used in the past. The day after, we got up and set off to our destination. I remember that year it took us over three hours to cross Paris, such was the traffic that day, which didn't do Poppy any favours. Still, she never complained. But apart from that we had a fantastic journey and arrived late afternoon. We did the minimum to get the house habitable, I started the fire on the wood stove, and I went to get some pizzas from another village just 10 minutes away, which we liked very much. That was our first night there, and of course, barring Poppy's pain which was already causing some serious limitations, we had a fantastic holiday.

Chapter 34

That break away gave us a chance to recharge our batteries, spend more time together, and talk a bit about the future. Not much, though, as we somehow never seemed to find the appropriate time to have a deep conversation about it, always procrastinating. Poppy was reluctant, and I'm not very good at talking either.

After the operation, Poppy's mobility in her stump had reduced, but the break helped her to regain some strength, and she was ready to start physio again. We also had the next appointment to follow up on her surgery in February, so we were optimistic that things would start improving again.

An appointment was given with the physio in mid-January, and unfortunately, she confirmed the reduced mobility as there was too much-scarred tissue in the area. She was given some exercises to do at home, and I would give Poppy a massage in the area every night for 4-5 weeks. With that, they and we were hoping they could do a cast for another prosthesis in a few weeks.

The problem is that following the operation, Poppy's stump ballooned and kept changing size, which made it impossible for the orthopaedics department to do another cast. The operation in November had been very intrusive, and the surgeons had removed a great number of lymph nodes. Poppy wasn't aware at the time, and neither was I, that the operation would have such life-changing implications. A side effect of the surgery meant that the lymphatic system was not doing its job now, and there was an excess of fluid collecting in the tissues. In Poppy's case, it went to her stump.

I know this was a big blow for Poppy. The prosthesis had given her more independence, and now we also had a car for her to drive. Without the prosthesis, everything was so much more difficult for Poppy, not to mention the extra pressure and stress on her leg and arms, mainly wrists and elbows. At this time, life was being quite difficult for Poppy. Again!

The problem with the stump really worried Poppy. I naively used to say to her not to worry, that it was just a matter of time. It had been a very intrusive operation, and her body needed the time to heal and readjust. In a few months, everything will be ok, as the surgeons had said. The reality was different, she knew very well, and I guess I did as well, although I didn't want to accept it. The lymph nodes had been removed, and the lymphedema was something she would need to endure for the rest of her life.

The first week of February, we were again at the hospital, this time for Poppy's surgery follow-up. From a surgical point of view, everything was going well. The scar had healed, and the surgeons were happy with the result of the operation. However, the last scan, which Poppy had had the week before, still showed signs of activity in the groin area and ascending now to the iliac area. Not the best news, but at least they didn't see any metastasis.

We were told that surgically there was nothing else they could do, and as the chemo-rad treatment had not been sufficient, they were going to discuss with the oncologist and multidisciplinary team to see what could be done. Another appointment was given to Poppy for two weeks after. We tried to keep our spirits up in the meantime, and I remember talking to our friends and family, explaining and saying that we still felt optimistic, but it was certainly taking its toll on Poppy.

Back we were at the hospital two weeks later. This time, we would see the oncologist. He really was a lovely man that seemed to care very much for his patients. It was over a year since we had met him, and he had always been very kind and considerate with Poppy. However, that didn't make the reality more palatable. He told us that, following the multidisciplinary meeting, the overall consensus was that the cancer was still active and now progressing to the pelvic and common left iliac area. In their hospital, there was nothing else they could do for Poppy, and she would now be referred to another hospital much more specialized in cancer treatment.

A timely coincidence perhaps, but in this other hospital, they had just started running a clinical trial with a new treatment, immunotherapy, and we would be contacted to see whether Poppy would fulfil the criteria to be accepted in the trial. One always hopes for a miracle, and I vividly recall thinking that perhaps this was the little miracle, or rather big by now, Poppy and I had been waiting for. After all, she had already had the physically and psychologically traumatic amputation, the aggressive and terribly debilitating chemo-rad, and the even more intrusive and traumatic surgery that had left her with a life-changing condition. Perhaps the time had come for my beautiful Poppy's luck to start changing.

Chapter 35

When waiting for this kind of phone calls, the days seem agonizingly long. We were completely at their mercy, and there was absolutely nothing we could do but wait. Nevertheless, we considered ourselves very fortunate that Poppy could perhaps have this treatment in such a well-renowned hospital, a centre of excellence in the treatment of cancer. Therefore, we didn't mind waiting a bit longer if there was a possibility of Poppy being admitted in the trial.

Eventually, Poppy received the phone call, and an appointment was made for her. It was already the end of April, and it had been a couple of difficult months for Poppy. The pain had been more acute of late, and she felt it over a larger area than before. It was increasingly more difficult for Poppy to have a good night's sleep, the pain usually waking her up in the middle of the night. I would give Poppy her medication, but it wasn't having the same effect anymore. Also, her stump was giving her trouble, even the change in temperature was affecting its size and shape, which made it extremely difficult to cast a new prosthetic leg.

The four weeks from the end of April until the end of May were some of the craziest and more challenging in Poppy's life. We just didn't stop. In the appointment with the clinical trial team, we were told about the kind of treatment it was, how it worked, what drugs they would be using, how they would be administered, and when. However, before Poppy could be accepted to the clinical trial, there were some tests they had to run.

The appointment was on a Tuesday, and as time was of the essence, a full body scan and other tests and explorations were arranged for Friday. The results would be discussed among the medical, surgical, and clinical teams, and if Poppy fulfiled the criteria, she would start treatment the month after. I remember praying very hard those days that the results of Poppy's explorations would make her eligible for the clinical trial.

She had the scan on Friday morning, and in the afternoon, she received a phone call confirming what we already knew, that the cancer had progressed since January. What we didn't know, however, is that the enlarged lymph nodes were now affecting the kidney and ureter. Being Friday, Poppy was given an urgent appointment for Monday, where she would have some blood and renal function tests done, and a stent would be inserted as well.

Looking back now, I can't believe it, but as usual, that weekend, we just did as normal, and we had our little celebration with a takeaway and a bottle of wine. Instead of thinking of the negative, we were always trying to think of the positive, as difficult as sometimes may be. That weekend, for instance, I couldn't really say what we were celebrating, but we always found an excuse. In fact, for us, just being together was a great cause for celebration.

Glad we did, though, as Monday was a very long day for Poppy in the hospital. The results from the blood tests were good, but the urologists were reluctant to operate and put a stent as it was the area where Poppy had had the radiotherapy treatment, and it was already quite damaged. They were going to discuss it among the medical team, and they would tell us the day after, as we nevertheless had to go for Poppy to sign some consent forms in order to have all the required tests and explorations done.

The following day we made our way to the hospital again, and they confirmed to us that cancer had grown and it was compressing slightly Poppy's left kidney and ureter, but her right kidney was working perfectly well, and the renal function was compensated. No stent, for the time being. Thank you very much. A lot of paperwork to sign, though, for the explorations to come, the most important of which was a head scan, as if the cancer was already in the brain, it was game over. Poppy would not have been accepted in the clinical trial.

By the middle of May, it was clear that Poppy's condition was deteriorating. In fact, it had been getting progressively worse since Christmas. The pain was much more intense, the painkillers now having little effect as her body was becoming more tolerant. One day, Poppy was in agony, and we had to go to the hospital, where the explorations concluded that the tumour was now compressing the sciatic and femoral nerves. She was administered intravenous steroids and prescribed a course of oral steroids over five days. Also, the pain Poppy was experiencing in her stump was much worse lately, and they significantly increased the dose of that particular painkiller. We were hoping that Poppy could be maintained stable and with the pain under control for the next two weeks. We were also praying that all results were favourable. If so, she was due to start the immunotherapy treatment at the end of May.

Fortunately, all scans, X-Rays, and tests were ok. Poppy fulfilled the criteria, and she would start the treatment. Sadly, part of the criteria was to have cancer that was terminal and inoperable, words that don't fill you with overconfidence for the future. But that was the reality. The overall condition of my beautiful Poppy had deteriorated significantly in the last few months. Her quality of life was severely compromised by now, and this was really her only and last chance.

Chapter 36

The day of the treatment came. Poppy had to go to the hospital the day before to have some blood tests done, and that would be the normal procedure every time before the treatment day.

As much as I wanted, it was impossible for me to accompany Poppy to all her medical appointments, but one of our neighbours, a retired lady and a good friend, could accompany her on some occasions or other friends sometimes if they were free, could give Poppy a lift. On other occasions, Poppy had to go to the hospital on her own and then I would pick her up or meet her there if there was an important appointment.

I must say that it was one of the hardest things for me not to be able to accompany Poppy to her medical appointments. But there were so many! I knew she was more than capable of taking a taxi on her own, but that was not the case. It was always on my mind, knowing how much pain she was in, being on one leg and struggling with the crutches. After all what she'd been through already and having to go on her own, with nobody to accompany her for a bit of moral support. That was hard for me, although nowhere near as hard as it was for Poppy, of course. Luckily, there weren't that many occasions in which she had to go on her own. As brave and capable as she was, I knew very well that she really appreciated my presence there with her, that tiny bit of help and moral support. As for me, it made me feel just a tiny bit less inadequate.

I took the day off, and we arrived at the hospital well before the due time for her treatment. We felt very optimistic and hopeful that this would make a difference in

Poppy's cancer. We had read a lot about this new type of cancer treatment, and in some cases, immunotherapy had been very successful for certain types of advanced cancers, some of them skin cancers like Poppy had. There had been remarkable results, with some people responding to the treatment extremely well to the point that the cancer had practically disappeared. And I guess one always thinks, why couldn't it be me? Why couldn't I be one of the lucky ones? Human nature, I suppose.

All the nurses in the team were absolutely amazing from day one; very kind, professional and supportive. Poppy sat in one of the comfy armchairs, and I sat next to her. The room was full of patients undergoing different treatments, and the nurses were very busy. One of them was allocated to Poppy and explained that they were waiting for the drugs to be ready and brought up to the treatment room. As soon as she got them, she would be back. A little while passed, and the nurse returned and administered the drugs to Poppy. It all went really well, from the moment we had arrived until the moment we left, and Poppy hadn't had any reaction. After the customary period of observation, we made our way home feeling very positive, as compared to the chemo-rad, this had been a doddle. However, we spoke too early! After a while, Poppy started complaining of pain in the area affected by the cancer: her stump, left groin, hip and lower back. The pain was excruciating, accompanied by very high temperature, incredible shivering and nausea. It was so bad that we thought we had to go back to the hospital. After a while, however, the pain and shivers started receding, and the temperature was eventually brought down with paracetamol. It really took Poppy by surprise, but for the next cycles, she knew what to expect, and we were ready.

We wanted to think that the fact that the pain was so localized in the area affected by the cancer was a good sign. That is because, a difference to traditional chemotherapy, that destroys all rapidly dividing cells, cancerous as well as healthy cells, immunotherapy uses the normal defensive killer cells of our immune system to attack the cancerous cells recognised as alien in our body. Therefore, it would make sense that where the cancer was active is where Poppy felt the pain.

I remember trying to explain this to our friends and families by saying that the treatment did not itself have a direct effect on cancer, but it helped to trigger the normal immunologic response of our body when fighting against disease. Of course, any treatment has side effects, and in this case, it could exacerbate the normal immune reactions of our body.

Poppy's treatment was as follows: the drug would be administered on a three-weekly cycle for a maximum duration of two years. In Poppy's case, she had her treatment on Thursdays, the Wednesday before she would have to go to the hospital for a blood test and other explorations, and there would be a scan every 3-6 weeks, depending. As it was a clinical trial, everything was paid for by the pharmaceutical company, but also everything was completely controlled, monitored and recorded. The caveat was that if the scan showed that the treatment was not effective, it would be stopped. We were praying that Poppy would respond well, and we were counting on another couple of years together. At least!

In my head, I was still arrogantly dispelling the horrible thought of Poppy not being here. She was a fighter, and if someone could defeat cancer, it was my beautiful Poppy!

Chapter 37

The first week of June, Poppy was given an appointment to insert a stent. The multidisciplinary team had decided to try, as although the area was already very affected by the radio and scar tissue and the renal function was maintained, the risk of Poppy's left ureter blocking and causing an infection or necrosis was potentially worse. Her immune system was already very compromised by now.

There were some complications on the day, and Poppy had to be admitted. It was a Monday, she had to stay overnight, and the procedure and other tests were successfully carried out on Tuesday. She was discharged in the afternoon, I picked her up from the hospital, and we went home.

On Thursday, Poppy had to go to the hospital again. This time for one of the regular blood tests that the pharmaceutical company was carrying out. I could not accompany her on this occasion. I remember talking to my brother and saying, "Poppy is a bit in a bad mood today," which was very rare with her. I wasn't surprised, though. Who could blame her: it was the third day in the hospital this week. Stent, tests, blood test, had to go on her own on Thursday feeling awful as she had a temperature in the morning... I knew it was all taking its toll, slowly eroding the greatest willpower and mental strength I have ever seen in anyone. And yet, she never complained, just a bit grumpier on the day. What a remarkable woman and an inspiration for me. I tried to finish work a bit early, rushed home and spent the rest of the day with my beautiful Poppy. Tomorrow would be Friday, and then the weekend when we could be together. Typical Poppy though. By Friday, she was back to normal, no longer grumpy. Truly amazing.

The second cycle went much better. Poppy knew what to expect, she had loaded herself with as much morphine as she could before the treatment, and the pain, shivers, and temperature were less. I used to joke that she took such doses of morphine that it would send an elephant to sleep, but joking apart, if I had taken it, I would have overdosed!

The week after, I accompanied Poppy to the hospice. She had received the 'invitation' a while back, but, not surprisingly, she had been postponing going to see it. I had said to her before, "Poppy, do you want to go at some point to the hospice just to see what it is like." "Not really. I don't think I want to go yet," she replied. If she didn't want to go, there was no point in pushing. I knew Poppy very well, and she was not going to go. It was her decision, and it was fine by me. The word hospice, perhaps mistakenly, conjures negative thoughts. Indeed, it was the centre for patients with terminal cancer in our catchment area, but in addition to end-of-life care, they were also providing some treatments of alternative medicine. I never pushed Poppy to go and see it, it was her prerogative, and I respected it. She would go when she was ready. The alternative therapies, however, I thought they may perhaps be of benefit to her, physically and mentally. We talked about it, and she agreed to go and see it. I accompanied her, we were shown the facilities and then she had a massage and a Reiki session for her pain, which she really enjoyed. It was the first session of many.

I remember thinking at the time when shown around, what a beautiful and peaceful garden. One could hardly hear any noise, just the sound of the birds coming down from the surrounding trees to the water feature in the centre, encircled by some wood benches, plants and trees. Little did I know then that I would be spending quite a bit of time there in the future.

I recall describing the hospice to my brother, how beautiful and serene it was, in particular, the garden. I explained that would be the place where Poppy may go to spend the last days of her life, but that I hoped it would be in many years to come. Poppy's family was great, they kept in touch all the time, and they would come down as often as they could to see Poppy, in particular her dad and partner. As for my family and friends in Spain, on the other hand, being so far away, I suppose it was difficult at times to understand all that was happening. Therefore, I always tried to keep them in the loop as much as possible.

But there was another reason, more selfish perhaps, for my explanations to other people. I had genuine and immense difficulty coming to terms with the reality of what was happening, as clear as it was in front of my eyes. I could not tell myself the cruel reality, I could not accept it, but I could tell someone else. That way, it was as if I could detach myself from it, and it wasn't really happening to us, to Poppy. It was less hurtful. We all have our ways of dealing with difficult or unpleasant situations, and that was mine.

I could easily say to other people, as I did that day to my brother: 'let's be clear, the cancer is terminal and inoperable, and she has deteriorated dramatically in the last few months. It's not looking promising. That's the reality, but miracles do happen, and I just hope they can give her a few more years with an acceptable quality of life. For the time being, I have to be optimistic and keep fighting for Poppy. I'm not throwing in the towel yet, and as long as Poppy is alive, I will always be by her side and will do everything I can for her. After that, I'll see what I do with my life. It doesn't bother me now'. This I could tell to our friends and family, but not to myself. It hurt too much. I was losing my beautiful Poppy.

Chapter 38

July was a very busy month for Poppy. I took two days off to accompany her to the hospital on pre-treatment and treatment days. It would be her third cycle. The day before the treatment was a long day for Poppy, and she was very tired by the end of it. We were in the hospital by 8:00 am, and she had a scan, blood test, urine tests, health check, measurements, and so many things that I can't really remember them all. After all that, and when the results were back and the team had had the chance to look at them and discuss them, we were seen by one of the doctors from the clinical trial team. They then explained the results of the tests to us and the effect the treatment was having on Poppy's cancer. It seemed that after the first two cycles, there was a halt in the progression of cancer. In other words: the cancer was stable. Alleluia! For the first time in the last few years, we were winning.

It was a very long day indeed for Poppy, and she was very tired at the end of it, but the positive news came at the right time, I feel. Poppy rested that night, and the day after, she was ready for treatment again, physically and mentally. And I was there with her, which for me had become something crucial. The side effects were again not as pronounced this time, and a couple of days after, she felt much better. Also, we were looking forward to our new bed that was being delivered that day. We had decided to replace our bed and mattress for something more ergonomic and hopefully more comfortable for Poppy, as she was having real difficulty lately getting comfy in bed. With the new bed, we were hoping Poppy could get a better night's sleep.

The week after, Poppy didn't have any treatment, but a scan had been arranged for her on Thursday, and an appointment had been made for the week after to discuss the results. On Friday that week, as Poppy felt a bit better, I accompanied her to a yoga class for disabled people. It was a bit far, over half an hour by car, but it was something she had been wanting to do for a while, but she hadn't felt well enough to do it up to now. A couple of days back, she had asked me, "I'm thinking of going to Yoga on Friday. Do you think you could take me?" "Of course, Poppy. That's great," I replied. Anything I could do for her to make me feel less useless. I was also very keen for her to do it as I thought it could maybe help her with her breathing, lymphatic drainage and postural problems she was experiencing lately due to having to be on one leg all the time, even perhaps with rechannelling the energy through the Chakra centres. At that time, I was reading a lot about everything and anything that could have a beneficial effect on Poppy.

The idea was for me to accompany her that first time, and if she liked it and hopefully felt better, she could go there on her own in the future. It was a bit of a drive for Poppy, but if she continued improving, there was no reason why she could not do it. And she was a very good driver nevertheless. That way, she could drive the car, go on her own if she wanted or with a friend, meet up with other people and maybe have a drink together after the session. All positive things for Poppy's body and mind.

The week after, we had the appointment with the clinical trial team to get the results from the last scan. You don't always get to see the same doctor as there are many on the team and constantly changing, it seems. However, this time we saw a doctor we had already seen a couple of times who was very pleasant. He confirmed that the cancer was stable, which was good news, but it also showed that the cancer was not shrinking, which was not that good news.

There was nothing we could do but for Poppy to continue with her treatment and hope for the best. I knew Poppy very well, and I knew she had already done her research. So had I. Therefore, we knew that if the treatment didn't cause the cancer to shrink in the first few cycles, it was extremely unlikely it would do so after. Furthermore, if it was stable, it was usually for around 6 months only, after which the cancer would continue its course, and that was it, game over. Again, not the best news we wanted to hear, but we could only be positive and keep fighting.

That weekend also, Poppy's family was coming down to see her, and I was delighted there would be someone else to try to distract her. On the other hand, it was starting to be increasingly more difficult for Poppy to be with people for long periods of time. She was getting more pain, and she was getting more and more tired. Mixed feelings, then. However, overall I always felt the benefit of having someone else around and some kind of normality to Poppy's life outweighed the pain, discomfort and tiredness. Not sure she would have agreed with me on certain occasions, though. I would say to her at the end of the day: "Poppy, wasn't it lovely to see your dad?" "Yes, but everything hurts so much," would be her answer. I had nothing to offer, the sheer feeling of impotence tearing me apart.

The week after, Poppy had the usual visits to the hospital for blood tests and check-ups. On Friday, however, she was going again to yoga. She had enjoyed the session two weeks before, and she wanted to continue. We had paid for the course, and she was looking forward to it. I took the day off and accompanied Poppy to the centre, as it was still too difficult for her to drive that far. For me, strangely, these were some of my happiest days, as I could do something for Poppy, be of some help and also spend more time with her. I would wait in the park while she had the class and then drive home together. Time is so precious, and once it is gone, you can never get it back. We both understood that very well, and perhaps that is why we always tried to spend so much of our available time together.

The week after, Poppy had treatment again: her forth cycle already. Time was flying, and it was already the end of July. We had been talking about taking some days off, but we were going to discuss it with the doctors and follow their advice. We were given the green light by the medical team and agreed that if Poppy was well enough and felt strong enough, we could go in between cycles. It would certainly be great for Poppy to switch off a bit, and we started planning our holidays: if Poppy was well enough to travel, we would not hesitate. In our minds, we were still those two kids full of love for each other, full of passion for life and full of energy for our next adventure. Poppy's body was telling us otherwise, though.

The first two weeks of August were hard. I was tutoring on a private course that had been arranged a while back, and, unfortunately, Poppy got ill during that time. She had a lot of pain and a high temperature, 39.9 at the time. She called the hospital and was asked to make her way to A&E. She was diagnosed with a urine and kidney infection, given intravenous antibiotics, prescribed oral ones and discharged with a note to go back for a check-up in a couple of days. Luckily, after a few days, she felt much better, and we made our decision: we were going away on holiday. Poppy, still as efficient as ever and the best PA, found us a great deal for the crossing and the hotel. The week after, on a Thursday as customary, she had her treatment and the day after, with the car washed and cleaned, levels and tyre pressure checked, loaded with whatever we were taking, not much anymore apart from the cats, we set off. Nothing had changed, at least in our minds.

Chapter 39

The journey was hard on Poppy, even with breaks and spending the night in a hotel. Apart from that, once we settled, we had a fantastic holiday, almost three weeks. With the cancer stable, the dose of painkillers increased, and of course, understanding the limitations that Poppy's condition imposed, we still managed to do most of what we wanted. More importantly, though, Poppy was away from the routine of hospitals and doctor appointments.

I was trying to work very hard on the house. We didn't have the money to contract a professional company to do everything. Therefore, structural work was always done by a contractor but everything else I tried to do it myself as much as I could. I remember saying to my brother that sometimes it felt like I was working more when I was on holiday in the house that when I was at home, but my dream was for Poppy to be able to see the house done and enjoy it. I could see, however, that I was running out of time, and it was extremely frustrating and demoralising, but again, there was nothing I could do, and clearly, I had to strike the right balance between working in the house and enjoying our holiday together. So I did what I could without trying to think too much about the unpalatable looming prospect of Poppy not seeing the house finished.

We had bought the house after my dad passed away. We were left with a few thousand pounds, and I said to Poppy we could either buy a very nice car or a little wreck somewhere habitable enough and do it up slowly. We had been to France many times and seen many houses for sale, and on one of our visits, we saw that particular house on Poppy's birthday. An omen, perhaps? We negotiated the price, and we bought it the day after! We knew it needed a lot of work, and the idea was that when we had enough money, we would get a company to do the work. We would agree on everything, the work would be timed to coincide with our holidays, and the rest, Poppy would stay there to manage the project, and I would fly down at the weekends. Unfortunately, as things didn't go according to plan, we were never in a financial situation where we could do that. Nevertheless, we still loved our holidays there.

Our love for France had started many years back. In 2000, to celebrate the Millennium, we took off the whole month of August, and we cycled from London to Barcelona. Yes, by bike! We also thought it would give us a break from the intensity of dancing, but at the same time, we would work on our fitness while travelling through France. Our bikes fully loaded, we set off on the 1st of August, and it was one of the greatest experiences of my life. We stayed in hotels, B&B, and gites, and if we couldn't find anything as an emergency, we had our camping gear. Glad to say we only had to camp twice, although at a campsite with all the facilities. However, after a few hours cycling in the heat, one really appreciates a nice little room, with a bath for Poppy if possible, a cold shower for me, and a nice and comfy bed.

People in France were much more used to cyclists, and we met so many that month. I remember one day staying in a little motel and we met four guys from the Netherlands doing the famous Pilgrimage route to Santiago de Compostela in Spain. They were travelling light and doing 60-70 miles a day easily in half a day and the rest of the day sightseeing wherever they were. In fact, we met quite a few from different countries doing the Pilgrimage by bike that summer. However, what I had never seen before and I have not come across again since is 'luxury cycling travel' at its best. We met two couples from the States, clearly very wealthy, spending three months in the summer touring Europe by bicycle. But they were travelling with a butler! He would arrange everything for them: where to eat, where to sleep, the suitcases they were carrying to be put in the train or taken by taxi to their next destination, so everything would be ready when they arrived, the clothes ironed and ready to wear for dinner in their 5* hotels. Remarkable!

Our rides were a bit different. I remember one day, we got very wet, and we arrived at this cute little hotel in Amiens. I said to Poppy, "Let me try here and see if they have a room." I was so drenched, dirty and smelly that I didn't even dare to go in. So embarrassed I was, just knocked at the door. A lady opened, and I guess she must have seen éall by then because, if she was surprised at the 'apparition' in front of her, she certainly didn't show it. With my best smile in the circumstances and also pointing at Poppy behind me, I said, "Madame. Avez-vous une chambre disponible pour deux personnes? Désolé, les vélos sont très sales!" I said to her that I was sorry the bikes were so dirty. In reality, we were dirtier than the bikes! In any case, that was most of my French at the time. The rest, as usual, was out of a phrase book, so I couldn't engage in lengthy explanations. By then, it had been almost 20 years since I had studied French at school.

With their usual 'joie de vivre' the landlady, perhaps taking compassion at our sorry state, waved her hand beckoning us to follow her while saying, "Pas de problème. C'est bon. Venez, venez avec les vélos," and she showed us the way to the garage. We left the bikes there, took from the panniers what we needed and off we went to the room. It's been over 20 years, and I still remember this most cosy, cute and beautiful room in the attic with a bath for Poppy. And I remember even more the happiness on Poppy's face when she saw that the room had a bath. It was the least my beautiful Poppy deserved after following this mad man she had for a husband cycling around France!

We saw and stayed in many beautiful places: Paris, Chartres, Versailles, the Palace, indeed one of the most wonderful buildings I have ever had the chance and be fortunate enough to visit. Absolutely mesmerising. No wonder it bankrupted the country! In any case, we had already spent over two weeks, and we were only in the Val the Loire, not great progress. We talked about it, and for the next six days, Poppy took the train to our next agreed destination, and I would cycle. I had to push a lot and do almost 600 miles in six days. The plan was: we would get up, have breakfast, go to the train station and put Poppy and her bike on the train. While I was doing all the crazy cycling, she would arrive at the destination and either go to the hotel already booked in advance if we had been able to, or she had to find one for us to spend the night. Again, she was the perfect PA: she always found us a room, even without speaking the language, just a few words. That's how remarkable Poppy was and how much trust I had in her.

In Perpignan, we had a funny episode. As that day we had not been able to book a room in advance, Poppy had to look for one. Unfortunately, she only managed to find a room in a rundown hotel close to the station, a bit of a seedy area and had a couple of 'unwanted' approaches. Poor little Poppy, but I knew she could handle herself, so I never worried too much about her being on her own in day time. In any case, she left the hotel and was waiting for me at the station as arranged. We went to the hotel together, and of course, there were no more advances from anyone. We had a pizza in a restaurant in the main square, and I spoke Catalan with the waiter. Interesting how people from Perpignan think of themselves as more Catalan than French, but I knew that, as I had been to Perpignan a few times when living in Spain.

The room in the hotel was as seedy as the area, so we used our imagination, and we made the most of it, a few shades of grey to the fore. Needless to say, my ride the next day was…mmm… long, hard and painful!

In any case, we made it to the border, crossed into Spain, and then made our way down to Barcelona on the beautiful coastal road of la Costa Brava. I knew la Costa Brava very well, having been to most of the places many times in the past, but this time felt different. We would stop at certain places, at the top of the coves, under the shade of the pine trees and marvel at the deep blue water beneath us, the sound of the waves crashing against the rocks, the salty air greeting us every time we stopped by the sea. I loved the sea, I loved the Mediterranean, and I loved the Costa Brava. But most of all, I loved Poppy, my beautiful Poppy, with all my heart.

Chapter 40

The rest of the year wasn't great for Poppy. From October, things started deteriorating for her again. She had a lot of pain in her left side, and we had to go to A&E. They did a scan, blood and urine tests. The explorations concluded that there was no infection and the stent was not blocked, which wasn't the greatest news as that meant that the tumours were most likely becoming enlarged and were compressing the nerves in the area.

By now, it was November, and still, the orthopaedic department hadn't been able to get the prosthesis working for Poppy. She had another appointment, more changes and adjustments, and was given another appointment in 2-3 weeks. Hopefully, by then, the prosthesis would be ready, and she would be able to wear it. It was very frustrating for Poppy but also for the technicians in the prosthetics department, who had always been superb form day one. The truth is that since Poppy had the intrusive surgery the year before, she hadn't been able to wear the prosthetic leg with ease. Part of it was Poppy not feeling well enough, but mostly due to the fluctuating changes in her stump due to the lymphedema.

Poppy never complained openly, but in view of how the disease was behaving, I know she regretted an operation that ultimately didn't seem to have made any difference in the progression of the cancer. So difficult to say, and of course, we will never know if not having the operation would have significantly altered the course of the disease. What we do know is that the side effect of the operation was a life-changing condition that ultimately would impair her ability to wear a prosthesis, and that, sadly, made a huge difference to Poppy's overall quality of life. It would be fair to say we are not always aware of the risks of the operations and treatments, nor their true benefits and costs. Ironically, in our life together, we always favoured quality over quantity and sadly, that would not be the case on this occasion.

That mid-week in November was very hard on Poppy. The previous week she had a lot of pain, and this week, it was full on. On Tuesday, she had the appointment for the prosthesis, with the frustration of the struggle of the previous year since the operation. On Wednesday, it was pre-treatment day, with the usual blood tests and the rest. On Thursday, it was treatment day. I remember texting my family to explain, the texts getting shorter as it was so repetitive. When they were asking how Poppy was, my reply of late seemed to be always the same: 'appointment, treatment, pain getting worse, infection, visit to A&E, more painkillers and antibiotics, home now, resting in bed'. It seemed to be our life, Poppy's life of late. Yet, I also recall saying that we were grateful she could still have treatment. I was not complaining. I still had Poppy in my life.

The day after the treatment, Poppy was in terrible pain and had to take enormous doses of painkillers, including morphine. Eventually, the pain receded, and she had a relatively good night's sleep. The day after, Saturday, I would carry out my ritual: get up early and do the stretching exercises. Otherwise, everything ached, particularly my back. Sort out the cats. Go and buy the paper at the corner shop, perhaps some milk, bread and biscuits as well. I would let Poppy sleep as much as possible, and at the right time, I would wake her up gently with her medication and a cup of tea. Still gave me enormous satisfaction to be able to do that for Poppy. After all, that was one of the little things I could do for her, and I know she would have done it for me much more and a thousand times better.

That week also, my uncle in Spain had died, one of my dearest. We had always gone on holiday together with my parents, and we were very close. As Poppy was going through the treatment and had been quite unwell, I couldn't go to the funeral. However, when she felt better a couple of weeks after, I went to pay my respects and spend the weekend with my auntie near Barcelona. That weekend also, Poppy's family was coming down to see her, and they would be with her most of the weekend. They would keep her company, and she wouldn't be that much on her own.

That weekend, in hindsight, I made, perhaps, one of the many mistakes I made with Poppy. She had mentioned about accompanying me. After all, I was just going on Friday and coming back on Sunday, as, on Monday, I was back at work. However, I dismissed the idea as I thought it would be too much for Poppy: going to the airport here, the flight to Barcelona, a car journey of over an hour from the airport, all the socialising, the many people I had to see and places to go. I made a mistake, one may say, of telling one of my cousins I was coming down: before I knew it, he had told my other cousins and rallied a group of almost 20 coming to see me at my auntie's on Saturday afternoon! Advantages and disadvantages of having a big family.

On Friday, after arriving at the airport and getting the hired car, I stopped on my way to see my best friend in Spain, who was now living just 2 blocks away from where I used to live. I had lunch with him in a bar-restaurant that I used to frequent 25 years back. Nothing had changed! After lunch, on the way to my auntie, I stopped at the Monastery of Montserrat, which has always had a special place in my heart. I talked to Poppy for a while, took photos of a few things in the shop and asked what she preferred. It was like she was there with me in a way.

In the monastery, I did my prayers and lit the candles, a big one for my uncle, who had just gone. Not that he would have cared: he didn't believe in God. In any case, I've always thought that prayer doesn't hurt anyone, but it may help someone.

I arrived at my auntie's on Friday afternoon. My cousin came for dinner with her husband and kids. My other uncle, who lives in the same town, also came. Saturday morning, my auntie accompanied me to buy a bunch of flowers from a florist, and we went to the cemetery where my mum and grandparents are buried together. I paid my respects, put the flowers in the vase and did my prayers for them. I also thanked them for what they had done for me. The wonderful images of my childhood and teenage years shared with them brought tears to my eyes. Difficult to believe, but it was over 30 years since my mum's death.

After the cemetery, it was shopping time. I had a list of things to buy for Poppy, and we went shopping with my auntie. Then it was lunch in the restaurant with my auntie and family with the kids. Of course, they invited me. After, it was back home to meet up with the troupe of cousins and their kids, some of them who I had never seen, that had driven over an hour to come to see me. My other auntie came as well; it had been years since I hadn't seen her. We went to a bar, all of us, and of course, they invited me. We were together for 2-3 hours, and they left. Then it was time to go out for dinner with my uncle. He is only nine years older than me, and I have the fondest memories when growing up with him. He took me to a lovely restaurant and, of course, he wouldn't hear of me paying! We spent a while together, and then he dropped me off at my auntie's place. I really enjoyed that time with him. It had been years. On Sunday, I got up, had breakfast with my auntie and left. I stopped at the cemetery again briefly and then made my way to the airport. I had to be there quite early, with plenty of time to return the car and meet up with other cousins who were coming to see me at the airport and have a drink together before my departure. Of course, they paid. The crazy life of a Spaniard with a big family, but I was used to it. However, it would have been too much for Poppy, no doubt about it, and we both knew that.

The problem is that I had said to Poppy that it wasn't the right time for her to come with me, as I knew what it would be like. But we would go next year once she felt better. I will have to apologise to my beautiful Poppy for the rest of my life as, sadly, I did not know at the time, but there would not be another chance.

Chapter 41

Unfortunately, the flight back was delayed, which wasn't great, as, in all honesty, I just wanted to get back home to Poppy. It had been great seeing my family, and it had to be done, although it was non-stop from the moment I had arrived at the airport on Friday morning until the moment I was taking the return flight Sunday afternoon. However, mostly I missed Poppy. We had been texting and talking on the phone several times a day, as we always did, so I knew she was fine, and she had a good time with her family, although she was very tired at the end of the day. The pain was more or less under control which was good. One less thing to worry about.

Every night we would chat on the phone for a while, UK time being an hour behind helping. I would tell Poppy who I had seen, where I had been, and what I had done. We always did that, making the other person, although far away, somehow a participant in the activities. Then she would tell me about her day.

Another reason we would chat at night is that Poppy didn't like sleeping alone in the dark. She would always have a dim light as a company when on her own as she wasn't comfortable in pitch black darkness. Also, chatting for a while at that time would make Poppy's night shorter, which was always a good thing with her constant pain now. But mostly, I just enjoyed talking to Poppy. Even after more than 20 years, it was a pleasure to hear her voice, even on the phone. I loved Poppy's voice, and I wasn't the only one. It was soothing and comforting.

I was talking, explaining about the Monastery of Montserrat and how much it had changed since I last visited.

Or about my cousins' crazy visit. Or about the restaurant that my uncle took me to and the delicious food we ate that Poppy would have loved. I would ask her about her day, and she would reply, and we would have this lovely conversation. Many things surely repeated over the years, and she would laugh at my silly jokes, most also repeated over the years. Poppy was one of the very few people I could really have good communication with and be totally relaxed. It was very easy to talk to her. After so much talking about the weekend, we were both excited at the prospect of going together next year when she felt better and with good weather. That was the plan.

The truth is that since I met Poppy, I hardly went anywhere without her. I cannot explain it, but I radically broke with my life of the past, my bad habits. I stopped going out drinking with my friends at night, I stopped going out with other women, and I just wanted to be with her. Interestingly, she never asked me to do or not do anything, apart from giving up smoking: she was worried because I was having respiratory infections ever more often and losing my teeth! In any case, I just did it because I loved her very much, I loved being with her, and I tried, for the first time in my life, to do it right, or at least not too wrong, for her.

There were occasions, of course, in which we would be apart, my week immersion course in France or hers when we were studying for our degrees, for instance, but somehow I always missed Poppy a lot! I could be having this wonderful time with my cousins or having dinner with my uncle, for instance, or out with friends on a special occasion. Suddenly I would think of Poppy and how she would have liked being there, doing that. I could say to my uncle, for instance, "I wish Poppy was here. She would have loved those prawns. Next time, we'll come together, and we'll all come here again. She must have these prawns next time. They're delicious." Poppy was always on my mind. It is very difficult to describe, but there was nobody else that made me feel like Poppy did. Being with her was so much more enjoyable for me. It was not only how she made me feel but also how I would feel without her, like something was always missing.

Since I met Poppy, I have always thought that it is not only how you feel when you are with your loved one but, almost more importantly, how you feel without that person when that person is not with you. It had never happened to me before, and it was new to me. When you are on your own and you feel lonely, who would you like to be with? When you have a bad day at work, who comes to your mind and you think, I'll rush home when I finish, and everything will be fine. When things don't go well in your life or unfortunate, sad events happen, who would you want to have by your side? Feel their presence, hear their voice, see their face, feel their touch. If you feel like that about someone, that's the person you have to be with, of course, if it is reciprocated. That person to me was Poppy, and I was very fortunate it was reciprocated. I always missed her very much.

Eventually, the plane departed from Barcelona airport, and when I arrived, I was delighted to see that Poppy had come to pick me up with the car. She hadn't driven as much as we wanted this last year, but that day, she did. She got in the car and drove more than half an hour to the airport, still without the prosthesis, still on one leg with the crutches, and still with the pain. She wanted to drive to the airport to pick me up, and she did it. She wanted me to see her there waiting for me when I came out of passport control, and she did it. She wanted us to drive back home together, and we did it. I was so proud of her. What a phenomenal woman she was!

The rest of the month was busy for Poppy. She didn't have treatment that week, but it wasn't going to be an easy week for her, either. On Monday, she had to go to the hospital for pre-operatory checks. One of our friends was free and could accompany her, as I had to work that day, for which I was always glad and truly grateful. I didn't want Poppy to have to go on her own if it could be helped.

On Thursday, she had a little operation. Little as the procedure itself, as they only had to replace the stent. However, as the surgeons could not access via the kidney as the area was far too damaged, the procedure had to be done under general anaesthetic. Nothing was easy for Poppy any more, her body so battered by now, it was remarkable that she still had that most beautiful smile of hers.

I dropped Poppy off in the hospital in the morning with a friend and went to work. As usual, the nurse would call me when the operation was done, and I would make my way to the hospital. "Remember, the nurse will call you when I go in, so answer the phone!!!" Poppy said to me. She knew that I never answered the phone at work. "Yes, Poppy, I know. I'll keep my phone with me." "Might come up as a private number," she said. "That's fine, no problem," I replied. The nurse would call, and I would make my way to the hospital. There, we would wait together in the room until she'd be discharged and then make our way home. Again, one of many, but together.

The week after, it was treatment week again. The usual routine; pre-treatment day to the hospital to do the bloods and check-ups, and on Thursday, Poppy had her treatment. The operation the week before had gone well, but of course, she had some pain following the operation that lasted a few days. Then, she had the treatment this week. On top, unfortunately, when I went to Spain, I caught a cold, minor for me, but of course, Poppy got it as well, and it made her feel quite unwell. We were always so extremely careful about where we were going and who we were with. But this time, I caught it, which made me feel awful just thinking of the risk to Poppy.

November blended into December, and to say that Poppy was not feeling great, would be an understatement. She continued with her immunotherapy cancer treatment. She was starting to feel quite worn out, more tired and with more pain as time was progressing. Every year since we bought the little house, we spent New Year's Eve in France. Most Christmas as well, but not all, as some initially I had to work or we had other commitments. But every New Year's Eve, we did. We just liked the fact of being abroad, doing our celebration, and welcoming the New Year in a different country.

That December was clearly different. I knew she was struggling. "I got some cash as I need to buy dad and B a present. And yours, too," she said. "Of course, Poppy, do what you have to do. But don't spend too much on me, you know that all I need for Christmas is… YOU!" I would say to her. I loved to say that to Poppy. "It's so much harder for me as I can't go to the shops…" "I know, Poppy, my love, but you're doing great!" "No, I'm not." "Yes, Poppy, you are. Of course, you are." It was so difficult to see Poppy struggling so much. Yet, at that point, I still thought something would happen and we would be fine.

We would have lots of little conversations during the day, mainly on WhatsApp. "How are you, Poppy? I didn't want to wake you up this morning when I left. You had a bit of a rough night. How's the pain now?" That night she had woken up a few times with pain, so from 2:00 am-4:00 am, we didn't sleep much. "The pain is better now. I slept ok after that. Did you get back to sleep?" "On and off, but it was ok. I'm so sorry you're having so much pain lately." "On and off? I wonder why…" "I don't know, Poppy. At least I didn't wake up until 5.30 am." "That's not great, though. You need to get more sleep." My beautiful Poppy, with terminal cancer and all that pain, still worried about me because I wasn't sleeping much. I said, "I know, Poppy, but I'm ok." "Well, I hope you have an easy day today." "Yes, Poppy, today is an easy day. Home by 5:30 pm, I think." "Excellent! At least we will have the evening together." And she meant it: it was so important and enjoyable for us to spend the evenings together, as much time as possible as we could, as always. But somehow, now it seemed more pressing…

"Beautiful day today, Poppy, cold but sunny. 1 degree when I left this morning for work," I said. "Did you have to scrape the car?" "No, just ok with the wipers. Poppy ok?" I must have asked that 1000 times a day. "Not great. I think the pain has started like this since the stent replacement." Unfortunately, that procedure caused Poppy a lot of pain in the days to come. But we could still talk about Christmas and presents. I said to Poppy, "I'll get you some lingerie for Christmas, Poppy." I knew it was getting more and more difficult for Poppy, but I still wanted her to feel feminine and attractive as she had always been. Even when she had the amputation, to me, she was still a very attractive woman, and I think it is important for a woman to feel attractive for her man. I might be wrong, but I have always tried that. I was always fishing for clues, though. "Have you seen anything you like?" I asked. She sent a few photos of different brands, colours, and styles. There were a couple she said, "These are pretty, from JL, don't you think?" I replied, "They're all very pretty, Poppy… on YOU!" Poppy was one of the most beautiful and feminine women I had ever met in my whole life, but cancer had slowly and insidiously been taking away her physical beauty. Yet, what pained me most was the fact that she was starting to see herself as not very feminine and attractive any more. Yes, the cancer may have been destroying her physically, but it could never destroy her beauty and femininity inside and her true essence as a woman. Never!

Chapter 42

Poppy had another operation 8 days before Christmas. "Testing, testing... all good here. Are you getting my texts?" I hadn't replied to her texts. "Sorry, Poppy, I had the phone in my coat. How's Poppy doing?" I asked. "Ok. Waiting for the consultant to come. Sats are still low. Are you ok? You didn't sleep much last night." "I'm ok, Poppy. The oncologist said they may keep you in observation for a while. Keep me posted," I said. "They've moved me to the oncology ward. Have my own room on the 11th floor!" Poppy said. "Wow! You must have an amazing view. 5* hotel?" "Ha-ha," Poppy still laughing at my silly jokes. "I may still be discharged, but at least it is much more comfortable. And I have a good signal too." A while after, Poppy texted, "The consultant just came in. They need to do a few checks and exclude a blood clot." "Are you feeling a bit better, Poppy?" "I'm ok, just tired." She continued, "Do you know what he said? He asked me what I wanted to do if I deteriorated under their care. I was shocked!!! The nurse said not to worry." "Yes, Poppy, the consultant is just covering himself, don't worry about it," I said. She was not overly worried by the comment, but nobody likes hearing that either, I guess. In any case, I knew my beautiful Poppy wasn't ready to throw in the towel. She was not going anywhere yet.

I was there for a while and then went home. Poppy was kept overnight as she wasn't breathing very well, her blood pressure was still quite low, and they gave her some fluids. We chatted and texted on the phone that night, as usual, with lots of kisses, until 1:00 am when she lost reception.

The day after, "Good morning. Are you ok? At work?" "Yes, Poppy, here now. How was the night?" I said. "Ok,

168

but I missed you and the 'gatitos' (little cats in Spanish)" "We missed you too, Poppy. I hope you can come home today. The flat always feels so empty when you're not there!" I never got used to it: every time Poppy wasn't there, the flat would feel so empty. She said, "I hope so. Apparently, the plan is to do another scan, and if everything is ok, they'll send me home." "That would be wonderful," I said.

After a while, "How's Poppy doing? Any news?" "No news yet. Poppy is a bit worried…" she said. "No, Poppy, my love, you don't have to worry. I really think it's just an infection. But of course, I understand that you worry about it. It's normal." Poppy was worried because of her low blood pressure, low oxygen in the blood, and not being able to breathe well, and they had found a suspicious mass in the base of her lungs in the scan they had done before. That's why they were going to do a different scan, and she was worried about the results. She was worried it could be a metastasis. "Try not to worry too much, Poppy. Everything will be fine, my love," I said, and then I sent her a photo of the cats. I knew that would cheer her up. Then I said, "They're waiting for you at home Poppy. Don't you think they look like BIG 'pestecillos'?" (A little pest in Spanish). Poppy replied, "They are the biggest, most wonderful, adorable, angelic, 'pestecillos' EVER!" she said. "Ha-ha. They are." With that, we continued chatting for a while, laughing, Poppy less worried now. Our cats were Poppy's salvation: she loved them so much.

The day after, I knew she was worried. Very worried. We were waiting for the results, and I asked her: "How are you feeling?" "Terrified," she said. "No, Poppy, don't worry, everything will be fine, but whatever happens, we'll brave the elements together." Luckily the scan showed it

169

was just most likely an infection: Poppy was treated with antibiotics, discharged, and home we went together.

In any case, that year, it was clear Poppy wouldn't be well enough to travel before Christmas, but we were hopeful we could make it for New Year. A few days after, she felt a bit better. I asked her, "Poppy, ok?" She replied, "Poppy good. But how are you? I'm a bit worried about you. I think a break will do you good." "No need to worry about me, Poppy. You and the 'gatitos' are worth fighting for and keep me going every day." That is true: since I met Poppy, I had something extremely valuable to fight for, and in a way, the three of them were my 'little family'. Poppy was my life.

The day after, the 23rd of December, although it was already very difficult for her, Poppy took the car and went shopping with our friend together. That filled me with so much happiness! We were staying at home for Christmas, and she went shopping, like she did so many times in the past, to get everything we needed for the celebrations. I stayed at home waiting for some parcels she had ordered. At some point, I texted her to see how they were doing: "Hi, Poppy, how are you getting on?" "So difficult, so busy everywhere, but we're doing well," she said. "Ok, Poppy, no rush. Take your time." A while after: "Hi Poppy, just got two parcels from Amazon. How are you getting on?" "Excellent. We've just finished in Sainsbury's. I tell you, it was hell there. We're on our way home already, but there is an enormous queue in the car park." "Oh, sorry, Poppy, but don't worry, you'll be here soon. Text me when you're here, and I'll come out to get the bags."

Clearly, we couldn't spend Christmas away, but we would try to do the best we could at home. However, for that, we needed a strong frame of mind, and I knew that

Poppy had been down a lot, not surprisingly, quite worried about everything and with so much pain lately. We had a little chat that night, and the day after, 24th of December, she sent me this message: "Just wanted to say I'm going to try very hard to enjoy each day. Of course, I'll have blips along the way, but I'll try my hardest. I may not be the strongest, best or anything else, but I am kind and care for people. The last few days, I've been trying very hard at being at peace. I vow to do whatever I need to do to achieve that. I think being happy is the greatest freedom. I believe, in happiness, you find health and healing. Xxx." It was so hard, but at least I knew the chat the night before had worked. I said, "Very well said, Poppy. To be happy and at peace inside is very important, although difficult to achieve. I'm still working on it, and we can only try a bit every day. That is all. Time will take care of the rest. You don't worry about anything, my love. Let's take it day by day." Poppy said, "I love you so much." "I love you too, Poppy, a lot."

Christmas that year was very hard for Poppy. Her pain was now more frequent, intense and longer-lasting than before. We stayed at home as we couldn't travel, but we still had our little Christmas tree and had our celebration at home. Our neighbour and friend joined us, and we talked to friends and family. As always, we still tried to make the most of it. With that, we had a Christmas as enjoyable as we possibly could, revelling in each other's company, savouring every moment, and creating more memories to add to the thousands and thousands we already had.

Christmas come and gone, and we thought we could perhaps go to France for New Year. On the 27th, Poppy had an appointment with the consultant, and we were going to speak to him. That morning at 7:00 am, Poppy was awake, and she asked me: "Did I take the painkillers at 4:00 am when we were awake?" "I think so, Poppy, so you said," I replied. "I'm sure I did." Poppy was taking oral morphine sometimes, now hourly. "I'm very sad," she said, "I know we don't say it much anymore, but I love you. Tons. To the moon and back." "I know, Poppy, don't worry. It's ok." She continued, "At the end of the day, to feel loved, cherished and wanted is life itself." I smiled and gave her a kiss. "And until I know otherwise, I truly believe I have years to live," she said. "So do I, Poppy. I truly believe in the healing power of love. That's why you are still here because you are much loved by so many people." I continued, "I love you very, very, very much, Poppy. That's why I don't give up. I'll never give up." "Neither will I," Poppy said, "I will not give up no matter my circumstances." I gave her a gentle cuddle, as by then, I could not hug Poppy hard anymore because of her pain. I also gave her another kiss, as I knew no matter how hard, Poppy would never give up. It would have to be taken away from her.

We went to the hospital. Poppy had the usual routine: blood tests and the rest, and then we spoke to the consultant. We asked him about the possibility of Poppy travelling, and again, we were told if she was up for it, we should do it. We went home a bit happier. Maybe, after all, we would still be able to spend New Year in France. We started looking at crossings and hotels, but sadly, Poppy got very unwell a couple of days after, and therefore, for the first time in 14 years, we would not be able to spend the New Year in France, in our little house, still a work in progress after all those years, very much a labour of love. I know Poppy felt truly awful about not being able to go, not for herself but for me. She knew how much I liked getting up in the morning on New Year's Day after the celebrations the night before. I would clean everything and get ready for her to get up. Then, I would light the fire on the wood stove and had my customary breakfast of smoked salmon on toast and a glass of champagne. It was a psychological way of welcoming the new year.

I always say the year is very long, lots of things can happen, and one can only hope to get to the end of it in the best condition one possibly can. There is no guarantee, though. That is why every single New Year's Eve, at midnight, I would open a bottle of champagne, letting the cork hit the ceiling as hard as it could. We would toast welcoming the New Year, and I would give Poppy a huge kiss as I hugged her, saying how much I loved her. I would thank God that we had reached the end of the year together and that we were given the opportunity to start a new one again together. Then, once we had the cats, I would chase them, grab them gently and also give them a kiss wishing them a Happy New Year also. What a silly thing to do as, of course, it didn't make any difference to them, they always looked at me in a funny way, but for me, it was extremely important. Through that kiss, I was expressing how fortunate I felt to be able to do that. I was alive and healthy, with a job, a wonderful wife and two silly little cats, which were invaluable to Poppy, and me. I had it all!

By mid-January, Poppy felt better, and we were considering perhaps going to France then. I recall mentioning to my brother that we were really looking forward to our little break, but we didn't want to raise our hopes too much, as with Poppy, anything could change dramatically very quickly. But life is too short, and as things were going, we had to try to make the most of every single opportunity left to us.

In any case, I wanted Poppy to feel pretty, to feel good, even more if we were going to be travelling, so as she felt a bit better, we arranged an appointment with the hairdresser. It had been a while since my beautiful Poppy hadn't been to one, as it was getting progressively more difficult for her to go places on her own, and she had been quite unwell lately. That day, however, she went accompanied by one of our friends. She texted me at 5:30 pm, "Done!" "Excellent, Poppy. How did it go?" I asked. "Very, very, very long," poor Poppy had forgotten how long it took but also, sitting in that position for such a long time, I knew it must have been very difficult for her. I said, "Well, maybe it was long, Poppy, but the important thing is that you've done it!" "Yes, all done now," she said. "I'm sure Poppy is very pretty now," I texted with a smiley emoji. "Can't wait to see you, Poppy. Coming home now?" I asked. "Yes, we're on our way now." "Ok, Poppy, see you soon." When I heard the key at the door, I rushed to the entrance to meet Poppy, and she looked beautiful!

The day after, I texted: "Poppy, before I forget, you know I've got a really bad memory, but…, have I told you lately that I love you… VERY MUCH!!!" She would text me back with emoji kisses. I didn't need more. I would do that many, many, many times, just out of the blue. Poppy was always on my mind, and I just loved her so much

That week it was her treatment week, on Thursday as usual, and if Poppy felt well enough, we would go on holiday for a couple of weeks. On Wednesday, it was pre-treatment day. Therefore, she had to go to the hospital for blood tests and regular check-ups. The nurses noticed that the oxygen saturation in her blood was 92%, which is pretty low, but they couldn't find a reason. Also, the X-Rays showed some nodes in the lungs, and they were going to investigate further. On the other hand, Poppy felt reasonably well, and there were no signs of infection. She would have her treatment on Thursday if all things go well.

Poppy had her treatment, we spoke to the doctors on the day, and we decided to go. The next scan would be in three weeks, and as Poppy's condition was progressing, we didn't know whether we would have another chance or when, for that matter. And I am so glad we did, as, unfortunately, my beautiful Poppy would not have another chance.

Chapter 43

We had a fantastic journey, and with the limitations imposed by Poppy's pain, we were very much enjoying ourselves. However, I know very well she did it more for me than for herself, as she did not feel that well anymore. It was the first time in the many occasions we had been there that I went to the supermarket on my own to do that first big shopping. I didn't realise it at the time, but this journey was very hard on Poppy, too hard.

I remember we had always very much enjoyed that first shopping, the different products in the supermarkets, planning ahead the meals, filling up the fridge. It was always very satisfying to think of the whole holiday ahead. But on this occasion, I went on my own, with Poppy's list in one hand and a heavy heart in the other. Of course, I had been to the supermarket many times on my own, but never when doing a big shopping, and certainly not the always very special first one: that would always be done together. It was very special for us. But Poppy could not do it anymore, and that broke my heart. It was certainly not the same without Poppy. I just went around the supermarket like in an automated pilot and with no enjoyment at all. How different from the other times. And yet, I still thought we would be fine, that we had a future, and that we could still do so many more things together. I wanted to still do so many things together with Poppy.

We had a few good days, Poppy's pain barring, doing absolutely nothing, just eating, drinking, sleeping and reading in front of the wood stove. Just being together, sharing that time, enjoying each other's company. I had become accustomed over the years to taking the two weeks over Christmas as my proper holiday, as in the summer, I usually worked in the house. It was not Christmas, it was the end of January by now, but for all intents and purposes, it was our Christmas holiday, just a bit delayed.

The weather forecast had predicted heavy snow for a few days, and I stocked up on the wood fire pile inside. Indeed, it snowed heavily for a few days, and it was wonderful to watch the snow falling outside, slowly covering everything with a white coat while sitting in our living room in front of the roaring fire. We had seen it many times, but that time it felt truly magical. Poppy loved it, and so did I.

I have always thought there is something mesmerising about sitting comfortably in front of a fire, your eyes unawarely bewitched by the dancing flames, unconsciously following their hypnotic ever-changing shapes and colours. It sends my brain into a semi-lethargic state, lowering my blood pressure and heart rate, and the breathing becomes slower and deeper. It almost instantly takes away the stress of your everyday life. However, it could also be something powerfully primeval that brings to you your most innate and wild sexual impulses and desires. I can attest to that, but that will remain between Poppy and I, and it would certainly be the scope of a different kind of book!

However, as wonderful as it was looking at the fire, every so often, I would find myself stealing a glance at Poppy, my beautiful Poppy, that didn't look that strong anymore. Every so often, also, negative thoughts would creep into my mind, trying to test my mettle and break my spirit. And every so often, I would need to fight the tears in front of Poppy at the thought of the inevitable if this treatment didn't work. But you keep fighting, negative thoughts, tears and whatever else may be, because there is absolutely nothing else you can do.

We didn't leave the house in four days, and we didn't move the car. How wonderful compared to the hectic life at home. I only went out to take some photos to send to our friends and families. I remember everybody saying how beautiful it looked, a picture-postcard cottage. Of course, that was on the outside. On the inside was a different matter. We had had the little house for 12 years already, and I remember saying to my brother at the time that I hope it would not take us another 12 to finish the house. It would have taken us only 24 years. They built many Cathedrals in less! We always tried to make fun of it, but the truth is that when Poppy started getting seriously ill all those years back, our priorities shifted, and we no longer had the time, money and energy to dedicate to the house. We had to adapt to our new circumstances. Again, Poppy was more important than any house, as well as she had been more important than dancing, and she was more important than anything else. At the end of the day, a house is just a house, something material that can be replaced. A person is irreplaceable.

Unfortunately, after a few days, Poppy felt very unwell, and our holiday was cut short. She was short of breath, with a high temperature and pain in her chest. We thought she may have an infection and started taking the antibiotics we had brought with us. She was adamant she did not want to go to the hospital this time in France, and I was not going to force her. I think deep down she felt very sick, and perhaps she thought that she may go in but not come out, and I'm sure she didn't want to spend her last days in a hospital abroad. Therefore, we called the hospital at home. She spoke to the cancer treatment team and were told to return as soon as she was able to travel. We started packing. Two days after, Poppy felt a bit better, and we had a pizza from our favourite place that night with a little glass of wine to celebrate, if one can say that, the end of our holiday. So different to how it used to be. In any case, we set off the day after and slowly made our way back, with an overnight stay, impossible otherwise for Poppy anymore. We arrived home, sorted the cats out, and unpacked. Poppy rested as much as she could as the day after it was back to the hospital. That sadly was to be our last holiday, but those days in front of the fire were worth it. They left a wonderful and indelible memory, forever printed in my mind: Poppy sitting on her red sofa in front of the fire, a book in her hands and the cats by her side. One more of thousands of memories Poppy gave me, created together, and which can never be taken away from me.

The clinical trial team had already arranged an emergency scan for Poppy. As I was still on my holiday period, I could accompany Poppy that day for her scan, blood tests and other explorations. The day after, she had an appointment with the oncologist to see the results. The explorations showed that Poppy had a pulmonary embolism, hence why she was so unwell the week before, and we had to come back. She was very lucky: it could had been so much worse! Again, she was immediately prescribed heparin, again daily injections for six months, again seeing her go through that. Poor Poppy, she was starting to look like a colander.

On top of that, she was due to have her next cycle of immunotherapy treatment the day after, but she was too unwell, and it was cancelled. Instead, the clinical team was going to meet up with the medical team and oncologists to discuss Poppy's case, and we were given an appointment in the afternoon. It was by now the beginning of February.

The appointment didn't bring good news to Poppy: the scan showed an increase in the pelvis and iliac area affected by cancer. She also had a collapse of the base of the lungs, most likely due to the embolism. The plan was to continue with the treatment for two more cycles, then reassess based on the results from the scan and MRI. These would determine whether the cancer was still very active and progressing. We were still full of hope. There was still a chance, never throw in the towel. She would do the next two cycles, hit the monster on the head, and then we would go to the appointment. That appointment in six weeks would turn out to be one of the most important and decisive appointments of Poppy's life.

Chapter 44

Poppy, as brave as ever, continued with the treatment and had the two cycles administered. It is true, she was as brave as ever, but my beautiful Poppy was no longer as strong, neither physically nor mentally, the last few years having taken their toll. It had now been two and a half years since Poppy had been diagnosed with cancer and had the amputation soon after. We knew what the statistics said if cancer behaved the way it had done with Poppy: three years since the moment of diagnosis. Scary thought.

In February, we had Valentine's Day. I texted: "Poppy ok?" one more of the millions of times I said it, I guess. "Happy Valentine's Day," as always, accompanied by lots of smileys and kissing emojis. She said, "Happy Valentine's Day! Love you lots xx. How are you getting on?" She was asking me because that day she was in hospital having treatment and I was at work. I couldn't take the day off, but our friend had accompanied her. The treatment was late morning, and Poppy would be there a few hours, but at least I had arranged to finish work a bit early. I would make my way to the hospital and wait with Poppy and our friend until the treatment was finished and then go home.

We were home by 5:00 pm, and although Poppy didn't feel great, we tried to celebrate. We always made a conscious effort to celebrate every single Valentine's day. Of course, every day is special when you are with your loved one, at least to us. But I used to say to Poppy that some days are a little bit more special: Birthdays, Christmas, Anniversary, Valentine, and anything else that could come to our mind. Those days we did something to make it that extra little bit more special.

At the beginning, when money was really tight, we could never afford to go to a restaurant on a day like this. However, the truth is that we didn't want it either, and even when we could afford it, we only did it once. We didn't feel we wanted to be surrounded by people on that day, and we preferred the intimacy of celebrating at home, on our own, cooking something we fancied and opening a bottle of wine we had chosen for the occasion. For us, being together, enjoying and sharing a little dinner at candlelight with the person you love was what made it special. Days like that made me realise even more how fortunate I was to have someone like Poppy in my life. Someone that was so much better than me, from who I learned so much, that completed me and who, with time, had helped me to find my inner peace, and to accept myself with my many weaknesses and limitations. Thanks to Poppy, I had found my internal, true happiness, which had eluded me for so many years. I had finally come to realize how important that was for me.

After Valentine's Day, many days followed, and we continued with our routine. Of course, I was much more involved in all the house chores as Poppy could do very little by then. She was already taking these huge doses of paracetamol, ibuprofen, quick-release oral morphine and then the slow-release one, and the rest of the pharmacy at home, but the pain was not really improving. Waking up in agony in the middle of the night, I would go round to her side of the bed, get the medicines from the box she had on the bedside table and give her as much as she could take to try to ease the pain and let her get some rest and sleep. This pattern had been going on for a while, but I had become accustomed and, at Poppy's slightest movement complaining of pain, I would jump, eyes wide open ready for action. Poppy used to joke, saying that it was as if I had a spring in my back, but it was so difficult and heartbreaking seeing Poppy going through that practically every night. It is true I didn't get much sleep, but I would not change it for the world. Every single minute that Poppy was not in pain and could rest was worth the effort.

Our life continued, but by then, Poppy was getting up later, around 10:00 am. It was difficult for her to get going early in the day, the medicines making her quite unwell at times, but also, if she was not getting much sleep through the night, even if she woke up earlier, she was dozing on and off. She would text some days in the morning saying: "Thank you for doing the dishes." She would sometimes send it with a photo of our cats next to her. She had got up at 10:00-10:30 am, gone to the kitchen and the cats have followed. I always made sure I would clean the litter trays, give the cats any medication if needed, and feed them before going to work. I would also clean and wash the dishes and leave everything ready for Poppy when she got up, so she could feed the cats easily. That's why she was thanking me. Something it would take me minutes, and Poppy still always so grateful.

One day at the end of February, I hadn't heard from Poppy by midday, so I sent her a text. You guessed it, "Poppy, ok?" which was my usual and very unimaginative way to check that everything was well. Poppy replied, "Yes. Have I told you lately that I love you? To the moon and back a trillion times! Thank you for all you do. Xxxxxxxxxxxxxx.." That was my beautiful Poppy: she had a rough night, felt very unwell, got up quite late, and still would find the strength to write a text like that to me. "Poppy, my love, that was a lovely text you just sent. No need to thank, and the truth is I don't do much either. I wish I could do so much more, my love...." "You do! And I do appreciate it even when it seems that I don't. You are amazing! Xx." I wasn't. Poppy was the amazing one, we all knew, but she always tried to make me feel good, to make me feel special. I continued trying to make her laugh: "Mmmm… Poppy, have you had a copita de tinto? (lit: little glass of red wine in Spanish). Isn't it a bit early, Poppy?" "Ha-ha! It's just so that next time I scream at you, you have a text to look at!" That was us: even when we had some terrible moments, we were always trying to make the other laugh, or at least to put a smile on their face to lighten the situation. Of course, I replied with a text with lots of emoji kisses.

I would usually call Poppy during my lunchtime and have a little chat. I would text with my typical: "Poppy ok?" and something else like "Beautiful day today." She would reply, "Gorgeous! I'm good. You ok?" Then I would call, and chat for a few minutes, really saying the same things: How are you feeling? How's the pain? Did you manage to do this or that she wanted to do? The truth is that Poppy was much, much better than me at all the bureaucratic staff, paperwork, phone calls, and emails! She had the skills and the patience, and I neither had one nor the other. I really valued what she did, and she knew. She always dealt with all the paperwork, and I wanted her to continue doing that; everything as before, like nothing had changed. I think it was important for her and perhaps even more for me. However, the truth is that unbeknown to me at the time, the medication, and I guess the cancer as well by now, had started affecting her cognitive skills, and later on, I realised some things had not been taken care of, and I had to deal with it. I was not angry or upset about unpaid bills or similar, just so utterly sad that I had not even recognised the deterioration she had been suffering over the last few months and that she was no longer capable of doing it as before. She kept it to herself and hid it so well that I was none the wiser.

It was now the beginning of March already. As difficult as it was sometimes, we still tried to be positive and cheerful. We would text: "Poppy, ok?" At lunchtime, that meant I was now on my break. If you are ok and awake, text me back, kind of. Most days, she would do it, and we would chat for a while. For others, a text would suffice. That day she replied, "Yes. Just to remind you that you are amazing! Xx." She was now saying these kinds of things more often. "Poppy, to what do I owe the honour?" "Just for being you!" "Oh, dear. Poppy, leave the bottle alone!" "Ha-ha." We could still make each other laugh. "By the way, Poppy," I said. "Yes?" "Mmm… have I told you lately how much I love you?" "I love you too! So very, very much!!! Xx. And thank you for the best kitchen ever!" "It's not the best, but I think it's a very nice little kitchen. That's the least Poppy deserves after putting up with me all this time!" "It is the best for me," she said.

Finally, after all those years without a kitchen in France, although we had managed perfectly well with a cooker, a table and a barbecue, we had saved enough for a basic but nice kitchen, and it had been fitted the year before, so it was the second time we had been there with a kitchen. But not any kitchen, a kitchen like Poppy wanted, the colour she wanted, the cupboards she wanted, the worktop she wanted, and for the first time in our lives, she had a dishwasher. I was so pleased about that.

We could have had a kitchen before, though. We had saved, and we had the money a few years back, but one of our cats got very ill. Terrible peritonitis, we almost lost him. He had a big operation and was at the vet for many days, with all the medication one could imagine, but I thank God to this day, he eventually pulled through. However, the bill was over nine thousand pounds, and our insurance was capped at six thousand pounds per condition. Therefore we had to pay the rest from our pocket. That is where the money for the kitchen went at the time. No regrets, though: our cat was worth much more than any kitchen. It just took us a bit longer.

We already had a bedroom. Now the open plan kitchen-dining-living room was also finished. Now we needed a bathroom. I had always dreamt of having this wonderful bathroom for Poppy, it was on my mind, and I had already spoken to the builder about what I wanted to do. I wanted Poppy to have this beautiful 'bath with bubbles', so she could soak for hours with a gentle massage, soothing her battered body. It was going to be a surprise for her. I said to Poppy: "Next project, a beautiful bathroom for Poppy. Let's start saving!" "You can have everything I have, but it's not much. But more important than a bathroom is you. Xx." "It's a lot, Poppy, but nothing compared to you." She then said something that really touched my heart: "You have given me nearly 23 years of love. You are everything and more I ever could have wished for. Thank you. Now, for a bit more!" Poppy said. "Another 23 will do, my love…" "What would I give for that! But whatever we have, I will appreciate and love. Time is precious!" "Probably neither you nor me will have 23. Vive la poetry! But we still have whatever we have, which is truly precious, and we have to make the most of it." Always making silly jokes when things were serious. "Beautifully said xx," Poppy replied, still laughing at my jokes, my not-very-good ones and the really bad ones. It was hurting so much to hear Poppy say these things, me just thinking of the prospect of not having Poppy another 23 years, or 15, or 10, or 5, or 1, month only, perhaps? That thought was killing me inside.

Chapter 45

A few days after, Poppy had an appointment with the oncologist team. Sadly, they didn't give us the news we hoped to hear, although I guess Poppy probably knew before being told. I remember that day driving home after the appointment being fairly quiet for both of us. And I remember getting home and trying to cheer Poppy up, trying to fight the sadness inside me after hearing the news. And I also remember having a very heavy heart and economy of words when I spoke to my brother and said, "No good news. The treatment hasn't worked, and they are going to stop it."

In the appointment, we were told that the most recent scan showed the cancer had grown significantly in the last six weeks, massively infiltrating the left pelvic area. That's why Poppy had much more pain in the area. The clinical trial team would now refer Poppy back to the medical and oncologist team to see whether she could have more radiotherapy in the area. However, we knew that was extremely unlikely as she had already had all the radio permitted when she was treated with chemo-rad two years before. That only left Poppy with the unpalatable option of chemotherapy. This one, however, was the typical and most traditional one, highly aggressive, indiscriminating and with well-known and very nasty side effects. It would be fair to say that we were not filled with overconfidence after the appointment, yet for as long as there was hope, we would keep fighting.

Our life continued the best we could, me still working but less now. We had always tried to save my days off for the big operations, post-operatory when I had to look after

Poppy, for more serious appointments or when she was really unwell.

The doctors didn't procrastinate, though. Poppy started her chemotherapy treatment almost immediately and had a weekly session. It was almost the middle of March now. As always, the room where the treatment was administered was very busy, and sometimes Poppy had to wait for ages, but the staff were amazing. Most days, I would have to go to work, but always tried to finish as early as possible and make my way to the hospital. Many times I would arrive, and Poppy would still have hours to go, but at least we could be together. Once finished, we would make our way home.

I always kissed Poppy in the morning before going to work. I used to leave before 6:30 am and tried not to wake her up. Some days though, she would wake up, perhaps just hearing the door shut and would send me a text: "Have I told you lately that I love you? Poppy, strong, and fighting!" "Oh, Poppy, I can't wait to finish work and come home. I miss you soooooooooo much!" "Just get through the morning, and you will soon be home. Won't be long. Xx." "Yes, I know, Poppy. Try to get some rest."

Poppy knew I didn't want to be at work, I wanted to be there with her, but she was always so gracious and supportive, even when she would have preferred to have me there. But she always made it look like everything was ok, like, don't worry, it's fine. You are at work for a few hours, and then you'll come home.

I used to say to Poppy if I woke her up when kissing her in the morning before going to work: "Sorry, Poppy, I woke you up." It rarely happened, though. However, Poppy knew I would always kiss her in the morning, and I would always kiss her goodnight. At the very beginning of our relationship, one night, we had a silly argument. I don't remember what, nothing too serious, I guess, but Poppy went to bed without saying goodnight. When I got up in the morning, I gave her a kiss before going to work, trying not to wake her up. When I got back home that day, she said, "You gave me a kiss this morning before you left." I said, "Of course I did, Poppy. But I tried not to wake you up, sorry." "I was awake, but I didn't open my eyes," she said. I had a temper, but almost as soon as it came, it went. It would pass quickly, and I didn't hold grudges. Poppy, however, didn't have a temper, but it would take her much longer to get back to normal. We were just different, and we learnt and adapted. But that day, I told her something that to me was very clear, "Poppy, let me tell you something for you to know. I will always give you a kiss in the morning before going to work in case something happens to me and I will never see your beautiful face again. Equally, I will always kiss you goodnight in case I am taken in my sleep, and I never see your beautiful face again, either. No matter what, I will always kiss you in the morning, and I will always kiss you at night." By then, Poppy was ok. She smiled at me and nodded. Since that day, she knew that regardless of how big an argument between us could be, she would still need to put up with my kiss!

Chapter 46

It was now towards the end of March, nearing Poppy's birthday. Sadly, the 21st of March was the beginning of a very hard period for Poppy. I had gone to work and left before 6:30 am as usual. Poppy texted at 6:40 am: "Love you loads xxx. Missing you. Getting worried." That was not normal. "Morning, Poppy. What's up? You ok?" "Missing you badly!" "Missing you too. Try to get some rest before you get up. It's very early," I said. Then Poppy said, "My turn to cry today." I called her, and we chatted for a few minutes. The truth is that Poppy was a very strong, brave, determined and positive woman, but we're not robots, and sometimes things get a bit too much. And God knows how much she had had already!

She was worried because that day, she would have a scan in the morning. And the scan would reveal whether the chemo was working or not. Our friend was coming at 9:00 to accompany her to the hospital, but in view of how worried I felt Poppy was, I requested at work to take the rest of the day off as annual leave, and then I texted Poppy: "Poppy ok? Are you at the hospital yet?" She replied, "Worst driver ever! About 10 minutes away. He got lost, and I'm going to be late." "Don't worry, Poppy, you're almost there, and they're always running late. Anyway, I have news for you. I hope good news." "What news?" she asked. "You don't need to take a cab home. You will be picked up by your own personal chauffeur! Is that ok?" "Ahh, fantastic," she said. "Just let me know how you're doing. I'll be leaving soon." "I'll let you know how they are doing, but I think I will be done by 11:00 am." "Ok, you might have to have a drink and wait for me a bit." The hospital was a good 30 minutes away from work, but if it was busy with traffic, it could take me longer. Poppy said,

"Ok, don't worry, it's quite busy, but they're running almost on time." "Ok, keep me posted," I said.

That was our life. For this scan, she needed a contrast to be administered and then wait a few minutes. She would let me know when the cannula was in, when she was going for the scan, and if I had not arrived, when she was done and ready to go. But that didn't matter because it was me who was picking her up, and then we would make our way home together, once again, one of many hundreds of times.

That day, however, was hard for Poppy. We arrived home, and I could see how worried she was. For the first time, we started talking very seriously about her condition. She could see that things were not going in the right direction: the treatments hadn't worked, her overall condition was deteriorating, and she could feel the lymph nodes getting bigger and pressing certain structures, reducing her mobility and causing her a lot of pain.

But until then, I am ashamed to say I had almost been blind and in complete denial of the reality that was unfolding in front of my eyes. I never wanted to accept that Poppy could not be cured. We used to say that we could fight and defeat everything together, anything that was thrown at us. But sometimes, it was almost impossible to keep up the spirits and be positive, and that was one of those days as I started to come to terms with the cruel realisation that perhaps this was a battle we could not win. It was a really sad day.

The day after, I went to work, and I received a text from Poppy at 11:00 am. That night had been even more difficult to get any sleep, so at some point, I got up and wrote a note to Poppy. I guess she had got up not long ago, taking her medications, seen my note and then think about what to say.

This is what my beautiful Poppy texted that day: "You are breaking my heart! I know you are worried. I see it in your eyes every day. I see the change from total belief in a cure to uncertainty. I wish I could stop time and stay here in this moment forever. I'm worried sick about you too. I have to believe we can keep going as long as possible. The pain is bad but manageable most of the time. I will fight as long as I can to be with you. You are my reason for living. Xx."

In that letter, I had written how much I loved her, how much she had done for me and what she meant to me. How fortunate I felt and how grateful I was to God that she had put Poppy in the journey of my life. How Poppy was now my life, and I could not conceive my life without Poppy anymore. How I was very worried about how things were going, but I would keep fighting for us and never give up. I also said that miracles do happen, and I had already had mine by meeting her and having 23 wonderful years. I was now praying to God that there was a miracle for Poppy as well. In any case, every day was precious, and we had to make the most of it. That was more or less it.

She continued, "I will keep that note and read it when I'm feeling desperate. I would have given up a long time ago without you. I just hope this chemo isn't too bad. Hairless is not a good look!" I read Poppy's message, and there was a big lump in my throat, tears coming to my eyes, and I really didn't know what to say. In the end, I just said, "I don't care about hairless. It's still you but with less hair." "True," Poppy said, "and you have enough for both of us!!" That is because I'm very hairy. I used to say jokingly that I'm a very good example that man comes from the ape. Jokes apart, I said, "And although I'm deeply saddened at the moment, I don't give up. I truly believe that there is still a future for us. Call you soon." "Good. I do too! Xx." As soon as I could, I called my beautiful Poppy, and we had a chat.

Chapter 47

A couple of days after, Poppy texted again at 6:40 am. "I'm starting to hate mornings... I know I'll be fine later. It's just the moment you go that's hard. Xxxxxxxxxxxxxx." I replied, "I know, my love, with daylight is more difficult for you." "I think I'm going to get up and watch tele for a bit. The pain is vicious this morning." I said, "Sorry I woke you up when I gave you a kiss this morning. You were sleeping so well." "I was already on and off awake. And anyway, I prefer to have a 'kissito' (little kiss)." "Ok, I'll give you lots of 'kissitos' when I get home," I said. "Good. I hope you are ok." "I'm fine, Poppy." "Ok, but promise me to eat well and go for a walk today." "Ok, that's a good plan." "I'm so worried about you. I couldn't be more worried. I love you so much! Xx." That was again my beautiful Poppy, with terminal cancer very advanced by now causing agonising pain, and still worried about me. I could only reply, "Poppy, don't worry about me. I'm fine. I'm more worried about you. You just worry about getting better, ok, my love?"

"My bowels have emptied completely," Poppy texted in the afternoon. "That's excellent news! That should help a lot," I said. Poppy was always very constipated, so much morphine and other medications having that effect. Sometimes she wouldn't go to the toilet for days, which surely added to the discomfort and pain she was already experiencing. When things were getting really bad, she had to take laxatives, but she didn't like that, so she tried all-natural remedies first.

The day after, I texted Poppy at lunchtime: "Poppy, ok? Can't wait to finish today and come home. I miss you so much!" "Yes, I miss you badly too... do you have any paracetamol? I've got only 2 left." "No, sorry, I don't have any, but I'll get you some on my way home," I said. I made friends in so many pharmacies. I was constantly buying paracetamol and ibuprofen for Poppy. "Thank you. Also, treatment is booked for Friday at 11:00 am." "Oh, Poppy, I'm so sorry it's your birthday," I said. "Never mind, treatment is more important. And if I feel ok, we can have Chinese takeaway." "That would be great, Poppy. A little celebration, Poppy and I," I said.

That was pretty much the story of our lives at the time. We had talked about whether I should give up work and just stay at home, but we somehow felt that overall it was perhaps better to continue as much as possible with some kind of normality and routine in our lives. In hindsight, I probably made a mistake and should have stayed at home at that time and not when we decided to do it later.

End of March now, and Poppy had just had another pulmonary infection, not too severe this time, but it made her feel a bit grotty for a few days. She had been prescribed some antibiotics and was starting to feel a tiny bit better, but the doctors had to cancel the chemo on her Birthday. Perhaps the best Birthday present after all that day!

In any case, on her birthday, she was too poorly to do too much, but we didn't want to just stay at home. In all honesty, I was perhaps more the one that didn't want to stay at home, the scary thought of that being Poppy's last birthday at the back of my mind. We always did something for our birthdays, regardless of how much or how little, but something meaningful, something different, something we could remember. I didn't want this year to be any different. Although I was still not prepared to accept the reality, denying what was clearly happening in front of my eyes, I found myself more and more often contemplating the idea

195

of Poppy 'losing the battle', that terrible expression again. And if this was going to be the last time we could be together on Poppy's birthday, share that day with her and enjoy her company, I wanted to have a better memory than just sitting at home.

We had to be realistic, though: going out for the day was already out of the equation. But a little outing perhaps could be managed. We had a quick search, and we found a house belonging to the National Trust, it wasn't too far, and it was open to visitors that time of the year. It was less than forty minutes away by car, but by now, that was already quite difficult for Poppy to manage. I guess, again, she did it for me. We were there a little while visiting the house and the grounds, but we had to come back because of the pain. On our way back, we got some Chinese takeaway, and we 'celebrated' Poppy's birthday the best we could.

That day also, I felt extremely sad when I asked Poppy to take a selfie of us in the gardens with the house as the background, and she reluctantly agreed. It was very rare for me to ask for a selfie together, extremely rare, Poppy being the one usually taking our selfies together. But something was telling me that I may not have that many more opportunities left. She was in quite a bit of pain, in one leg and with the crutches, but that wasn't the main reason. I realised at that moment it had been a long time already since Poppy would take photos as we did before. We had hundreds of photos together. Poppy always so natural, so photogenic, and so beautiful. She didn't look like that anymore...

April came, and our life continued. Some days, Poppy would have a reasonably good night's sleep, not waking up too much in pain, and that would lift her spirits, but it wasn't very often. Rather more often, she would have a bad night, the pain would wake her up, I would give her as much medication as we safely could, and we would wait for it to take effect. The day after, I would probably get a text like: "I miss you so much!!" with lots of crying emojis. "I miss you too, Poppy," I would reply. Often now, just to take her mind off things, I would be looking for offers on line, so she could distract herself for a few minutes at least. I would text: "Hey, Poppy. I've seen an advert. M&S online sale of up to 70% ends today. Maybe you want to have a look if you need anything?" "Yes, thank you, I'll have a look," she would say. The truth, however, is that by now, Poppy really didn't have that much interest in anything. Every so often, she would send me a list to do the shopping. It was becoming increasingly more and more difficult for Poppy to go out.

On the 10th of April, she texted me at 7:50 am: "Started vomiting out of nowhere. Had my coffee, and whoosh, it came back up!" "Oh, poor Poppy, I'm so sorry. So you didn't fall back to sleep when I left," I said. "Not yet, but I may doze off. Not as much pain as yesterday, which is good." The day before, the pain had been really bad. "That's wonderful news, Poppy. So pleased to hear." "Don't worry about rushing home today. Just do what you can. I'll be ok." That was Poppy, never putting any pressure on me, always saying she'd be ok. Later on, I texted: "How's Poppy doing?" "Bad. Sick and in pain. Resting," she replied. "Ok, Poppy, I'll finish as soon as I can and come home." And so I did. I was home soon after. Sadly, that was becoming the norm, and the side effects from the chemo were starting to affect her.

The next day was even worse. I texted Poppy at 12:30 as I hadn't heard from her: "Poppy, ok? I haven't heard from you. Resting?" "Sick, sick, sick! Very thirsty…" was her reply. The day after, again, I hadn't heard from her. She always let me know when she was up. I texted at 11:00 am:

"How's Poppy today? A little bit better?" (no reply). I texted at 12:10 pm: "Poppy there? Not very well, I guess?" (still no reply). Again I texted at 1:30 pm: "Poppy ok?" She eventually replied at 1:45 pm: "Just woken up," she said. That was happening more and more often.

We were now in the middle of April. She texted me one day: "How are you feeling this morning?" I hadn't been very well for a few days. The stress, constant worry, and lack of sleep, I guess, eventually all take its toll, and sometimes one feels a bit under the weather. "I'm fine, Poppy. Just a bit tired. Can't wait for my days off," I replied. I had arranged a few days off to spend more time with Poppy. I said, "But most importantly, how's Poppy?" "Poppy is good! Feeling less grumpy, less sore and generally good! The pain, as usual, bothered me around 5:00 am, but it settled," she said. "Poppy, you weren't grumpy, my love, just in pain and fed up. I'm sure I would be much worse!" She continued, "I was particularly grumpy with H (H and S were our cats). He seemed to manage to hurt me, scratch me, etc., every single time. Plus, I worry about sticking my fingers in his mouth every night because he bites down. Cats' mouths are full of bacteria!"

Unfortunately, our cats were used to climbing on us when in bed or jumping on our laps when sitting on the sofa. They had done it since day one, and of course, it had never been an issue. However, now it was becoming a problem increasingly, as when jumping on Poppy, they would press on the tumours and cause a lot of pain. Also, our cats were getting quite old and had developed some medical conditions which required treatment and daily administration of an oral pill for their advanced renal failure, among others. Therefore, we had to administer a tablet every night, which meant holding them, which I always did, and then opening their mouths and putting the tablet at the back of their mouths, which Poppy did. Poppy was getting worried about that as well. I said to Poppy, "H is being a bit of a pest, and you weren't well. It's not your fault, Poppy, but neither is his. He's not going to understand why he can't jump now. We'll see what we can do." Then she said, "And you don't like doing the tablets. I'm worried he'll bite me." That was true. She had always done it because she was so much better than me. In any case, now things had to change. I said, "I know, Poppy, you're right. But maybe I'll have to start doing the tablets for them from now on." And that's how it came that from that day I gave the tablets to our cats; one less worry for Poppy. Also, I took those days off, and I could spend the whole day, every day, with my beautiful Poppy. Priceless.

Chapter 48

Our life continued, we were now at the end of April, and I was back at work. It was always very difficult the first day back at work, leaving Poppy at home on her own. I texted her in the morning: "Poppy, ok?" She replied, "The pain is bad this morning. I've taken all my tablets, so hopefully, soon, it will settle." "Oh, poor Poppy. I'm so sorry you're in so much pain, and there is nothing I can do…" She said, "You can give me lots of 'kissitos'. "Don't worry, Poppy. I will. I still have millions for you!" I continued, "Today, my papa would have been 81!" "No way! My goodness. I know you miss him so much, but today we will say Happy Birthday Papa. Xx." Poppy always knew what to say to make me feel better. "I do, and my mum. I know my dad was so much stronger and wiser than me and my mum so kind and patient: I just ask them to guide me because Poppy, my love, I really don't know what to do…" She said, "They are guiding you very well. However, you are doing a brilliant job, better than you think. I know they are looking out for you and sending you love and kindness. Xx." That was Poppy: even if I felt utterly useless and desperately impotent that I couldn't do more for her, she would still always be so gracious. "I miss you. Come home soon," she said. And, of course, as soon as I could, I rushed home to Poppy. I had always done it from day one. Nothing had changed there. And now we would have the weekend together.

April came to an end and gave way to May. I texted Poppy: "Hi Poppy, how are you doing?" "I'm just resting! Not too sick, but the post-chemo pain is yuck. Taken lots of painkillers, and they are definitely helping. Xx." "That's good. The more you rest, the better," I said. A couple of days after: "How's Poppy? I gave you a 'kissito' but didn't want to wake you up. You were sleeping so well." "I did sleep well after a while. You slept well too! I don't think you heard H being sick around 2:30 am," she said. "Oh! I didn't hear anything, although I kept waking up."

It had started happening to me a while back, once every few weeks. Sometimes, my body was so tired that I would just collapse and be completely gone for 2-3 hours. I guess that night had happened, and I must have been completely oblivious to the world for a while! Then I would wake up in a panic.

Poppy sent me a picture of a ham sandwich she had made herself and taken to bed. She had taken 2 bites and texted: "Breakfast in bed." "Wonderful, Poppy. Did you enjoy it?" "Yes, I enjoyed it. I was hungry. But now I feel sick… can't win!" she said. I asked her, "Oh, poor Poppy. Did you take your nausea tablets?" "Yep. Still got more to go, but the headache they give is as bad as nausea. Need to keep my fluids up too. Although what helps best is 'kissitos'. Lots of them!" "Keep drinking. Very important. Hopefully, today should be the last bad day, and from tomorrow, you should start feeling a bit better. Hopefully!" Then I sent another message with lots and lots of kisses. I would never run out of kisses for Poppy.

The day after, I texted: "How's Poppy today?" "The pain still bad, but I'm managing." Sometimes, I would just think about all she had gone through already and what she was going through now, and I would say: "You're so brave and strong. You never cease to amaze me." And then she would say, "Only as strong as the team around me = YOU! Nobody can do this alone." She was right. Nobody can do it alone, but I was doing so little, and she was doing so much. There wasn't much equality in the partnership.

Sometimes she would text in the morning, 7-7:30 am: "Just dozed off again! We need bread. Only 3 or 4 slices left. Xx." "Ok, Poppy, I'll get some on my way. Anything else?" I wouldn't get a reply. My beautiful Poppy had just dozed off again, just like that.

I would still always text on my lunch hour: "How's Poppy doing?" Sometimes after a while, I would get a reply: "Just woke up." It was 1:00 pm. Poppy was sleeping more and more.

Some days she would text: "Got a temperature of 38.8. Taken paracetamol. Feel ok." She always said she was ok, so I didn't worry, but I knew that most of the time, she was not that ok. Of course, I worried, but I tried not to think too much, and I certainly tried not to show it.

The chemo was supposed to prolong Poppy's life a bit more and give her a minimum quality of life. In reality, it made Poppy feel very unwell and did not prolong Poppy's life. We tried, though. Her family came to visit her in the middle of May, a few hours on Friday and longer on Saturday, and at the end of it, poor Poppy was absolutely destroyed, totally exhausted, and she spent practically all Sunday asleep in bed. By then, I was spending as much time at home as possible, still working, although less. The weekends were a blessing as I could be at home all day with Poppy, keep her company, prepare her medication and make her a cup of tea.

We continued with our life, always the best we could, always texting. How are you today? How's your pain? I miss you lots. I can't wait to finish work and come home. The pharmacy would call, saying the prescription was ready for collection, and I would go and pick it up. Can you get bread or this or that on your way home? I've run out of cheese slices. Not urgent, but can you get me some in the next few days? Any are fine. Can you please get me some broccoli as well? No rush and not much as I'm not eating much yet, and we don't want to waste food. I've also fancied that pâté again.

It was now towards the end of May, and Poppy had already the third cycle of chemotherapy. She wasn't eating much, that's for sure, so anything she fancied, I would rush to get it for her. At least she could eat something she enjoyed. The chemo had been very hard on her, making her feel very sick and tired, and of course, she lost her hair. Her hair is something I always remember when I first met Poppy: she had this straight long black hair gently cascading over her shoulders to the middle of her back, and it was absolutely stunning. Now it didn't look anything like Poppy's hair of all those years back, with more and more falling and leaving bald patches. She had lost most of her hair by then, and on the 24th of May, I shaved Poppy's head. It made me feel extremely sad, but it was the best for her.

Interestingly, on one of my last visits to our best friends just a few weeks ago, they gave me a photo that they had printed specially for me of Poppy and I on one of the dinners in their place many, many years back. We reckoned it must have been around 2002, we were sitting at the table, and she was wearing this red top front open, just insinuating her beautifully shaped body. But it was the long black hair and her radiating smile that put a lump in my throat. She looked so much like the Poppy I had met all those years back, happy, casual and relaxed, almost without make-up and so naturally beautiful. And with that long black hair! Yet, I was the one who shaved Poppy's head. I had to.

I remember saying to my brother at the time how horrible the effects of this chemotherapy were, how unwell they made Poppy feel and how I had that day shaved Poppy's head. He said not to worry as the hair will grow back, and I distinctly recall saying to him that I truly hoped to see Poppy's hair grow back. Unpleasant thoughts were coming to my head more often now.

However, we still tried to play it down. Poppy texted me: "We're running out of milk. Can you get some on your way home?" As usual, I would reply: "Of course, Poppy, no problem." She said, "I've eaten one of your cakes." "Oh, naughty girl." "Yes, very naughty. Actually, I think it was my bald head that ate it, not me!" "Ah, the egghead. Naughty egghead. Then it's not your fault."

That last chemotherapy treatment had been very hard on Poppy. Her body was already so battered, and it didn't really do much for her. At least the Bank Holiday in May blessed us with good weather, and we decided to do a barbecue. We ate, and then Poppy sat on the sofa to rest. As she was sitting on the sofa, dozing, and I was doing the washing up, I was looking at her, and she was starting to look so poorly: I could see the merciless cancer inexorably languishing my beautiful Poppy in front of my eyes. I'm glad she was asleep so she couldn't see the tears in my eyes.

Chapter 49

On the 1st of June, I cut the grass and started making the garden look beautiful for Poppy. Don't ask me why. Poppy was this independent, strong and brave woman that loved life and the outdoors, but also this quiet and timid person, very kind and gentle, that was very happy spending hours indoors on her own with a book, her kindle or watching telly.

When she was well, we always had a beautiful garden. Sometimes we would go together to get some plants. I loved accompanying Poppy to the garden centre. She knew quite a bit about gardening, but I didn't have a clue. Other times she would go on her own or with one of her friends, and then she would show me what she had bought or planted. In any case, we always had a beautiful garden in the summer. And she was superb at growing tomatoes.

By now, however, she could do very little, and gardening was out of the question. But I thought that if the garden was beautiful, she would be tempted to spend more time there instead of indoors, and that would be beneficial to her. In all honesty, it was almost coming to the point that I felt totally useless and didn't know what to do to improve her quality of life. It was so utterly frustrating and depressing, but I could not let it get me down, and neither could I show it to her.

That week Poppy had the scan. The day before the scan she had said to me: "I don't want to go tomorrow! I hate this scan business!" I replied, "Don't think too much about it, Poppy. Let's just do it and get it out of the way." Poor Poppy, she was already so tired of so many scans, so many medical appointments, so many operations, so many procedures, so many treatments, in fact, so much of everything over so many years that it was no wonder that sometimes she would feel completely fed up with everything. Who wouldn't?

In any case, she replied, "Yeah…" "Of course, Poppy, then, with a bit of luck, this weekend will be your good weekend. Maybe we can celebrate a bit, cook something nice…" "Yummy!" The truth is that we were no longer cooking as before, we didn't have the mood sometimes, and also Poppy wasn't eating that much or enjoying her food anymore. No, we weren't cooking that much anymore, but I could still say: "Poppy… mmm… I don't remember. Have I told you lately how much I love you?" That and a few 'kissitos' always made it a bit better for Poppy.

Again, for that scan, I could not take time off from work that day, and there was nobody else available to accompany her, so she had to go on her own by taxi. I remember saying to my brother how awful it made me feel, as I knew how difficult it was for Poppy by now. My brother kindly said to me that I was doing all I could and couldn't do more, but he understood it must be 'very hard' for me. To what I replied, you cannot imagine how 'very fucking hard'. I very rarely swear, so I guess I didn't feel that great that day.

At least I finished a bit early and went to the hospital to pick her up. We always did that, but sometimes I would get stuck in traffic, and she would have to wait for ages. Yet, we always preferred to do it that way: for her, it was important because she was accompanied by me on the way home instead of by taxi on her own. For me, however, it meant so much more: I was picking up my wife, the most important person in my life. There is nothing like picking up your loved one from work or, in our case, unfortunately, from the hospital, as we had to do many times, or from wherever she is. There is something very special in picking up your loved one and making your way home together. At least, so it was for us.

Interestingly, I always did that in Spain with my 'good' relationships. With the 'bad' ones, you don't bother. Not every day, of course, but for instance, when working late, if possible, I would pick up my girlfriends after work and then spend some time together. It cannot be underestimated how much good it does for a relationship, even if it's just half-hour together. To see each other that day, that otherwise you probably wouldn't see each other. To talk, the physical connection, perhaps a little drink somewhere, but together. Apart from very few occasions, if it could be done, wherever Poppy was, I would pick her up, or she would pick me up if that was the case, and we would make our way home together. It worked for us.

That day, as usual, I picked her up and made our way home together. The day after, she had an appointment with the oncologist to see the results. As it was a late appointment, - we always asked for the latest appointment available - I finished work, rushed home, picked Poppy up and then rushed again to the hospital. I would usually drop Poppy off at the entrance and then go, park the car, run back to the hospital to meet her and then make our way up to the clinic. Hopefully, we would make it to the appointment on time, and we practically always did, not least helped by the fact that usually the clinic was very busy and doctors were running a bit late, very late on some occasions.

"We did get the results from the scan today, and it wasn't good news," I remember saying to my brother. "This horrible chemotherapy hasn't worked, and the cancer has grown. Therefore they're going to stop the treatment." That was the news we were given that day when we saw the oncologist. Not the news we wanted to hear, and yet when my brother asked me how we were, I said we were fine within the circumstances and tried to be positive. Even more, that day, I still said to Poppy, "don't worry, I will be playing the guitar soon, you'll see."

The story of 'playing the guitar again' started when Poppy was diagnosed with cancer and had the amputation. The previous years I didn't have too much time, so I wasn't playing much the guitar, but I would still do it a few times a week, perhaps gently playing something for a while when watching a movie on the telly to keep my fingers moving, just going through the cords. It was very relaxing for me. Then I had one of my silly things. When Poppy was diagnosed with cancer, I said to her that I would play the guitar again when she was well, fully recovered, with her prosthesis, and we could go for a walk holding hands. We anticipated that to be just a few months. That was because after having the amputation, we thought Poppy was cured, but then soon after, we realised she was not cancer free as we had imagined. The cancer had already made its way up to the lymph nodes in her left groin. I then said to Poppy I will play the guitar again when you are cancer free, when we hear the magic two words 'all clear'. Before starting the chemo-rad, I said to Poppy, "you'll see, I'll be playing the guitar soon." The same happened before the big operation and again before the immunotherapy. Even this time, after that news, I still said it. I guess it was my way of keeping some hope. We still had time, something would happen, and I would play the guitar again.

That day, they also gave Poppy another appointment for the week after to discuss the options, which were clearly running out. Yet, I still thought that a miracle would occur and Poppy, my beautiful Poppy, would make it.

Chapter 50

That appointment never happened. Poppy received a phone call from the hospital the day after saying that there was nothing else they could do for her there and she was going to be referred to an experimental centre in another hospital south of London, hoping they could offer some help. They would contact Poppy to make an appointment, and as usual, we could do nothing but wait. In the meantime, interestingly, we were not talking much about it, and we were really trying not to think too much about it either. I think it was our way of coping with it, and in all honesty, we did not know what they could offer Poppy, neither there was anything we could do in the meantime. I guess after so many years, we had learnt to use that valuable time and energy in doing more positive things than just worrying!

One day, Poppy texted: "Remember that I love you very, very much. During tough times I just want to be there for you just like you are there for me. A problem shared is a problem halved, said someone very clever (not like ME!!!). Let's have some good days now I'm feeling better. You don't have to keep asking if I'm feeling ok if you don't want to: it must get very boring. Lots of love, Poppy the hedgehog!" It had been quite a few days since the last chemo session, so she was starting to feel a bit better. And for the record, she was very clever, not like me. She was, without a doubt, the clever and sensible one. Poppy also sent me a photo of her that day: she had put a bit of makeup on, mascara, lipstick and earrings, and she looked beautiful, regardless of being hairless. As for the hedgehog, well, as usual, our way to play things down. As hair was growing, the tiny bit of hair would be sticking out, prickly, so she had been promoted from an egghead to a hedgehog. How silly, I guess, but again, it worked for us.

I was still working, but it was getting harder and harder. One day I texted: "I miss you VERY much. I usually miss you a lot on Mondays, so in a way, it was nice the Mondays we were in the hospital. However, of course, it is better you don't have the chemo." Going back to work on Monday after having spent the whole weekend at home together was psychologically very difficult.

We continued with our routine. Poppy would text: "We'll need milk this evening. Not sure we can stretch it till tomorrow. Xx." I would reply: "Hi, Poppy. No problem, I'll get some." We still tried to be cheerful, and Poppy still tried to do what she could: "Big mountain in litter tray! Evidence was unclear as to the culprit." I loved Poppy's sense of humour. She always made me laugh. She continued, "Just fed them as both noisily asking when I made coffee." Our cats could be very noisy and persistent when hungry. "Going to try some ironing today. That's my hardest task. Xx." "No need to do the ironing, Poppy, I'll do it, or Ewe can do it for you." Ewe was our wonderful cleaner. "I don't mind at all doing a bit of ironing. It was good. But we need a new iron. It is steaming a little but not much." "Ok, Poppy, just have a look and order what you need." By now, it was almost impossible for Poppy to go to the shops, but at least she could still order on line. She had always most efficiently taken care of everything to do with the house, including all appliances. She would do her research, she would show me, and then we would 'decide together' what she had already chosen. Ha-ha. But I really appreciated she did that. Nothing had changed.

Another day she texted: "I started cutting the fuchsia but only a bit. I'm hopeless." It was so sad to see Poppy, that for years and years, had made sure we had a beautiful garden in the summer, could now do so little. I never knew what to say: "I'm sure you did what you could, Poppy. I'm very proud of you!" "Not really. I only cut a few twigs." That was the reality: by now, even on a good day, that was all Poppy could manage, just cut a few twigs.

On the 19th of June, as usual, around lunchtime, I texted: "Poppy ok?" She was awake, so she replied immediately: "Yep. Don't cry. We have to enjoy every day. Xx." The last few days had been quite hard, seeing how Poppy was deteriorating so much. Nothing was working, she could do very little, and she was in so much pain. It was so extremely difficult to see her like this, yet, I always tried to be as positive as I could. Some days I couldn't, and I would cry a lot. I tried not to do it in front of Poppy, but that day she saw me crying when I was in the garden. Memories came to me of the many years she had had a beautiful garden in the summer for us, going to buy plants, growing the tomatoes, and now she was hardly coming out, and the most she could manage was to cut a few twigs. I felt very sad inside, and I started crying.

I replied, "Sorry, Poppy, I just feel so very sad and frustrated sometimes because I cannot concentrate enough positive energy on you. I don't know if it makes any sense." I believe that through love and kindness, we have the power to heal, but I guess that this cancer was stronger than my love, my kindness and my positive energy, and I was losing the battle. I continued, "But you are right, Poppy, my love, every day is precious, and the last thing I want is to argue for something that we cannot change. As always, we'll adapt and do our best together. That's the most important thing for me." A couple of days back, I had said to her that we needed to keep positive and bring positive thoughts to our minds. Looking in hindsight, I guess it was very easy for me to say that, but not as easy for Poppy to do it. She said, "But I know I have to be positive myself. You can't do everything." She continued, "It is very important. I love you

211

so much, and this devastates me." I knew how much she loved me and how much it hurt her also to see me like this. "I love you very much too, Poppy."

Then she said something for the first time that broke my heart: "Actually, I feel bloody angry! All our plans and this comes along and changes our lives. It's very shitty!" I had no reply to that, just sheer sadness at the reality of Poppy's words. All the hard work over the years, all the sacrifices, all the plans for the future and this horrible disease just comes along and takes everything away from you. That was the unpalatable truth for my beautiful Poppy.

Chapter 51

Our lives continued, as usual, Poppy sending me lists to do the shopping. Then I would say: "On my way to the supermarket. Do you need anything else?" She would usually add something, and then I would text: "Shopping done. Got everything, and I did well. I think!" "I'm sure you did! I have complete faith in you!" No matter how bad, we still tried to have our little jokes. I think they are so incredibly important in a relationship, but in our case, perhaps even more because of our particular situation. All the silly comments, all the silly jokes, just kept us going.

"The meds aren't in yet, but Ros will text when they arrive. Xx," Poppy would text. Ros was the most wonderful and professional veterinary assistant you could ever imagine, and Poppy and she got on extremely well. No surprise there: Poppy got on well with everybody. But I knew she liked Ros very much because it had been many years since we were going to the same vet, and it had always been Poppy who had dealt with anything to do with the cats, from vaccinations to consultations to operations and Ros had been there from day one. It was only when I was off, or something serious, or mostly when Poppy started struggling, that I would take a more active role. Otherwise, I trusted her 100% with our little monsters. "Meds are in, except S' ear cream, which we don't need for a week or so." "Ok, Poppy, thanks. I'll pick them up after work."

A few days after, Poppy was contacted by the experimental centre and was given an appointment for the week after. In the meantime, however, she received a phone call from her normal hospital. She spoke to one of the oncologists in the team that used to treat her, and he said that there was a possibility they could offer Poppy another clinical trial, and she was also given an appointment for the week after. Another week full-on for Poppy and, again, perhaps, another chance. You never throw in the towel, no matter what, no matter how hard it is. We were still hopeful, and my beautiful Poppy wasn't ready to go. We would fight till the end.

The week after came, and we went to the appointment in our hospital. The oncologist explained that for this clinical trial, they were looking for patients with the same cancer that Poppy had but presenting a specific genetic mutation. The cancerous tissue available in Poppy's case was the one almost two years back, which is not ideal, but that could not be changed. The tissue from the biopsies would be requested from the hospital where she had the operation, and the samples would be sent to a highly specialised centre in Belgium where they could analyse it and determine the genetic code. Unfortunately, only 5-10% of the patients had that mutation, but again, we were praying for a miracle. Why couldn't Poppy be one of the lucky ones?

We were now around mid-June and would have to wait three to four weeks for the results. If Poppy presented the mutation, there would be a series of tests and explorations to see whether she fulfilled all the criteria to be admitted to the new clinical trial. The wait was agonising, to say the least, for both of us, but again we wouldn't talk much about it. Just wait and see.

In the meantime, she was contacted by the team in the experimental centre and given an appointment for the first week in July. Poppy also contacted the pain control unit to see whether they could do something to reduce the pain and, in this way, at least improve her quality of life. By now, Poppy was waking up every night in pain, usually between 2:00 and 4:00 in the morning. The new bed and mattress hadn't helped that much, neither the increased medications. We tried to deny it, perhaps, or we truly didn't realise, but the reality is that the cancer was by now much more advanced than we thought, and the pain was excruciating.

As Poppy was waking up in agony, I would get up and give Poppy her medication, then lie in bed next to her, turn to her, looking at her, with my fingers gently touching her arm, totally impotent, unable to do anything to take that pain away, just looking at her, her face distorted in pain, waiting for the medication to take effect, slowly, very slowly, so awfully slow at times, to ease that pain, that insufferable pain, by now hurting so much in her stump, in her hip, in her tummy, that wouldn't let my beautiful Poppy find a comfortable position to rest. Eventually, sometimes it could take over half an hour, the pain would start decreasing, the huge doses of morphine and painkillers slowly working their way through her body, but every time taking longer to act and having less effect. And yes, eventually, sometimes, 1-2 hours after the medication, Poppy would fall asleep. Then she would be asleep for a few good hours, at least three or four, and she would not be in pain.

It was now the end of June, and Poppy had been given an appointment for the week after on Friday in the experimental centre. Still hoping, trying anything available. The worse side effects from the chemotherapy were gone, she felt a bit better, and we decided to do something Poppy had wanted to do for a long time but we hadn't been able to do: we were going to the beach!

Poppy loved the sea, and she wanted to see the sea, smell the saltiness in the air, and dip her toes in the water, perhaps for the last time. Oh God, that scary thought again. I think she knew she didn't have much time, and she definitely would not have many more opportunities. Yet, I still didn't want to believe it. I just wanted to keep fighting, to try anything we could.

In any case, I was so glad we did go to the beach that weekend, as with all the sadness of the circumstances, it is nevertheless one of my happiest memories, not least because I did something right and meaningful for Poppy for a change. We were going to see her dad living on the coast, and we would stay overnight with them. They had always been very good to me, very kind and very supportive of Poppy, and it is a beautiful part of the world. But we had to get there first, a good three hours by car, already so hard for my beautiful Poppy.

Chapter 52

We left on a Sunday, and I remember talking to my brother before we left. I said, "We'll be leaving soon for Poppy's dad, and if we don't get much traffic, we should be there in around three hours." "And how is Poppy doing with the pain," he asked. "Well, pretty bad, to be honest," I said, "but she'll take as many painkillers as she can and hope for the best." I continued, "I know it's going to be hard on Poppy physically, very demanding and very painful, but mentally will do her an awful lot of good. And they're all very excited."

It took us over three hours to get to Poppy's dad. We had to stop twice on the way as, by then, it was very difficult for Poppy to be in the car for long periods of time, the tumour compressing the area around her lower abdomen and groin. The sitting position in the car was just too uncomfortable for her, and we had long given up on long journeys as the pain was just too severe, even with all the painkillers she was already taking.

It was one more thing that saddened me enormously. Over the years, we had had many driving holidays, we had been to many countries in Europe by car, and uncountable times to France, and she had always been the most wonderful travelling companion, always so organised and so patient with me. We had driven no thousands but hundreds of thousands of miles together, and there we were, after all the damage that the cancer had caused to Poppy, unable to go abroad anymore, and even a journey of 2-3 hours was agony for her.

This journey, however, was different. She wanted to do it. She needed to do it, and so did I, perhaps even more than

217

her. No matter how much pain she was in, it had to be done. It had been a long time since we hadn't been able to go to the beach, smell the air by the sea, with its unmistakable saltiness, dip our toes into the water, all the things we used to do and took for granted. Yes, it had been a very long time indeed.

I have made many mistakes in my life, and there are many things I regret, but it is usually the things that I have not done that hurt the most. I deeply lament not having taken Poppy earlier to the beach. It had been years, in fact. I think we were so busy with medical appointments, treatments, operations, trying to finish the house, and all in between Poppy feeling quite unwell that we almost forgot to live!

However, I believe it was not down to Poppy. She already had enough on her plate. I think it should have been me a bit more forceful in proposing certain things, like going to spend a day on the beach when she might have still been able to travel without so much discomfort and pain. I will blame myself for the rest of my life for always thinking that she would be cured, the next treatment would work, and she would feel better to travel, and one day she would get the all clear and 'I'll play the guitar again'. Then we could travel again, see our friends again, go to a restaurant again, and live our lives like before, again!

The stupidly eternal optimistic and often unrealistic person that I am did not conceive that Poppy would not be able to fight the cancer and be victorious. It was a thought that I had such great difficulty accepting that anytime it would come to my head, I would dispel it, almost with conscious arrogance. We were 23 years together, and then you're faced with the possibility of not being together another 23, or 10, or 1. It was awful because this completely changes your future, and I just didn't want to accept it. I could not conceive the idea of Poppy being defeated by the cancer and the dreadful prospect of her not being here, not being part of my life anymore.

The truth is that I feel words like fight, defeat, win or lose, when applied to cancer, are not really appropriate. We use them because we are brought up with the idea that we have to fight for what we want and never throw the towel; therefore, we are used to them. I agree, in principle, that one should never throw the towel as then the fight is over. But with cancer, somehow, I feel it is different. Nobody chooses that fight. It's the luck of the draw. After what I saw with Poppy and her relationship with cancer, I don't think you fight cancer in the sense that it is usually understood.

I have never met anyone in my entire life as mentally strong and determined as Poppy was, and anyone that knew Poppy would confirm that. Furthermore, she was extremely healthy, hardly ever even getting a cold. If someone ever put up a fight against cancer, Poppy did. But even then, it came to the point that she could no longer keep up. Her fighting spirit continued, but her ailing body was failing her. Would one then assume she gave up in her fight against that most horrible and insidious disease that, for years, would plague her? No, you can't fight cancer. You just accept, adapt, do your hard damn best and hopefully overcome.

That was my beautiful Poppy, having had all possible treatments available to her, knowing that the disease was irreversibly progressing, feeling the cancer growing inside her, the pain every time more unbearable and still not giving up. That is why that day, we made our way to her dad for Poppy to be by the sea. The journey, however, had already taken its toll on Poppy, and it was decided sensibly to rest at her dad's place that day and go to the beach the day after.

That night we had a little barbecue, chatted for a while, and then we went to bed. Poppy didn't have a good night's sleep, waking a few times with the pain, but that by now was sadly the norm. We got up in the morning, had some breakfast and then made our way the four of us to a different beach close by, sandy and most easily accessible for Poppy.

By then, her mobility was truly compromised, and she was unable to walk unaided for more than a few metres. We had the wheelchair with us, so it was ok, but even then, she could not be comfortable in the wheelchair anymore in that sitting position for too long. In any case, she wanted to do it, and it would certainly be done!

We drove in Poppy's dad's car, so we put the wheelchair in the boot and off we went. When we arrived, I got the wheelchair out, opened it and set up the foot supports. Still, I would unconsciously put both in, although I would usually quickly realise and take the left one off. Not always, though. Funny how your brain works. She didn't really need the left one, did she?

Poppy sat, and I pushed the wheelchair for a while on the pavement along the beach, slowly and gently, as every bump would make her jolt, and that was very painful. We were talking, enjoying those moments, those very precious moments, as thousands of many others, we had already shared and enjoyed together. But we weren't talking much, though. I think in both our minds the awful thought of that perhaps being the last time we could enjoy the sea together. After a while, when Poppy was ready, I pushed the wheelchair down the ramp onto the beach, helped Poppy to stand up on her crutches on the sand and slowly we walked together towards the seashore.

It wasn't very hot that day, 22 degrees, and there was hardly anyone in the water, probably feeling even colder as it was covered with clouds and a bit windy. That didn't matter to us, though. As we were approaching the water, we could see the waves capriciously and leisurely moving in and out, gently foaming and splashing when breaking.

We got to the water. I took Poppy's crutches from her and dropped them behind on the sand, clearly useless now in the water. I was holding her gently but firmly while she was enjoying the moment, the salty air in her face and the water dancing around her toes, up to her ankle, cold and making her feel alive, truly alive. At that moment, Poppy could feel like the independent, strong and brave woman I had met over 20 years ago, and she had always been.

We stood there, looking at the horizon, savouring the moment, trying to take every tiny sensation on board, the smell, the sounds, the air on our faces, the image engraved on our minds forever. We couldn't be too long, just a few minutes, the pain searing through Poppy's left side. Then, when it was getting too difficult to stand, Poppy turned to me, and looking at me with her beautiful blue eyes, she said, "Thank you, thank you for doing this for me. I love you so very much!" With that, I could see her eyes watering and a little tear delicately rolling down her cheek. I raised my hand, softly drying her tear away with my thumb, and said, "Don't cry, my love. Let's just enjoy this moment as if it was everlasting. We don't know what will happen tomorrow, and we can't predict the future, but I know what has happened in the past, and since I met you, you have made me the happiest man in the world. Nothing will ever change that." I gave her a kiss, and with that, as she was smiling at me, another tear rolled down Poppy's beautiful eyes, this time met with one from mine.

We had to go. We knew we had to go, the pain becoming unbearable. Yet, we didn't want to go, we just wanted time to stand still for us and that moment to last forever, a picture of us in the sea frozen in time. We spent a few more seconds looking in front of us, our eyes lost in the horizon and our minds lost in our thoughts. Then, with a deep breath, I gave Poppy her crutches, helped her out of the water and slowly made our way to the wheelchair. As she sat in the wheelchair and I was pushing her up the ramp, she turned her head to the sea, the last look before leaving. I am so glad she did, as that would be the last time my beautiful Poppy would see her beloved sea.

Chapter 53

We made our way back to the village and had lunch in one of the local pubs. Then we went to Poppy's dad for a while, and before it was too late, we set off. I remember that night explaining to my brother what we had done, how it all went, and that the weather hadn't been great, but it hadn't rained. Ultimately what was important is that we had done what Poppy wanted to do, and as my brother said, I had fulfilled a promise.

That was true. I had promised myself a few months back that I would do my very best to ensure that Poppy would see the sea, and I had told a few people. That was my promise to myself, and it was now fulfilled. However, it is interesting how other people perceive what you do in relation to how you see it yourself. Everybody, our families and friends, colleagues at work, and even acquaintances, would always comment on how very well I was doing in the circumstances, that I was doing everything I could, that I was giving Poppy all the help, support, and love. Yet, why did I feel I always came short, very short at times, it was never enough what I did for Poppy, and I felt so terribly useless and inadequate. The answer, I suppose, is that, regardless of how much you do, it's not enough. All your help, support, and love are not enough. All the medications I gave Poppy, and all the cups of tea I prepared for her, was not enough. All the times I accompanied her to the hospital for treatment was not enough. No matter how much I did, it always felt like it wasn't enough.

The married couple living next to us in France are hard-working country people who are loving and caring. After seeing Poppy struggle for so many years, having had the amputation and the many treatments, she said to me one day that I was an angel put on earth to look after Poppy! What a strange comment to make: I certainly was no angel in my life before I met Poppy and I hadn't, up to then, be of much help to Poppy regarding her cancer. No angel and no miracles, sadly…

People, women, in particular, would comment on how great a husband I was, so loving and supporting and caring. Yet, every time they said that I would sadly smile inside, thinking how little they knew, how little I did in comparison to how much I wanted to do, and how little anything I did was making any difference to Poppy's cancer progression.

Also, women, in particular, again would mention how fortunate Poppy was to have a husband like me, looking after her so well. Again, I would smile inside, thinking how little they knew, and I would tell them that I was, in fact, the fortunate one to have someone like Poppy in my life, and she would have done the same for me, only 1000 times better.

Again, people would comment, women again mostly, that many husbands would have left by now after all, we had gone through. What they did not realise is that my life with Poppy, even as it was at the time, was far richer than it had been without her. There was no comparison. Perhaps, not many people would understand that. Then I would reply that when you really love someone, that's what you do, and I was sure their husbands/wives would do the same in my case. I would never leave Poppy. There was only one thing that would separate us.

Interestingly, twice Poppy had mentioned that she would understand if I left her. I recall perfectly well the first time: it was when I picked her up from the hospital after the amputation. We drove home. I had made a banner at home and hung it on the corridor at the entrance with hearts, kisses and cat paws. In it, it was simply written, 'Welcome home. Now, we are complete'.

As we got in, I gave her a big kiss and pointed out to the banner on the ceiling. I said to her: "I love you very much, Poppy. That is my message to you." It is true, the flat always felt empty on the many occasions she had been in hospital, but this time, perhaps because of being diagnosed with cancer and having had such a traumatic operation as the amputation, it just felt worse, everything more 'incomplete'. I had never made a banner before.

It had been only a week since Poppy had the amputation, all still very raw, physically and mentally, an emotional roller-coaster and, undeniably, a big fight ahead of us. I made her a cup of tea, we sat on the sofa and then, out of the blue, she said, "I understand if you want to leave me," and pointing to her missing leg, she continued, "Look at me, I will never be the same again, but if you want me I'm still the same Poppy inside." I cannot describe with words how much it hurt hearing those words being pronounced, but I understand why she said it. 20 years back, I had met this beautiful young girl at a dance studio. We had danced our way to the top together, we had travelled thousands of miles together, and we had done everything together. Now, her look had been compromised physically, she knew her condition would impose limitations on our life in the future, and she was not sure how much we could do together anymore. She must have been terribly worried and scared, understandably so. The truth is, she was probably just terrified of our future ahead. That was all.

However, it never crossed my mind, even for a fraction of a second, to leave Poppy. I have walked out of many relationships, but that was because they did not offer what I wanted, and I didn't like wasting my time. Maybe I have too high expectations, I don't know, but I certainly don't compromise on basic values and principles. In any case, since I met Poppy, she was not only all that I wanted but all that I needed. How could I ever leave her? Trying not to sound too crossed, which is very easy for me sometimes, I said to her: "Poppy, don't say that. You know how much I love you, and you know that you are everything to me." Then, meaning it better than it came out: "With or without a leg, you are still more of a woman than many, and I will never leave you. I will only leave you if I'm carried out feet first. Otherwise, you'll still have to put up with me for a long time!" I tend to make silly little jokes when things are very serious. That's how I cope with them. Much more gently now, as my 'moments' usually last just a few seconds, I continued, "Poppy, my love, I know it's not going to be easy, but we are still together, and that is what matters. You are still the same Poppy to me, and we'll do it together. We just have to take one day at a time, and before we know it, things will get better. We also have the little monsters to look after, and they'll keep you busy and entertained, don't you worry." Another little joke as I used to affectionately call our cats little monsters. Then, to finish, I said, "and you know, because we've already talked about it, there is no reason that we cannot do more or less as we did before, you'll see." It is true, we had already talked about it, but I think it was the realisation of Poppy's new life when she got in the flat that shocked her the most. Of course, at the time, we thought that following her amputation, she was cured. One way or another, I was going to fight as hard as ever for Poppy. We had so much to live for.

The second time that Poppy mentioned leaving her, she did not say she would understand if I left her. She said I should leave her as things were going to get quite bad. It was once she had had all the treatments available, and nothing had worked. It must have been after her birthday, possibly April, when she was having the last chemotherapy treatment. It was making her feel very unwell. By then, she was already quite poorly, and she knew very well what the last few weeks of a terminal cancer patient are like when the stage is already very advanced and starts affecting their brain. As always, she said it with all the love in the world, but again those words hurt so much when pronounced. I know she was just trying to protect me, always shielding me from the worse, so I didn't suffer. She didn't want me to have to go through it all with her, seeing her suffer, seeing her deteriorate, but how could she think that I would even consider leaving her? Didn't she know me by now? Of course, she did, yet, she still had to say it because she didn't want me to see her waste before my eyes, her physical and mental faculties compromised, deteriorating and being taken slowly away from her. She didn't want me to see her suffer, as she knew that would make me suffer. Sometimes I think that if she had been strong enough, she would have disappeared to spare me what was to come. A silly thought, perhaps, my Poppy would have never left me as I was never going to leave her. It's just the idea of avoiding your loved one going through that most awfully painful experience. In any case, there was still a lot we could do, and now we had to deal with the next appointment first week of July.

Chapter 54

The first Friday of July came, and we made our way to the experimental hospital. We left early as Poppy had an appointment at 10:00 am. As usual, we arrived, she gave her name to the receptionist, and we were asked to wait in the reception area. We weren't kept waiting too long, and a nurse called her name. We accompanied her to the consulting room, and soon, a doctor came accompanied by a nurse. The doctor, a consultant in the hospital, told Poppy they had gone through all the medical history and test results of late, but they wanted to carry out some tests themselves: blood, urine, ECG, the usual. The doctor left, and the nurse arranged everything for Poppy. Now, we had to wait for the results.

When the results were ready, we were called back to the room, and Poppy was told that she had anaemia, quite advanced, and she required transfusions. That would be arranged at her normal hospital as it was much easier for Poppy to get to. In the meantime, they were going to look into treatment options available to Poppy. The problem is that they had tried every possible treatment available, and so far, nothing had worked: Poppy's cancer wasn't responding to anything and was inexorably taking Poppy's life away, relentless, insidious, unstoppable.

I remember explaining to my brother about the visit to this centre and the fact that any treatment they could offer Poppy would be experimental, phase 1. She would be a guinea pig. But we need people like Poppy, for whom nothing else has worked, to be the first ones on which to experiment with new treatments that, if successful, can go a long way in the future to help other patients. She was up for it, no doubt about that. In any case, we knew there was nothing else on offer.

The following Monday, I went to work, and Poppy texted around 10:30 am: "Thank you. You are the only reason I can open my eyes and get through the day. I love you beyond reason. Xxx." After the appointment on Friday, we had spent the weekend together, trying not to think too much about appointments, hospitals and treatments. We just wanted to enjoy the time we had together. I texted back a few minutes after: "Oh Poppy, my love, what a lovely text. And how's Poppy today?" She didn't reply. Her next text was at 2:30 pm: "Sorry I fell asleep." I replied, "Ha-ha! Good 'napita" (little nap)? "Yes, wonderful!" she said.

The day after, I must have woken Poppy up when I left for work, as I got her text at 6:30 am: "I love you. I would never, ever have chosen to have this happen to us. I'm waiting for that miracle but in the meantime, remember you must live life. It's too short not to. You are my dream husband, and you will be ok. You must be. The 'gatitos' need you!!! Xx." I replied with a lump in my throat: "Poppy, my love, they need you too. Everybody needs you more than they need me, so you must keep fighting together with me. And Poppy, I'm living my life, much more than I could have ever imagined and deserve, with you by my side, 23 wonderful years. What else can I ask for? Many things in life are not chosen, my love, but given. We just have to do the best we can with what we've got." Poppy said, "Very true! I told you Tuesday is my bad day! The tears keep dropping on Tuesdays. S is here to dry them, though." Our cat would keep Poppy company, he was the cuddly one, and his presence was invaluable to Poppy. Also, funnily enough, Monday used to be my bad day if I had to go to work, and Tuesday used to be Poppy's bad day.

The following day Poppy texted: "Where is your running stuff for washing? The doctor is coming from hospice at 10 for pain." Still, she would try to do her bit, as much as she could, put the washing machine on and hang the clothes after for drying if it wasn't too big or heavy. Also, by now, Poppy was under the pain control team from the hospice and the palliative care team, and they had arranged for a visit. After the doctor left, she texted me: "Blood transfusion tomorrow at 10:00 am." I hadn't replied to her texts, so at 12:30, she texted again: "So, have you seen your WhatsApp??" "Sorry, Poppy," I said, "Just saw your 'whats' as soon as I turned mobile data on. Thank you." Unbeknown to me at the time, our Wi-Fi at work was down. "Excellent," she said.

The day after, Poppy had the transfusion at 10:00 am. I couldn't go with her, but our friend would accompany her. I didn't want Poppy to fall asleep and be late, so I texted at 7:30 am: "Poppy... mmm..., have I told you lately how much I love you?" No reply. Another text 5 minutes after: "I love you LOTS!!!" Still no reply. At 8:00 am: "Poppy up?" At 8:30 am: "Hello. Earth to Poppy. Do you copy?" Always my silly jokes. A few minutes after, Poppy replied, "Ouf, just woke up. Love you too!!" "Ok, I'll let you get ready. Speak soon." 'Quick coffee and go." "Ok, keep me posted. Miss you!" "Miss you too. Wish you were coming but see you soon." "Me too. Sorry... my fault." A while after: "Taxi here. Speak later." That day I had to go to work for a few hours, but as soon as I was done, I would make my way to the hospital. She kept me posted as usual: "Here now, just arrived." "Had blood samples done, going to put in the cannula." "2-hour wait while blood is prepared. Don't know how many bags there are yet. Each bag takes two hours. So minimum finish around 3:00 pm." Poppy would always keep me posted, which helped enormously, and I worried that little bit less. We would chat when possible, mainly depending on how good the reception was in that part of the hospital. I would make my way to the car park near the hospital that we had pre-booked for a few hours and then walk to the hospital. I would always bring her something nice to drink from the cafeteria, and we would sit there until Poppy was done. That day, there were some complications preparing the blood for Poppy's transfusion and didn't leave until past 7:00 pm. A very long day for Poppy, but it had to be done. In any case, she had just finished, we made our way down to the entrance, and I went to fetch the car while Poppy and our friend were waiting. I picked them up, and then, as always, we would make our way home together.

Chapter 55

I have never been deeply religious, but I believe in God, and I believe that somehow I have been given help at very difficult times in my life. Until this day, I still wonder why. In any case, I remember praying a lot during that period of Poppy's life, clearly by now asking for a miracle. I would go to a local Catholic Church after the mass, when it was quiet and with few people around. Poppy would accompany me - she being Church of England didn't matter to us. On the rare occasion that Poppy went to her Church, I would accompany her gladly if she wanted me to do so. She was even less religious than me. I believe in God, but not that much in religions, as I feel that there is only one God for all of us, and all religions preach peace and love. The rest is secondary, our interpretation as human beings, and it's when it gets messy. I have friends from all religions, and I respect them all.

I trust in God, but sometimes things don't go the way you plan them to. In church, I would do my prayers holding Poppy's hand as she sat next to me. Somehow, I always kept my faith, and I thought that something would happen. However, the reality was telling me otherwise, Poppy was getting weaker and her body more consumed by the day, her pain every time worse, the doses of painkillers increased again by the pain control team and yet, some days having very little effect. Before leaving, we would always light a candle for Poppy and us and one for our loved ones gone. It might not help, but it won't hurt anyone, either.

It was now the middle of July, and I remember that Sunday being the Wimbledon final. We had watched it on the telly for many years and made a kind of special occasion day. We always looked for any excuse to celebrate, Poppy and me. We would do a barbecue, or a takeaway, or perhaps a pizza that Poppy used to do a long time ago with some dough bought from a delicatessen - and were delicious.

That Sunday, after eating, we sat on the sofa, and Poppy fell asleep. She had been much more tired and sleepy the last few weeks, her body very weak by now. I remember sitting there looking at her, completely uninterested in the final on the telly, just looking at her, how peaceful she looked, how beautiful she still looked to me, and how fortunate and grateful I was to have Poppy in my life. I also remember thinking that perhaps that would be, after 23 years, the last Wimbledon final we would watch together. And I also remember just having my eyes fixed on her, unable to take my gaze away, thinking how much I loved her, how much I still needed her and how much I could not conceive my life without her. My eyes still transfixed and unable to fight the tears any longer, I let them quietly flow at the thought of no longer having my beautiful Poppy in my life.

Chapter 56

The next week wasn't easy for Poppy. She had quite a lot of pain on Monday, and on Tuesday, her dad came to visit her for a couple of days. Again, I was always grateful when someone else could spend time with Poppy, her dad, family, friends, neighbour or even the cleaning lady, a lovely young Polish woman that became a friend. A while after Poppy had the amputation, we decided to get a cleaning lady a couple of hours a week to assist a bit. She recently told me how she felt immediately at ease the first time she met Poppy, and it was a pleasure to come home. She was not coming for the money but to spend time with Poppy. She found her truly inspirational. That was the effect that my beautiful Poppy had on people, always pleasant to everybody, always a pleasure to be with, and always an inspiration.

Her dad was here for a couple of days, and that made Poppy very tired at the end of the day. Yet, I still thought that the positive mental effect of having someone else around outweighed the negative impact on her body. Yes, she was more tired, but at least she had been with other people, talked to other people, and laughed with other people, and that was good.

The day after, Poppy had been given an appointment in the hospital, late once again, thankfully. Usual routine: I rushed home, picked her up, rushed to the hospital, dropped her off at the entrance, parked in the car park previously booked a few minutes' walk away, rushed back to meet Poppy, made our way up to the clinic, give her name to the receptionist and wait to be seen.

The oncologist team told us that they had received the biopsy sample requested from the other hospital, and it would now be sent to Belgium for analysis. The results would be in 2-3 weeks, and Poppy was given an appointment for the first week of August. That day she also had some blood tests and other explorations and tests done.

I remember talking to my brother that night, explaining, and I could not emphasize enough how important the results from the analysis of the biopsy samples were. We felt at this point that it definitely was Poppy's last chance. Everything hung on those results, even more given the fact that the experimental hospital could not offer anything to Poppy. They had contacted Poppy just a few days before and said that, regrettably, there were no experimental treatments they could offer Poppy with the type of cancer she had. That door was closed, one more and one less opportunity for Poppy.

There was still hope with the biopsy, though. If Poppy had the mutation, there was a possibility of her being admitted to the new clinical trial, but if she didn't have the mutation, that was it, the end of the road. Again, I was praying a lot around this time. I said to my brother, "The oncologist is also going to contact other hospitals to check whether they are running a clinical trial that can help Poppy. The next 2-3 weeks are crucial." "I understand. We pray every day for her." Interestingly, nobody in my family is very religious, but we were all praying a lot around this time! "Now we really need a miracle." I still wanted to believe that something would happen and said, "I keep my faith in the Almighty, and I have a bit of hope. Miracles do sometimes happen; I just hope it happens to Poppy." "Of course, miracles do happen. And you deserve it more than anyone else. After all, what Poppy has gone through and suffered." Everybody always so supportive, so wanting to help, and so kind with their words, but words sadly weren't doing much for Poppy's pain.

We continued with our lives, as always, the best we could. Another transfusion had been arranged for her, as last time there had been some problems, and they could not administer all the bags. Another time that I couldn't accompany Poppy, but our friend was with her. Another long day for Poppy. As usual, she kept me in the loop: "Journey was fine. We're here now." "How are you feeling?" "Ok. Got to drink lots of water because BP is low." That was one of the issues with her blood pressure, and sometimes the nurses would struggle to find a vein suitable to insert the cannula in. "Ok, Poppy, please keep drinking. Have you got something to read and drinks and food?" "Will do. Love you." "Love you too." A bit later, I texted: "How's Poppy doing?" "Eating a prawn sandwich!" she said. "Oh, I see. You're in the VIP section. The maximum I get is an egg mayo or tuna sandwich! Any good?" "Delicious!" she said. And we would continue our conversations every so often. When I finished work, I would go to the hospital and wait until Poppy was done. Then, as always, we would make our way home together.

It was by now approaching the end of July, and the pain was getting worse and worse. A doctor from the palliative care team from the hospice had phoned Poppy to check and doubled the dose again of one of the medicines. That night Poppy slept better, and the pain was manageable the day after, but it made her feel quite sleepy. I was talking to my brother every night, explaining how things were going, and I said, "at least she slept better last night." It was a blessing now when Poppy had a night when she could sleep more or less well. I remember my brother asking how I was doing and saying that those days I was very tired and I didn't have the energy for anything. In reality, I felt exhausted, I guess all those years were finally taking their toll on me as well. But I was still cutting the grass and doing the garden so it would look a bit better for Poppy, apart from working and doing the cleaning, cooking and the rest at home. Poppy could do very little by now.

I knew I was very run down and felt my immune system very low, but my greatest concern was to fall ill because then there was nobody that could look after Poppy. That really worried me, so I tried my very best to keep as well and healthy as I could within the circumstances. I prayed to be given strength and not to fall ill, and again, some strength was given to me, I don't know where from, and I was kept healthy, so I kept going.

The nurse from the hospice came to visit Poppy and checked on her. With the medication increased, Poppy managed the pain better. Just as well as that weekend, her family was coming to visit her. They were coming on Friday, and at lunchtime, I texted Poppy as usual: "Poppy ok?" "Yes," she replied. I knew she was awake, so we chatted for a while. Before I left work, I asked her, "Poppy, send me the list, please. I'll be leaving soon." I was supposed to do the shopping as her family was coming down, and we needed a few bits. "Yes, I'll send it now, but no rush. Dad texted, they're stuck in horrendous traffic." "Oh, poor little things, what happened?" I asked. "Fire on bus and crashes," she said. "Oh, dear." They eventually arrived, spent Friday and Saturday and left on Sunday. I could see the difference from even a few weeks back. By now, Poppy was quite weak, and that visit drained her. But it was good for her and her family, and again, she never complained. Just the pain, and yet, Poppy still had her beautiful smile ready for everybody. Truly remarkable.

Chapter 57

The first week of August didn't bring us good news. We had a late appointment and, again, the usual routine, rushing from work to get to the hospital on time. The doctor told us that, unfortunately, the result from the analysis of the samples sent to Belgium had come back negative. That was it, there was absolutely nothing else they could do for Poppy, and she would now be referred entirely to the hospice for palliative care. I remember that day in the clinic, not being able to hide my frustration, almost anger, at those words, "there is nothing else we can do for you, and we can only offer palliative care at this stage." I know it was not meant that way, but it almost felt like, "there is nothing else we can do for you. Now go and die." That frustration and anger, I think, is the result of the raw emotions that you feel inside: nothing has worked, no treatment has had the desired effect, and there is only one way this will end up, losing your loved one, Poppy dying! I was probably being unreasonable, and I don't blame anyone for their choice of words: it had to be said, and I don't think it can be said much better than that, in all honesty. But I think it is the first time that I felt very angry, really angry inside, towards the practitioners, even knowing that it wasn't their fault. Difficult to explain what I felt that day at that time, but it got very dark inside me. Fortunately, it passed very quickly. I had Poppy to look after and keep fighting for. No time to waste with dark thoughts.

During the next couple of weeks, Poppy was becoming increasingly more tired. Some days the pain was excruciating, and some nights, she was unable to sleep, so unbearable it was. By now, she would sometimes wake up in agonising pain at 4:00-5:00 am, take as many painkillers as she safely could, sleep for a few hours and then again wake up with the pain and drenched in sweat. The cancer would give her these uncontrollable sweats, and I would need to put towels for her to continue in bed until the morning when she would get up, and I would change the sheets. Everything was happening now more often and more intense: the pain, it was almost impossible to move Poppy now in bed because of the pain; the medication, now more often and in greater doses; the sweats, everything was getting worse for Poppy.

Still, we tried to continue the best we could. "Don't forget I need to get the sample to the doctors today and pick up a prescription," Poppy said. "Yes, I know. I'll take it when you're ready." "Thank you. I'm going to pee in the pot very soon!" "That would help enormously, Poppy: there's no point in me taking an empty pot for analysis!" We always tried to keep it light, with our little jokes. I took the pot for urine analysis to the doctors, picked up the prescription and went to the pharmacy to collect her medication. One of many.

"How's the pain today, Poppy?" I asked. "The pain is bad today, vicious," she said. Poppy continued, "But I've taken all the meds. I just have to wait until they start having an effect." "I'm so worried about you, my love. Are you ok for me to go and do the shopping?" "Yes, of course, I'll be fine." Poppy was always fine...

I remember being in the supermarket so sad, so wanting to cry, but of course, I didn't do it. We had been going to that supermarket for over 20 years. Usually, Poppy would do the shopping, but when I was off, on holidays or when doing a big shopping, we would go together. When she had the amputation, once she was ok, we would go together most of the time until we bought the automatic car, when she could again go on her own or with a friend. As she started deteriorating, we started using the mobility car in the supermarket. She could sit and drive around with me by her side, so we would still do the shopping together. Now, she couldn't even come, and there would not be more shopping together. Ever again.

It was now towards the end of August, approaching my birthday. My brother came to visit us with his partner for a few days. We hadn't seen each other for many years now, and I said to him that I wanted to spend my birthday the 4 of us together as I knew there would not be another chance. Poppy couldn't come to the airport to pick them up that night, but the day after, on my birthday, we had breakfast together. Then I left Poppy at home to rest, and we went sightseeing with my brother. I wanted Poppy to rest as much as possible, as we were going out for dinner!

In the past, that had always been very enjoyable. We were always excited when we were going out for dinner, just the two of us or with friends and family. I have so many memories of so many birthdays with Poppy: she always managed to make my birthday a truly special and memorable day, whatever we did. This time, however, we didn't have the usual enjoyment and excitement of past years. Again I know Poppy did it for me: she loaded herself with painkillers, and off we went, not too late this time. She was wearing a pretty dress and a bit of make-up, the first time in a long time, and she did it for me. All for me, as always, and she still looked so beautiful to me, but also by now so terribly fragile. I just wanted to have the memory of my last birthday with Poppy in a restaurant with people I loved, as we had done so, so, so many times over the years, always with friends and family, or the 2 of us in a special place. Unfortunately, halfway through the meal, the pain got very intense, and we had to leave without having desserts and coffee. That didn't matter though. Poppy had given me again a wonderful memory, a special shared moment in time, one more to add to the thousands I already had, forged over 23 wonderful years together, a celebration of my birthday in a restaurant with my beautiful Poppy and my loved ones. Now I can cherish that forever.

Chapter 58

A couple of days after, my brother left. This time Poppy accompanied us to the airport. She wanted to come, and she did it. We all knew it was the last time they would see each other, but nobody was making any comment, all casual conversation, although it was in our minds. I knew it was going to be difficult for Poppy, but she wanted to come, and I certainly was not going to say no to her. Now that I come to think of it, in 23 years together, I think it could be counted with the fingers of one hand the times I said no to Poppy. One was when my uncle died, and I didn't really want her to come that weekend. I went to Barcelona to pay my respects to my auntie and I still thought we could make it the year after. How wrong I was though. In any case, Poppy never really asked for much in the first place, but she gave me so much in my life! Poppy was this amazing woman that needed very little in material items, and she valued much more other things and certain qualities in a person: she showed me what those were, and she changed and enriched my life forever.

That day she wanted to come, and she came. It was difficult though, when we had to say goodbye to my brother and partner, fighting the tears as they knew they would not see Poppy again. Yet, I remember saying to my brother that if by any miracle Poppy was still with us at Christmas, I would pay for their tickets again to come and spend Christmas together. In reality, we all knew that was overoptimistic and extremely unlikely, no need to rush to save my pennies. Even Poppy - I know she had spoken to my brother's partner and told her she knew she didn't have much time left - but she was trying to hide it from me as much as she could, as she was worried about me and didn't want me to suffer. Poppy was worried about me: she was dying, she was actually dying and still worried about me… unbelievable, but that was my beautiful Poppy.

The day after, I spoke to my brother. After all these years of me just explaining things over the phone or with texts, they now had a very clear picture of the situation. I thanked him for coming, apologising because we couldn't do much on this occasion, but the important thing was that we had seen each other after all those years. Most importantly though, they had seen Poppy, and we had spent that time together, likely to be the last time.

He also asked me whether I had heard from my contact. It had all started because I was so desperate to get Poppy out of pain, the massive doses of morphine and painkillers now having very little effect: she was drinking oral morphine as I drank water, the cancer growing inside, causing her unbearable pain. I could see her every day in agony, not sleeping at night, unable to find a comfortable position in bed that would allow her to rest, and believe me, we tried it all. I could see the pain just searing through her body as she was moving. I had to do something about it. I was determined to do something about it. We did our research, and it seemed that cannabis could have a beneficial effect in the treatment of pain in certain cancers, so we decided to try it. However, I knew nothing about drugs, not even weed, as even in my difficult times when my mum died, I tried to keep away from it. That's probably the only good thing I did in those 5 years. However, now it was different.

Therefore, the contact my brother was referring to is a person I knew and trusted and was going to put me in contact with someone who supplied cannabis, not the usual one that you smoke, but one in a raw state that I could prepare as a liquid potion for Poppy.

Before bothering anyone, I had done some research on the internet and ordered from abroad, paid online and never received it. That was a risk I had to take, probably kept at customs, although I wish I could have explained at the time why it was done. In any case, plan A didn't work. We had to resort to plan B. Of course, I knew people who smoked, acquaintances only, nobody I could really trust, and I just didn't have a clue of what I needed and how to make it. I wanted the best possible quality and asked some people I trusted. One of them had contacts in the medical world and knew of some patients that had used it in the past and benefited from it. He also knew where to source the best quality one for my purpose, and I ordered a certain amount. I did the transfer to their account and was waiting for them to call me once it was ready for collection. That was the contact my brother was referring to, and I was waiting for.

By now, Poppy's quality of life was very poor. That day, for instance, I was saying to my brother that the night before, she was asleep on the sofa by 9:00 pm. I had woken her up at 9:30, gave her the medication and helped her to bed. Even with the massive doses of painkillers, Poppy woke up at 5:00 pm in pain, so I gave more, and then after a while, she fell asleep again. It was 11:30 when I was talking to my brother, and I said to him that usually I would have got her up by now, but she was so tired after these days that I wanted her to sleep a bit more. "After all, while she's asleep, she's not suffering," I said to him. Also, I wanted Poppy to recover as much as possible, as, on Sunday, her dad and partner were coming to visit her. But I would wake her up soon to give her the meds. "It was great to see you and to see Poppy," said my brother. "We're so happy we came." "Yes, we're very happy too. I don't think you'll see Poppy again, but at least we could spend some time together, and to me, that's priceless," I replied. "Life is so unfair," my brother said. "Yes, it is, and with Poppy, more unfair than with anyone else I know." Then I continued, "but there is nothing we can do. Just keep fighting, just praying for a miracle now." "Yes, we'll keep praying for you," my brother said. One could almost laugh now. I have never seen so many people who are not particularly religious praying so much. Of course, it didn't make me laugh at the time.

On Sunday, her family came, we had a takeaway, and then I was going to take them to the airport as they were flying to the States to visit family. Poppy wanted to accompany us to the airport, and of course, she did. We had a drink with them and then we came back. Unfortunately, Poppy forgot her medication at home, and by the time we got back, she was in agony and absolutely destroyed. The day after, she was in bed until the afternoon, so tired she was. In any case, it had been worth it: she wanted to do it, she wanted to accompany us to the airport, and she had done it. And it was great coming back together as, after that many trips and thousands and thousands of miles together, that sadly would be the last little journey in the car together with my beautiful Poppy.

Chapter 59

The end of August came. I kept doing the shopping, picking up Poppy's medications, and talking to my family and friends. I remember saying to my brother, "I'm ok, but Poppy gets worse every time." In just a week since my brother left, she had deteriorated so much! Yes, the pain was every time worse, and I recall on the 30th of August, I was saying to my brother, "Last night, it was very difficult for Poppy." Indeed, that had been a really bad night for Poppy. Between 2:10 am and 4:40 pm, I had to get up five times because of how much pain Poppy was in, and give her something else, give her something more, give her something, anything, that would help her with her pain. And she was boiling, her skin so hot, and nothing I was doing had any effect. No matter how much I tried, I couldn't keep her skin cool, her temperature down, or her pain under control. The fucking cancer was just so advanced now, and it was so difficult seeing my beautiful Poppy like that. I certainly felt like swearing that night.

The pain certainly was every time worse, but luckily that day, the doctor from the palliative care unit of the hospice visited Poppy and increased the dose of some drugs and prescribed a different one, again a prescription controlled drug that I would have to order from a different pharmacy and collect the day after. Being Friday afternoon, I rushed to the pharmacy and luckily, I got there on time. On the other hand, as they were unable to find the right strategy in terms of drugs and doses, the doctor suggested that Poppy be admitted to the hospice the first week of September to monitor the drugs 24/7, try different ones and see which combination and at what dose would manage to control Poppy's pain. They would call us on Monday to let us know. I remember thinking that this should have been done a while back, but again, I don't blame anyone or criticize them. I know very well my beautiful Poppy could be very stubborn sometimes, and I know she didn't really want to go into the hospice, so she probably played it down in front of the nurses. It's only when it got so unbearably painful that she agreed to it.

By now, it was the 1st of September, and the new medicine had helped a bit. I picked it up on Saturday, and Poppy took it. That, together with the increased dose of the other drugs and all the rest of the painkillers she was taking that night, Poppy slept better. She only woke up a couple of times during the night with the pain, but moderate in comparison, and she continued sleeping until 7:30 am when I gave her more meds. In fact, I had forgotten when it was the last time that Poppy had not woken up several times at night with agonising pain that would require massive doses of drugs and an eternity for it to settle. And that day at 9:00 am, she was hungry. I had also forgotten when it was the last time that Poppy had some appetite in the morning. I was so happy I even texted my brother to tell him. Funny how little things become so enormously important, like Poppy feeling a bit hungry in the morning. We just, totally unaware, of course, take so many things for granted.

As that day Poppy was hungry, with all the pleasure in the world, I took her some breakfast in bed. She ate a bit, and then she slept a bit more. By now, Poppy was sleeping a lot during the day, dozing on and off, her body very weak, the terrible illness sapping her energy, the cancer slowly draining her life away, like a vampire a victim's blood. That, coupled with all the drugs she was taking, made her constantly feel tired and lethargic. Her brain, by now, was also affected, and she would be quite forgetful, which was certainly not Poppy, as she had this amazing memory. She tried to hide it extremely well, and I would hardly ever mention it, but she was also getting more confused and disorientated at times.

I remember once I got very crossed with her, again, my temper. God forgive me. I asked her whether she had taken her meds, and she said that she didn't remember. She wasn't sure. I got crossed because she was in a lot of pain, and she had to take something, but if she had just taken it already or recently, and I gave her the same again, she could overdose. Poor little Poppy, she was taking so much medication, with different doses and at different times. My being cross with Poppy was brief, but I think I was in a way more cross with myself, and I vented my frustration at her because of how things were going. You cannot imagine how worried you get. I never thought I could get so frustrated at something as I got at seeing how things were slowly but surely being taken completely outside our control. After all what Poppy had gone through, all the operations and treatments, all the medication she was taking and still nothing was working. Nothing seemed to be heading in the right direction. I was losing Poppy, and the utter frustration, disappointment and worry at the sheer impotence in that situation, well, sometimes got the best of me.

In any case, I knew how much she was taking, I knew she was starting to have difficulty remembering things, and I still hadn't taken a more active role. That day I did. I made a chart, and in a box, I separated, labelled and coloured each medication differently, dividing it into the different times at which they had to be taken and with a box at the end of the chart to tick when it had been taken. That made me feel better, and we didn't miss any more medications.

At the same time, I had heard from my contact, and I could go to pick up the 'merchandise' on Sunday. It was not far from home, less than half an hour by car, but I remember being extremely nervous on my way back in case I was stopped by the police. I have the utmost respect for the police forces and any emergency service. In fact, I think they are truly exceptional individuals that risk their lives on a daily basis, and I admire them for the work they do. However, with the amount I had in the car, if well prepared would last at least 3 months, they would have thought I was a drug dealer! I think I would have had some explaining to do, and I would much prefer not to be in that situation.

I have probably never been so cautious and prudent in all my life when driving, and neither have I checked the rearview mirrors so much! In any case, I got home in the afternoon without any mishaps, and I said to Poppy, "Tomorrow, I'll make it for you." That is because the 'raw material' had to be roasted in the oven, mixed and cooked with other ingredients and followed by other procedures which take hours, all causing a very potent and perhaps rather suspicious smell. I didn't want to do it on a Sunday afternoon, with all the neighbours at home with their windows open and families with kids passing by. It would have to wait until Monday.

Chapter 60

Poppy hadn't been out of the flat the whole week and, as she was feeling a bit better that day, we decided to go for a little 'walk'. It was early in the evening, around 6:00 pm, and the temperature was very pleasant. I wanted Poppy to have a bit of fresh air, so I got the wheelchair out on the pavement, as by now, she could not walk more than a few metres with the crutches. We went around the block and onto the park behind. I was delighted to get Poppy out and go for a walk together. I know it may sound terribly stupid, but in my mind, nothing had changed: she was always and still my beautiful Poppy, and there was nobody in the world I'd rather be with, nobody in the world I'd rather go for a walk with, and nobody in the world I loved more. Unfortunately, soon into our little walk, we had to return: even just sitting in the wheelchair and moving around was too painful for Poppy.

By now, the pain was almost constant. It only varied in intensity, even with the enormous doses of many drugs and painkillers Poppy was taking. She would have some periods of medium-intensity pain, followed by high-intensity to excruciating. We just tried to manage it the best we could: I would load Poppy up with as much as she could safely take before going to bed and hoping she would get a few hours of rest before the pain would wake her up in the middle of the night. It was also difficult by now to take Poppy from the sofa to the bed, every step shooting sharp pain up her body, the few metres from the living room to the bedroom an agonising procession. We were just desperate to receive that phone call from the hospice to admit her and see how they could manage to control her pain.

The day after, we received a phone call from the nurse allocated to Poppy from the palliative care team at the hospice. She phoned in the morning and said that, unfortunately, they didn't have a bed available for Poppy, but they would try towards the end of the week. Clearly, Poppy wasn't going to the hospice for a few days to try to help her with her pain. Therefore, we resorted to Plan B. Everything was ready, and we were going to execute it.

Needless to say, we were quite concerned with the 'concoction', as I was just following the instructions we had found online. There were a few 'recipes', which used different ingredients and followed a different procedure. Unfortunately, I didn't know anyone who had actually done it, who had prepared the 'magic' potion that could be administered. Therefore, I just followed the recipe that seemed more reliable and trustworthy, constantly checking with Poppy, who was always so much better at these things than me. If I made a mistake, it would need to be thrown away and start again. In any case, I had so much that I could afford to get it wrong even a few times. I just used 10% of what I had to start with, and if it went wrong, I would try again, and again, and again until I got it right. I just wanted Poppy out of pain as soon as possible. In any case, we followed the instructions, and we got lucky the first time: six hours after I started, I had in a jar the product that could be administered to Poppy. And we couldn't wait to try it! Now it was a matter of how much she should take, and unfortunately, that would be just a matter of trial and error.

That night my brother was asking me about it. It was after 9:00 pm, and Poppy had just taken it. Once I had finished 'cooking', we had to wait for the potion to cool down. I remember saying to my brother about the smell when I was preparing it and that I hoped that my neighbours didn't get too high. "It almost knocked Poppy down!" I said.

Always the silly little jokes in the difficult times. I also remember saying to him, on a more serious note, that, without being pessimistic, things were looking quite bad. Really bad, in fact, by now. And I remember as well saying to him that I just wanted Poppy out of pain. Whatever she had left, I just wanted her with less pain. That was all I wanted. But that wasn't really true, was it? What I wanted, what I really wanted, was Poppy cured and back to being the amazing woman she always was. However, that was extremely unlikely by now. The next best thing was to get Poppy out of pain.

The potion could help with the pain, but some research indicated that it could take days or weeks for the patient to notice any significant difference. I didn't know whether Poppy had that long, and in all honesty, I just wanted her out of pain now. Also, we had read online that occasionally the use of cannabis could halt the progression of cancer or even reduce it, but we were taking that with a pinch of salt, and we weren't raising our hopes too much on that. Yet, you always hope for a miracle, don't you?

Poppy took her normal meds, and she also drank the liquid cannabis I had prepared. We didn't know how much exactly she should take, but we followed some guidelines, and Poppy took the full recommended dose. I didn't want her to take the full dose as she had already taken all her other meds, but she insisted, and to be honest, I wasn't going to argue with her. I didn't usually win, and with time we had learnt not to waste too much of our time and energy arguing: one will concede, and that was it. Sometimes it would be Poppy. Sometimes, it would be me, depending on how strongly we felt about something. This time it was me who conceded, and rightly so, which is not to say that I was in agreement, but that was what Poppy wanted, and that is what we did. It was her body, it was her pain, and it was her choice. In any case, she took all her meds around 9:00 pm AND the full dose of the liquid: to put it mildly, that night was epic!

I recall when my brother texted the day after to check how Poppy was and saying to him, "Oh my God, what a night. Too much to explain by text. I'll call you later to explain." I'll never forget that night. Soon after Poppy took everything, she fell asleep. Usually, if she was asleep on the sofa after dinner, I would wake her up around 10:00-10:30 pm and help her to bed. That day, I tried to wake her up, and I couldn't. I was trying to move her, poking her, and she wasn't reacting. I was asking her questions, and she wasn't responding. She couldn't hear me. I sat on the sofa next to her and gave her some time. Another hour passed, and still no response from Poppy. I thought I would give her a bit more time, it was midnight by now, and still, it was like she was completely drugged. Although I was starting to be a bit worried, I remember thinking at least in that state, she was not aware of anything, and she was not suffering. How sad, I guess.

I kept checking her vitals every so often, and it was all fine. She was just completely out of this world. I gave her a bit more time, 2:00 am, 3:00 am, 4:00 am, and still, I couldn't wake her up. By now, I was starting to get quite worried. I was sitting next to Poppy, my beautiful Poppy, just looking at her, thinking, hoping rather, that I had not overdosed her. Her vitals were ok, though. She was just in a deep sleep, very deep sleep, almost comatose, I guess. Another couple of hours went by, just sitting next to Poppy, constantly looking, checking that she was still breathing. It was, without a doubt, one of the longest nights of my life. I didn't dare to move from Poppy's side. It truly felt like an eternity, but around 6:30 am, Poppy moved: I knew at that moment that everything was fine, and I couldn't help but heave a huge sigh of relief.

I gave her some time, and then I started talking to her: she could hear me now, and she was starting to be a bit more responsive. She was very thirsty, so I brought her some water. She started sipping, a bit more aware of her surroundings and more awake now. After a few minutes, she asked me the time, and I said to her, "It's almost 7:00 am, Poppy." She looked at me in amazement, like she could not understand, and then she said, "Have I been asleep all this time?" "Yes, Poppy," I said. "And you have been here all this time?" she asked. "Of course!" I replied. She didn't say anything, just looked at me and smiled at me, my Poppy already so emaciated and still her beautiful smile. And in those beautiful eyes and that smile, I could see all her love for me, her unconditional love of all those years, love that didn't need any words at the time, and most sadly and regrettably, I will never be able to return. Looking at her with a gentle voice, I said, "Poppy, my love, you know you've given me a bit of a scare. How are you feeling?" With a mischievous smile, like a naughty girl caught doing something she wasn't supposed to do, she said, "I'm fine. I've never slept so well in my life!" With that, we started laughing as if we were the two kids we had met all those years back and didn't have a care in the world.

Chapter 61

We talked for a while, unaware of the time, and then reality set in again. It was almost 7:30 am, and I helped Poppy to bed. I asked her, "How was your pain through the night, Poppy? You were completely gone." "I didn't feel anything, and I didn't have any pain." At that moment, I knew we had done the right thing. It was the first night in a very, very long time that my beautiful Poppy had slept all through the night, without waking up a single time and without pain. We knew now that the potion would be of help in treating Poppy's pain. She had just taken too much with all the other medication she was taking as well. It was a matter of fine-tuning. I knew how much I had given her. I had a chart now where all was recorded: the drug/medicine/painkiller taken, the dose, the time and now included the potion. It was almost 8:00 am. I gave her the morning meds and, this time, just half of the recommended full dose of the potion. Poppy slept until 2:00 pm. Again, she didn't wake up and with no pain.

When Poppy woke up, I gave her the meds with water, made her a cup of tea and then she got up. She sat on the sofa, and around 6:00 pm, the pain was very intense again. However, we still had to wait a bit longer until she could take all her meds. By 8:30 pm, with excruciating pain by now and having eaten a little something I had prepared for her so she would not take her meds on an empty stomach, I gave her everything she could safely take and half a dose of the potion. Soon after, she fell asleep on the sofa. I would wake her up in a while and help her to bed. With the meds, we hoped that Poppy would get a few hours of respite, at least until 2:00-3:00 am.

I remember those days sitting next to Poppy on the sofa, looking at her as she slept, just looking at her, my mind lost in thought, feeling half-dead. It's like you are living in a dream, but you know it's real. Your mind wants to think it's not happening, but your brain, through your eyes, tells you otherwise. I can't really explain it very well, but you feel so sombre inside and lifeless.

Those days were very difficult for Poppy. I remember on Thursday that week talking to my brother late that night, and I said to him, "Now, these days, the pain starts getting really bad from 5:00- 6:00 pm, but we have to wait until she can take her strong meds, around 8:00- 8:30 pm. Those 2-3 hours are sheer agony, then I give her everything, as much as I can, including half a dose of the potion, and she is asleep on the sofa now." Then, with a very heavy heart, fighting the tears, I continued, "We really need a miracle now. It's so hard seeing Poppy like this, my poor Poppy. She's just being taken away from me, little by little, day by day." My brother replied, "We pray every day, but it doesn't seem to be enough." Again, the non-religious people were in constant prayer. "No, not really. Poor Poppy, she sleeps most of the day now, doesn't have much appetite and eats very little...," the lump on my throat getting bigger, "she's lost so much weight, poor little thing, and she's getting so thin, so fragile, she's just a few little bones now...," taking a deep breath, "she moves very little, the pain is now really bad, and her head is gone. It is just getting so bad now." Half sobbing, half crying, I continued the best I could, "and the other day she weed herself without realising." When that happened, it really broke my heart, as Poppy had always been this most clean lady, and I knew how much embarrassment it caused her those few drips of urine she could not hold. She almost looked at me in horror, and the best I could manage, as inadequate and useless as ever, looking at her with sheer impotence and sadness inside, was

to say, "Don't worry, Poppy, my love, it's ok. I'll help you."
I said it with all the kindness and love in the world, but that
was all I could say, that was all I could do, and it felt so little
in the circumstances. By now, the cancer was so advanced,
pressing everywhere, internal organs, nerves, blood vessels,
everything, and it was starting to affect the control of her
bodily functions.

It may be difficult to understand, but for Poppy, until
then, she had always maintained her utmost dignity
regardless of how bad the pain was, her amputation, the loss
of her hair or whatever else. Now, if she was starting to be
incontinent, it just felt like the last thing that she could still
have some control over it was taken away from her. I know
she found that extremely hard, so embarrassing and
shameful almost. Poppy always so clean and now weeing
herself. Luckily that didn't happen very often, and it was no
problem when she was standing up: gravity would do her
job, and I would do mine cleaning after. The problem was
when happening in bed at night, as by now, it was extremely
difficult to manipulate Poppy without causing her
excruciating pain. It always made me feel awful, inflicting
so much pain when I had to change the towels that, by now,
I was putting in bed every night in case the incontinent pads
did not work too well. The pads were too tight for her and
were pressing, so we had to make some cuts for Poppy to
wear them

I remember saying to my brother that it really broke my
heart and tore my soul apart almost more than anything else
seeing her like that because I knew how much it meant to
Poppy. I also said, "but I have to keep my strength so I can
be with Poppy and help her until the end." So hard to
pronounce those words. My brother asked: "Sorry to say it,
but why don't you get Poppy in the hospice? I know you
don't want to, but it could help." They knew I never wanted

257

to have Poppy in the hospice unless absolutely necessary, but mostly because of her. However, the time had come now. "Yes," I said to my brother, "I have spoken to the nurse this afternoon, and she'll come with the doctor tomorrow morning. They couldn't get a bed for Poppy this week, but they are trying to get one ready as soon as possible," I replied.

The day after, the nurse and doctor from the hospice came and spoke to us. Poppy still not keen to go to the hospice when told that the bed would be ready for her that afternoon: being Friday, she said that she wanted to spend the weekend at home and start on Monday. As always, I supported her decision: after all she'd gone through, a weekend would not make any difference, and the doctor and nurse were relatively in agreement. In any case, it wouldn't have mattered. I would have fought the battle for Poppy because if that is what she wanted to do, that is what we were going to do. Full stop. No questions asked.

Interestingly, just a few days back, we were chatting for a while on one of her lucid and not-too-painful moments, and she said to me, "I feel so cheated. All the sacrifices, all the hard work, all our plans for the future and now we won't be able to enjoy it." That again broke my heart, and I couldn't say anything. I had no words. I had worked so hard, so many hours, so many years, and we had sacrificed so much, so I could provide Poppy with an early and enjoyable retirement. I just wanted the last years of her life happily living together wherever she wanted, most likely in Spain near the sea. I didn't mind, in all honesty, as long as it was with her. I would have gone to the North Pole to live in an igloo as long as it was with Poppy. Poppy never complained, but that day, through that comment, I could feel the sadness and resignation at her fate. She was the most determined person I have ever met, but she knew she didn't have too long. Again, I had no words, only tears...

That day, she had also said to me: "When the time comes, if you see that I get very ill and it's approaching the end, please, don't take me to a hospital. I want to be here with you and the cats." She said it, looking at me with the most loving and kind look as if knowing how much it would hurt to hear those words. She continued, "I don't want to die in a hospital or in the hospice. I just want to die here, at home, with you." Again, words didn't come to me, I just looked at Poppy with a huge lump on my throat and tears in my eyes, and with my right hand, I caressed her face and I just nodded to her. I left my hand there, almost unable to remove it from her face. Poppy gently leaned her face into it, put her left hand on top of mine and closed her eyes briefly so as to savour that moment and engrave it in her memory forever. So did I, one more of a million. She then opened her eyes, and we just stayed there, looking at each other with a gentle smile, feeling each other's touch: words weren't needed. In that look, that smile and that touch, we were saying how much we loved each other: with all the love in the world!

Chapter 62

When the nurse and doctor were leaving, I accompanied them to the door and stepped outside with them, so Poppy couldn't hear what I was going to ask. I said to them I wanted to know, in their opinion, how bad Poppy was. They told me that she was very poorly, she had been hiding it from me to spare me the worrying and suffering, but they didn't think she had long. By now, being the beginning of September, still, stupidly, I asked, "What do you think? Is there any chance we can spend another Christmas together?" Trying to avoid the question, they said, "Let's get Poppy in the hospice next week and take it from there." I said as calmly as I could, as still my temper and short fuse could sometimes ignite, "Look, I know nobody can predict the future, but please tell me how long realistically you think Poppy's got left. That's all I ask. I want to know, and I need to know." They looked at each other, and with compassionate looks on their faces, they said, "Seeing how much she has deteriorated lately, we guess a few weeks, two, three, maybe four, but you never know, she might recover a bit and perhaps a couple of months." With that, and realising that for Poppy and I to spend another Christmas together would definitely require a miraculous intervention from someone, I thanked them very much for their honesty and bid them goodbye, saying I would see them on Monday at the hospice.

Needless to say, I didn't mention anything to Poppy when she asked what I was talking about with the doctors: I know very well she knew what I had asked, but I lied to her, saying that I was asking about the hospice, what we should take with us for her admission and what time we should be there. I also sadly know very well she knew deep inside what was the answer I had been given. I never lied to

Poppy. That day, I did. It could also be counted on the fingers of one hand when I lied to Poppy in 23 years, and it was only perhaps when I had been preparing a surprise for her and didn't want her to find out, or little white lies to do with chocolates mainly: I have a very sweet tooth. That was also something I learnt from my beautiful Poppy: in the past, I had lied so much to so many women so many times, but with her, I tried to do it right.

That afternoon Poppy and I were talking about her going to the hospice. It was clear her admission was to enable the palliative care team from the hospice to monitor 24/7 the effect of different drugs and doses in the treatment of Poppy's pain. She would be in the hospice for a week or ten days, and then she would be discharged and back home with the right medication to control her pain and improve her quality of life more effectively. At least, that was the plan.

We were just sitting on the sofa talking about it, and out of the blue, she said to me: "You know why I didn't want to go to the hospice today, don't you?" I had my suspicion, but I didn't want to say it. "Well, it's better to start on Monday, the beginning of the week," I said. She looked at me with extremely sad eyes, and gently placing her hand, by now very thin and pale, on my forearm, she said, "I want to spend this weekend here with you and the cats, in case it's my last weekend at home." And with the saddest smile I ever saw on Poppy's face and weepy eyes, she continued, "Just you and the cats, that's all I want, only you and the cats." Hearing those words hurt so much. I knew how much she loved us, how much she loved our little furry monsters and how much she loved the big hairy one.

Our cats, by now, were starting to get quite old. It was one day in November 2002 that I went home after work, and

Poppy had a 'surprise' for me. Normally, I would open the door and ask as usual, "Where is Poppy?" to which she would reply as customary, "Here," from wherever she was. I loved arriving home, I loved coming back home to Poppy, and she loved my arriving home. I cannot explain it, but since I met Poppy, we both felt something very special when getting home to the other, being reunited again, being together again. As I said, I can't explain it, but that is how it felt. That is how it was. I never got tired of it, and neither did she, and I know very well because she told me many times. Every single time, every single day, year after year, going back home to Poppy was enormously comforting and satisfying.

I would always give her a kiss and ask, "How's Poppy today?" or "How was your day?" or whatever. That day though, she took me to the kitchen and, pointing to a cardboard box on the floor, she said, "Look what I have here. I found it. Can we keep him?" There in the box, there was this tiny, scruffy and skinny creature that looked like a cat, his ears almost bigger than his body. I looked at the cat, then at Poppy, then at the cat again to make sure I wasn't dreaming and then at Poppy again. I didn't say anything. Looking at me, Poppy continued, "I found him in the rubbish bin when I took the rubbish out. There were three little kittens, two were dead, but this one is still alive." Looking at her, I said, "Poppy, are you sure? You've never had pets. It's a big responsibility." It is true Poppy had never had pets, but I had had two family dogs when growing up, and I knew very well pets need looking after a lot. I continued, "If we are going to keep him, we have to look after him well, which means vaccines, medicals, and insurance apart from the normal everyday care. Are you sure? Also, it might scratch the furniture, you'll have hairs everywhere, and it will never be clean and tidy anymore!" I was trying to put her off as much as possible, as I knew how big a responsibility it is, how attached you get to them and how eventually, they almost rule your life.

At the same time, I could see in Poppy's beautiful eyes how much it meant to her, how much she wanted it. Perhaps it would also fill the void that giving up dancing had left in our lives. Without mentioning the positive effect that a pet could have on Poppy's health and give her some companionship when she didn't feel that well. We also didn't have kids. I had no choice but to say, "Look, Poppy, let's do this: we take him to the vet, have him checked out properly and see what they say. If he's too ill already and cannot be saved, the vet can do the kind thing for him. But if there is a chance he can pull through, think about it well tonight, and if you still want him tomorrow, then go and get him." And so we did. We took him to the vet, where we were told he was around five weeks old, in a very poor state, terribly malnourished, with a bit of a displaced hip, blocked left tear duct, drippy eye causing a sore on his skin and a mild heart murmur. They would keep him overnight, give him proper food and medication, and there was a chance he would be ok. With that, we left the little cat at the vet, and we went home.

Needless to say that Poppy didn't have to think about it that night: I knew she had already made up her mind, and therefore I knew if the cat made it through the night, I would have a little furry friend at home when back from work the day after. Deep inside, although I didn't say it to Poppy, I was praying that would be the case. It would do wonders for Poppy. She phoned the vet in the morning and was told the cat would be ok. She went to pick him up, and that is how we came to have the most inappropriately named cat in the world at the time: Hercules!

It was a pleasure having H around: back from work and siting on the sofa, he would come to me. He was so tiny he would fit in the palm of my hand. I loved it. That's only half the story, though! Two weeks after, back from work again, I got in. Poppy was already there, kissed as normal, and asked about H, and Poppy said he was in the kitchen. Then I heard this most strange noise coming from the bathroom. I asked Poppy, and she said to go and have a look. I went to the bathroom, opened the door, turned the light on and there it was, a tiny black blob, a thousand times furrier than H, looking at me with crossed eyes, making these funny noises: I couldn't believe my eyes! Poppy had followed me to the bathroom and was standing behind me. I looked at her and, not really knowing what to say, the first words that came to me were, "Poppy, what's going on here?" And then Poppy said, "I went to the vet to take H for a check-up, and he said that he should have a friend of his age to play. It helps them to develop better as they can play together and keep each other company."

A minute ago, I could not believe my eyes, and now I could not believe my ears. "But Poppy, you realise this is double the hassle, double the expense, double everything!" I said. Poppy, with her characteristic gentleness, said, "I know, but the vet said that they had this litter of five kittens, the other four were quickly taken, but nobody wants this one. He's so black and hides so well that nobody can find him. He's a real Houdini. Also, he was the least attractive of the litter and made these funny noises, so nobody wanted him. It'll be good for H to have a friend to play with, and they can cuddle together." I was speechless. I just looked at Poppy, her beautiful face, her beautiful eyes, her kind and gentle manners, patiently waiting for me to say something. Again, I saw in her eyes how much it meant to her and how much she loved me; I also knew how much she had already done for me and how much I loved her. How could I say no to my beautiful Poppy? That is how it came that we got Samson to keep Hercules company!

Our cats gave us so much. Words are threadbare to explain how much they did for Poppy. Their unconditional love and companionship for so many years cannot be underestimated. I personally love animals, sometimes even more than humans, I regret to say, based on our behaviour. I think we are the only species that derive pleasure from hurting and making suffer other humans and animals. Deplorable for a species that consider themselves so superior.

We live in a materialistic society, and looks seem to be everything. The younger we are, the more important our external appearance. When someone is missing a leg or an arm or has some facial disfigurement, for instance, we almost look at them in disgust, and we don't think of the internal qualities of that person. It happened to Poppy quite a few times, people staring at her because of her missing a leg. Animals don't judge us for our external appearance and give us that unconditional love, even if we are not 'perfect', like missing a leg. We have a lot to learn from our pets.

On the other hand, I used to say to Poppy that pets are like kids that never grow up. They always need to be looked after. They'll never fly the nest, make a life for themselves and come to visit you every so often. On the contrary, they will always be dependent on you, and we will always be their servants. But that is not a chore. It is done with pleasure and love, as their presence enriches our lives beyond words.

Therefore, when Poppy said that she wanted to spend the weekend at home with me and the cats, I understood perfectly well. The bond she had with our cats was just incredible, forged over many hours of being together over the years, and helping her with their company and love in the difficult times, that sadly were many and very prolonged. It's all about love, and perhaps, it can only be truly understood and appreciated by someone that has experienced it.

Poppy was all love for others and for us, and I learned so much about loving and true love from her. But just thinking that she thought her end was so near broke my heart so much. Nevertheless, I also wanted to be with Poppy that weekend, just be close to her, feel her presence, and talk to her, although by now, she wasn't awake that much and also, she was not very coherent at times. That didn't matter: I could still be with her, hold hands on the sofa and have our little conversation. And Poppy would be with her beloved cats.

When Poppy had said that, however, I felt I had a lump in my throat. I didn't know what to say. As usual, my choice of words was never the most appropriate, "Poppy, don't be silly, my love. You'll see, we'll go to the hospice on Monday. It'll be like a 5* hotel for a few days, and maybe even by next weekend back home. All sorted with the meds, and you'll feel much better." As usual, she just smiled at my silly comment and didn't say anything: she didn't have to. I could see all in Poppy's eyes, mostly her love for me. And sadly, again, although unknown to us at the time, it happened as she feared: that was to be the last weekend of my beautiful Poppy at home. I'm so grateful she could spend it at home as she wanted, with me and her beloved cats.

Chapter 63

That night Poppy woke up in pain at 3:30 pm. Clearly, I hadn't given her enough of the potion. However, following the incident of the first night when I gave her the full dose, I had since spoken with a cancer specialist I knew, all off the record, of course, and explained what I had done and what had been the outcome. She made some recommendations, which I followed. I had reduced the dose of the potion, and we were also playing with the times it was administered so Poppy could have less pain during the day.

That night she woke a few times, and also, afraid of being incontinent in bed, she wanted to go to the toilet a couple of times. By now, it was very difficult for Poppy to go on her own, incredible as it may seem, but those 10-12 steps were already extremely difficult on her own, so I just helped her. Luckily, after a while, she fell asleep for a few hours until the morning. I would then give her the meds, and she would hopefully sleep until midday or 1:00 o'clock without pain. I was desperate for Poppy to go into the hospice to see what could be done for her. On one hand, Monday couldn't come quickly enough; on the other, I just wanted to spend as much time as possible with Poppy that weekend, as I could see that we didn't have that much left.

The night after, I remember texting my brother explaining we had dinner around 7:30, then I had given Poppy her meds at 8:00 pm, and then after a while, I had helped her to bed. It was 9:30 pm, and I was saying to my brother, "I'm sitting on the bed next to Poppy. She's falling asleep now. I'll call you later." Those nights I would help Poppy to bed and wait, sitting next to her until she fell asleep. Every single moment we could spend together now was so very precious. I remember thinking how much the cancer had taken its toll on Poppy. It had destroyed her beautiful looks and was now taking away the little she had left. Yet, I remember being there just looking at her. I still loved looking at Poppy, having her by my side, and feeling her smell and her touch. She was my wife, such a wonderful word, and even until that day, she made me feel special just being by her side.

Once she fell asleep, I would sit on the sofa watching telly for a while, perhaps reading something, but not much anymore as it was very difficult to concentrate. I would find myself often going back to the beginning of the page a few times, as it was not registering what I was reading. Therefore, I used to read very little. I had almost given up reading completely. By then also, I was sleeping less than ever, many nights no more than 3-4 hours of broken sleep at most: first of all, it was very difficult to fall asleep, I just constantly worried about what was happening. Mainly at night, you find your brain going into overdrive with negative thoughts. Then as soon as Poppy woke up in pain, I would get up, give her the meds and hope for the best. Sometimes it would be an hour until she fell asleep again, so intense the pain was sometimes and so little effect anything she was taking would have by now. I would help her to the toilet or change the towels on the bed if required. Also, I had a lot of pain in one of my shoulders, a chronic injury from the past, and it would wake me up in pain. That was not the problem. I was used to it after 40 years. The problem is that the pain would make me agitated in my sleep, and then I would disturb my beautiful Poppy, and that was a problem. So I preferred to sit on the sofa at times, while she was asleep, with an ear always tuned to the bedroom for when she was starting to moan with pain and just checking on her every so often.

To this day, I still thank God for the strength He gave me, even with such little sleep over so many years. I will be eternally grateful for that and for keeping me healthy during those very difficult times so I could help Poppy. "Try to get some sleep tonight," my friends and family would say to me, and I would always reply, "I can't sleep, it's very difficult now, but I rest enough, so I'm well." I didn't realise at the time, but people were also worried about me.

That weekend we just managed the best we could, and on Monday morning, I got a phone call from the hospice. The nurse confirmed they had a bed ready for Poppy and to be there by 2:00 pm. After a while, I woke Poppy up to give her the meds and let her know. She woke up later, and I took her a cup of tea to bed. I was really looking forward to having Poppy in the hospice well looked after, but still, I knew she wasn't that keen. At least we had had our weekend together, and she had been with the cats.

We packed everything needed, and we made our way to the hospice, not too far from home. We arrived just before 2:00 pm, went in, and Poppy gave her name to the lady at the reception. She asked us to wait while she called the nurse. A few minutes after, the nurse came, and we accompanied her to a ward with four beds: three were occupied, and the last one at the end by the window was empty. That would be Poppy's bed for the next 7-10 days while they were trying different drugs and doses to keep her pain under control.

Everybody was very professional and pleasant, and after a while, the doctor that would be in charge of Poppy came. She introduced herself and explained what they were going to do, how and when. We had a bit of a chat, and then she started asking the questions we were so used to in order to fill out Poppy's medical history. However, from 3:00 pm until 5:30 Poppy had terrible pain and a high temperature of 39. She was given the normal meds we had, and didn't really had that much effect. Therefore, the doctor revised all the medicines Poppy was taking: some were replaced, others the dose modified, and high-strength oral morphine administered for quick pain relief, but in a much higher dose than she was already taking. They also connected a pump to Poppy 24/7 with a morphine-based drug administered directly into the blood so they could monitor and make changes quickly depending on the effect.

My brother texted, "How's Poppy? Are you in the hospice?" I explained what they had done, and he said, "That's great. You'll see, she'll be back home in no time, like new." I replied, "That's the miracle I have been asking for, already, for a long time." I continued, "Anyway, I'll leave you now. I have to go home to sort the cats out. Call you later." Our cats, by now quite old and with many health issues, were both on daily medication. I went home, did the food, litter trays and meds, back to the hospice at 8:30, and I was there until 11:30 when Poppy fell asleep. All staff in the hospice were absolutely amazing from the moment we arrived: nurses, doctors and non-medical. So I could stay till late, provided I did not disturb anyone. I just stayed in a little corner out of everybody's way and delighted I could be there with Poppy.

I went home, sat on the sofa, and one of our cats came and jumped on my lap. Our cats had completely different personalities. S loved cuddles and contact with people. H was much more detached, but interestingly the more loyal and also the one that always knew when Poppy wasn't well and wouldn't leave her side.

I was emotionally drained but still wide awake, my mind a roller-coaster of thoughts and emotions. In any case, eventually, I felt very tired and went to bed. It was past 1:00 am, and must have fallen asleep immediately as I don't remember anything else. I slept like a log that night and didn't wake up until close to 7:00 am. I was amazed. I had slept over 5 hours that night, a record for me. I woke up like new!

As soon as I opened my eyes, I was thinking of Poppy. How was her night? Had she been in much pain? Still, after all these years and the many times she was in the hospital, I missed Poppy so much when she wasn't at home, this time probably even more. I just wanted her pain sorted and my beautiful Poppy back home.

I texted at 7:15 am: "How's Poppy? How was the night?" No reply. I thought maybe she had a bit of a bad night, and she was asleep now. I also knew that the first thing she would do when awake would be to check her phone, and any messages from me, friends or family. As she still hadn't replied an hour after, I texted again: "Poppy ok? Poppy awake yet?" No reply. I thought she would be asleep, which was good. I would see her in a while anyway.

It was Tuesday already: the first day done! I sorted the cats out at home, did what needed doing, and I was at the hospice around 10:00 am. I didn't want to go earlier as I would be there the whole day but mostly not to get in the way of the nurses' job as they're usually very busy from 8:00-10:00 am. When I arrived, I saw that Poppy was in quite a lot of pain and not very happy. She had woken up at 5:30 am in pain, but we couldn't communicate as the Wi-Fi in the hospice was down. In any case, I knew it was difficult for her physically and mentally being in the hospice, but we had to give them a bit of time. I helped Poppy to the shower, and I washed her hair, that's to say, the little bit she had that was slowly growing after she lost it following the last

271

chemotherapy treatment. I loved touching Poppy's head and giving her 'kissitos' on her little head. Showered and with a clean change of clothes, Poppy felt a bit better. One of the ladies doing alternative therapies offered Poppy an aromatherapy session and a massage, and I was delighted Poppy agreed, as that could loosen up her stump that by now was very contracted at the top because of all the operations she had had, the radiotherapy and scar tissue.

Also, I was hoping she would eat a little as she hadn't had much appetite of late, and she hadn't eaten since 5:30 pm the day before when she had half a sandwich. I used to say to Poppy: "Poppy, you have to eat a bit if you want to get better." "I know, but I'm not hungry." "I know, my love, but you have to make an effort. You need food in your body to make you better." "I know…" That was one of our typical conversations. My beautiful Poppy, by now, had so little appetite and was so thin and fragile.

Chapter 64

Poppy had a bad afternoon, but they administered a different painkiller, and she felt a bit better. Therefore, being such a beautiful evening, I helped Poppy onto the wheelchair, and we went out in the garden. The garden in the hospice is magnificent, so peaceful, serene, calm: just beautiful. She perked up a bit and ate a little more that evening. We were joking, and I was saying to Poppy that the first thing we would do when she came out was to have a Mcdonald's. We hadn't had one for years, I think, and that would be her reward for being such a good girl in the hospice. Because everything else would be 'second best', I would take her to a good restaurant to eat a big steak if she was a 'naughty girl'! She just smiled at my silly joke, still smiling at my silly jokes, still that beautiful smile.

That night I was talking to my best friend in Spain, and he said, "You seem a bit more optimistic today." It is true. I had been quite down of late, everything going so wrong, crying a lot when Poppy was not around, yet still hopeful. Part of me wanted to pretend that it was not really happening, the inevitability of it all getting to you sometimes. I said to my friend: "I still pray every day for a miracle. The day I stop praying is the day I will have lost all hope, and that will be when Poppy is gone. Until then, I'll keep praying and fighting." My friend, who has known me for almost 40 years, replied, "Well done. You've always been a fighter. Keep going." People always so supportive, meaning so well, yet nothing we did seem to work.

That evening I did the same, and went quickly home to sort the cats out and back to the hospice. I was with Poppy for a while, and when she was falling asleep, I left. Back home, the usual routine, cats, coffee and sofa. I had slept so much, and so well the night before that it took me ages to fall asleep, and I kept waking up.

In any case, I knew that Poppy wasn't very happy, so I sent her a text just before midnight: "Home. Litter trays done, 'gatitos' done, both meds and fed. Very content. Washing machine on, ate something and now resting." Poppy always wanted to know how our cats were doing. I continued, "Poppy, I'm going to send this now, but I really hope not to get a reply until tomorrow morning, which would mean you fell asleep when I left and then slept the whole night without pain. I know you don't want to be there, my love, but I really think it can help you enough to improve your quality of life. The rest we'll do it when you come home, and we'll leave it in the hands of the Almighty. I love you VERY much. Let's keep fighting. I'll do the prayers for both." Poppy wasn't very religious and prayed even less than me.

I waited for a while, still wide awake, and then I went to bed. I kept waking up and checking the phone in case Poppy had replied. She didn't. That was wonderful. She was probably asleep. In the morning, she texted at 7:15 am: "I fell asleep immediately after you left! Just woke up. Xx." "Hi, Poppy. Did you have a good night's sleep?" I asked. "Yes. Did you?" "Yes, perfect. How's the pain?" "Didn't wake up at all. But fell over, and my BP dropped again. Cats, ok?" "Cats, little pests!!! Ha-ha. Anyway, did you get hurt when you fell?" "No, only my dignity." "Ok, no harm done then. Wait until I come, and I'll help you to the shower room like yesterday if you want." "Will do." "Excellent. Finishing a few things, and I'll make my way. See you soon."

Yes, I didn't sleep very well that night, I kept waking up. But that was nothing in comparison to Poppy's night.

Of course, she didn't tell me until I got to the hospice. She slept quite well until 5:00 am. Then she woke up and had to go to the toilet. I loved my beautiful Poppy to bits, but she could be so determined and stubborn sometimes! That night, instead of calling the nurse to help her to go to the toilet, she got up on her own and fell. She probably was half asleep, lost balance and tried to hold onto the arm of an armchair without realising that it folded out of the way; therefore, before she knew it, my poor little Poppy was on the floor. Typical Poppy, she didn't want to disturb anyone.

When I got to the hospice around 10:00 am, she was a bit disorientated, and she told me what had happened. In the past, I would probably have said something like, "What the hell were you thinking?", the tone of my voice denoting my anger inside. That day, however, I just said, "Poppy, why did you do that, my love? You know the nurses are here to help you, they won't mind, and you could have hurt yourself." I said it very nicely, but inside I was fuming because I knew she could have hurt herself badly, hit her head or caused internal bleeding. Perhaps she did: the nurses told me she was not only disorientated, but her blood pressure and oxygenation were pretty low, and they were waiting for the doctors to come to investigate.

However, that day Poppy started feeling a bit better in the afternoon. The blood pressure was almost normal, and the pain wasn't too bad. It seemed we had dodged the bullet. Just as well as our best friends came to visit her in the evening. I got Poppy on the wheelchair and out to the garden again for a while: another lovely evening, beautiful temperature. It was wonderful to be there with them, sharing that time together. It really helped Poppy. She was so much happier and brighter when they left, although tired.

When our friends left, I accompanied Poppy to the bath. She had a wash and a change of clothes, also feeling much better for it, and then went back to bed. Wait for the night medication, chat for a while, and around 10:30-11:00 pm, I would make my way home. The nurses were very good, but I didn't want to take advantage of their kindness. And also, Poppy was very tired after the excitement of the visit from our friends. At that time, there was no traffic, so I was home in 15-20 minutes.

The day after, Thursday, I had arranged to go to work quickly in the morning as I needed to do some paperwork. I was there by 7:00 am and out before 11:00. On my way to the hospice, I quickly stopped at home to check and sort out the cats: all good, five minutes, and to the hospice. When I got there I saw that Poppy wasn't great: she had a bad night, with a lot of pain, but she hadn't said anything to me because she didn't want me to worry! That was my incredible Poppy: she was dying and still trying to protect me. Unbelievable. She was taking a lot of oral morphine, and during the day, she was half asleep. Also, being her blood pressure quite low again, her blood vessels were collapsing, and it was difficult to put a line on her arm. They were trying in different places to no avail, so she looked like a drug addict, poor Poppy.

That day her dad came to visit her in the afternoon. He would stay for a couple of nights and leave on Saturday. We had a quick dinner together. I dropped him at the hotel and went back to the hospice. When I got back, the nurses had managed to put a line, and Poppy had the drip connected. She was half asleep. I just sat there next to the bed, and we spent a couple of hours together before I left around 11:00 pm.

At night, if Poppy woke up, we would text a bit. I never slept much, anyway. She would mainly ask me about the cats, where they were, what they were doing, and what they had eaten. I know she missed them terribly, and I couldn't wait for the doctors in the hospice to get the right medication at the right doses to have Poppy back at home again with her cats. It may sound weird, as I was with Poppy all day, but I was missing her also terribly at home at night. The truth is that nothing ever felt the same without Poppy. Nothing was ever the same without Poppy. There was always something missing at home without Poppy. Without Poppy, the flat felt empty.

The day after was Friday the 13th, and I did something that, again, I will regret my whole life.

Chapter 65

That Friday was a beautiful day. The weather forecast for the weekend was excellent, and I was thinking if Poppy was ok, they would perhaps allow her to go out for a few hours. We could go to the park or somewhere, just to give her something to look forward to and not be at the hospice the whole weekend. Perhaps a little takeaway if she felt like it? I would speak to the doctors and see what they thought, and then I would have a chat with Poppy.

I went to work again at 7:00 am to finish some paperwork. Just before 10:30 am, I was all done and about to leave when someone asked me for a favour. I agreed because I thought it would take me 10-15 minutes. However, there were some complications, and it took me much longer, and by the time I left, it was past 11:15 am. I rushed home to quickly sort out the cats and then rushed to the hospice. I really had to rush because in the morning, while I was at work, Poppy was told that the blood results the day before showed she was very anaemic, and the doctors had decided to do a transfusion. Being Friday and not wanting to leave it until after the weekend, they had arranged for an ambulance to take Poppy to the nearest hospital. The ambulance would be at the hospice between 12-12:30. That's why I was rushing so much, as I was going to accompany Poppy to the hospital for the transfusion, and I didn't want to keep anyone waiting for me.

I texted Poppy at 7:00 am: "Good morning, Poppy. I just wanted to say I love you. How was the night, my love?" No reply. At 8:30 am: "How's Poppy today? I hope you feel better today. Yesterday was a bit rough…" No reply. At 10:30 am: "Poppy, ok?" After a while, she replied, "Really bad night. Not well, BP very low, going to the hospital for a transfusion. Ambulance around 12-12:30." I said, "Ok, Poppy, hang in there my love and be strong. Love you very much. On my way." Unknown to me at the time, that would be the last text that my beautiful Poppy would ever send.

When I arrived at the hospice, the ambulance was already parked outside. I thought, 'Shit, they're already waiting for me'. It was around 12:10 pm, and I quickly made my way to the ward. However, as I was approaching Poppy's bed, I was met by a scene that I had not anticipated, and I will remember it for the rest of my life, as it changed everything.

Around Poppy's bed, there were so many people that I could not even see Poppy: two doctors, three nurses and the ambulance driver. They had also drawn half the curtain. I knew immediately that something had happened, and although I obviously didn't know what, I knew it couldn't be very good with so many people around. One of the nurses saw me arriving and told the doctor, who turned to me. I asked the doctor, who had been wonderful these few days with Poppy, "What's going on, what happened?" and then she told me, "We don't know, 10 minutes ago, just before the ambulance arrived, Poppy complained of pain and headache and lost consciousness. We still don't know what happened, but we're just checking now." I looked at Poppy, lying in bed unconscious, and said to the doctor: "Ok, I understand, thank you." There was no more I could say, and they had work to do. Then I continued looking at Poppy while a million thoughts, none of them positive, were bombarding my head at the same time.

While the doctors and the nurses were doing their job and not wanting to be on their way, I went to the coffee machine at the reception and got myself a coffee and some water. I sat there, sipping the water and the coffee with

Poppy's image lying unconscious on the bed engraved in my mind, going through the possible scenarios. It clearly wasn't good that she was unconscious, but we didn't know why that had happened. First, they needed to investigate, get a diagnosis and then hopefully treat it. Let's not jump the gun. Let's wait to have the right information, and then we'll take it from there. It's not all lost yet. That was me trying to use my logical mind to reason to still keep a tiny bit of hope. My gut feeling was telling me otherwise, though.

It is so extremely difficult to be in that situation and to keep your mind strong, positive and sane, not to throw in the towel. Yet, I was still praying for a miracle. How stupid of me, I guess.

While waiting, I vividly remember thinking about how I should have been there that morning. Clearly, if we had known she was going to have the transfusion that morning, I wouldn't have gone into work, but we didn't know. My mind now playing games: If I had left work at 10:30 am, if the little favour hadn't taken that long, if I hadn't stopped at home to check on the cats, if I had driven faster, if I had taken a different route, whatever, who knows, most likely I would have seen Poppy before she was unconscious. I could have given her a kiss while she was awake, and she would have given me a kiss back. I could have spoken to her, and I could have heard her beautiful voice talking back at me. I could have touch her when leaning down to kiss her, and she could have touched me back. But it was not to be.

I also remember thinking that I didn't have the chance to say goodbye to my mum, neither to my dad, and now I missed Poppy by 10 minutes. I just couldn't believe it! But it was nobody's fault: neither the person that asked me for a favour, not the cats at home, nor the drivers on the road. If anything, it was my fault, and I was wondering whether I would ever be able to see Poppy's wonderful blue eyes again looking at me, hear her soothing voice talking to me and see her beautiful face smiling at me. I was praying that would be the case, but would it? I was wondering, and I was so scared. What I had been fearing these last few years seemed suddenly now to be on top of me: the sheer realisation of Poppy dying. How will I be able to live without my beautiful Poppy?

Chapter 66

A couple of hours went by, and then the doctor asked me to accompany her to a private room as she wanted to talk to me. That's never a very good sign. She said that they didn't know exactly what had happened, but it seemed that the tumour had ruptured, and Poppy had massive internal bleeding. Interestingly, that's what we had been told, quite bluntly, to be honest, by a junior doctor in the experimental hospital a couple of months back. A bit more tact by the young doctor that day wouldn't have gone amiss. Unfortunately, she seemed to be right, though.

The doctor continued by saying that Poppy hadn't regained consciousness and she was too poorly to take her to the hospital as she probably would not make it. Poppy's best chance was to keep her in the hospice sedated. I asked her: "Is she likely to recover? What are the chances?" The doctor, with a compassionate look, said, "It is very difficult to say. The next few hours are crucial. If she regains consciousness soon, it will be very positive, but the longer she's unconscious, the worse the prognosis." "Will she make it through the night?" I asked. "She might. She's very strong. Poppy is young and healthy, and her body will put up a fight," the doctor said. There was no more to ask, no more answers they could give. We just continued talking for a few minutes. They asked me whether I needed someone to stay with me, someone to talk to, or anything I needed. There was no point in me saying the only thing I needed was my beautiful Poppy. They couldn't give her to me. Then I realised I hadn't eaten anything the whole day, so I said, "No, thank you, I'm fine. I don't need anyone to stay with me, but could I possibly have a coffee and a biscuit, please?" I knew I had to keep my sugar levels up. They said, "Have you eaten? Would you like us to bring you a sandwich?" I said, "Yes, thank you very much, that would be great." A few minutes after, a nurse came with a coffee and a tuna sandwich. I forced myself to have half, as in all honestly, I didn't have much appetite.

Later on, Poppy's dad came with her sister. She had come by train, and her dad had gone to pick her up at the station, so they came together late afternoon. They were also not prepared for what met their eyes on their arrival: there, lying in bed, was our beautiful Poppy, unconscious, with her skin boiling due to her high temperature and me next to Poppy, applying damp cloths to her forehead to try to keep her cool and more comfortable. It was a shock for them, and mostly for Poppy's sister, as I knew they had not had the greatest relationship in the past and hadn't had much contact for a long time. A while back, I'm glad to say they had reconnected. Everybody was happy and thinking they would have the opportunity to compensate for lost time. At least they had that contact the last few years, and I know Poppy very much appreciated that. She loved her nephew and niece more than she let show. She was always talking about them and buying things for them. A few months back, the last time that her sister came home to visit her, Poppy gave her a special piece of jewellery that she had been given by her grandma at her communion. It had a very special meaning for Poppy, and she wanted her niece to have it. She had asked me, "Do you think I'm doing the right thing, giving it to her now?" I said, "Well, it depends on how you feel, Poppy. If you really want it to go to your niece, today is as good a day as any other. But if you are not sure, wait and see how you feel in the future." "I think I'll do it now," Poppy said. "Very well," I said, and I'm glad she did. Poppy gave it to her sister that day to be passed to her niece; that was the last time they would see each other, Poppy being conscious.

We were all there, looking at Poppy, in reality now just waiting for a miracle, having difficulty accepting the reality in front of our eyes. When the time came, Poppy's Dad and sister left to go back to the hotel: on this occasion, I didn't feel like accompanying them for dinner, so I just stayed in the hospice with Poppy. Sadly, as they were returning home the day after, that was the last time they would see our beautiful Poppy.

At some point in the evening, I sent a text to my brother and friends explaining the situation: "For you to know, Poppy deteriorated a lot this morning, and the doctors decided to take her to the hospital to do a transfusion. They arranged for an ambulance, but 10 minutes before it arrived, she got very ill and lost consciousness. She is actually unconscious now, and the doctor told me that tonight it could go either way. But I keep fighting and praying and not throwing in the towel. I'm just going to pray like mad tonight. Please pray for Poppy."

Later that evening, my brother texted: "Just read your message, and I don't know what to say. Thanks for telling me. How is Poppy now?" "She's very poorly. I can't believe it, such a beautiful day and it's going to be a wonderful weekend. I was saying to Poppy's dad that it's not really a good day to die." What a silly thing to say: if we think about it, it never is a good day to die, I suppose. I continued, "In any case, we have to wait and see what happens tonight. She is sedated now, so at least she is not suffering." "I'm so sorry. It must be so hard. We'll keep praying." "Yes, me too. Now it is clearly in the hands of the One up there. There is nothing else I can do, absolutely nothing. Nothing has worked." Fighting the tears, I said, "I just love her so much. I don't know what I'm gonna do without her. I really don't know." "Don't worry about it now. Just try to rest a bit. You need to rest as well." "I can't rest…." "Just try. Think of the

284

good times with Poppy, those dreams you had together."
"Yes, I have thousands of wonderful moments together that I will cherish forever, but all the dreams we had for the future, now, it seems very unlikely that they will ever materialize." With sad tears freely flowing, I said, "We had so many plans, so many dreams. All shattered now. Well, at least I'm next to her. I'm holding her hand in my hand and stroking her little head. I talk to her, but she's not saying anything. Maybe she can't even hear me when I tell her how much I love her." I could certainly say those three words now, the most beautiful three words you can say to someone from your heart, 'I love you'. I learnt that from Poppy, and maybe Poppy couldn't even hear them now when I said it to her. My brother kindly replied, "She can hear you, but she can't respond. Talk to her, tell her beautiful things, about your holidays, about the cats, about France. The brain responds." That is exactly what I did. I just kept talking to Poppy, holding her hand, as if we were going for a walk on the beach…

Chapter 67

That day I didn't want to leave and go home to feed the cats. Our very good neighbour and friend did it for us. The cats were very used to her, so it was no problem. My only concern was them not having their medication, but for one day, it would be ok. I was just so afraid that I would leave and Poppy would go while I was away.

I had spoken to the doctor about it, and she had said some people almost preferred not to be there at the precise moment that our loved one passes, as it is very hard the last few hours of a dying person and even more when they take their last breath. However, I said to her that I would like to be with Poppy until the end, and if they didn't have any objection, I would just stay there. As things were going, Poppy may not make it through the night. However, as the doctor had said, she was young and healthy, and her body may put up a fight. And didn't it put up a fight, my beautiful Poppy!

Poppy had been unconscious for almost nine hours now, and that wasn't a good sign. She was still breathing, the breathing a bit more laborious at times, but she was also moaning in pain every so often. I mentioned it to the nurses, but they assured me she was not in pain, as she was sedated. Hour after hour, the night was passing, me sitting next to Poppy, looking at her, holding her hand, talking to her. In any case, I didn't want to leave Poppy's side, and I was there the whole night.

With the light of the day, everything seems brighter, the dark thoughts of the night gently giving way to more positive ones. With more positive thoughts comes hope, and with hope, you start praying again for a miracle. At the same time, your eyes and ears don't lie: Poppy was sedated. They had tried to wake her up a while back but to no avail. By now also, the mucus was building in her lungs, compromising her breathing, and she was having involuntary contractions in her arms. It didn't look very promising: it was coming up to 20 hours, and Poppy hadn't regained consciousness.

I had spoken to the doctor that morning when she came: she was not entirely surprised Poppy was still with us. Poppy could still go on for a few hours, but she thought that the fact that she hadn't regained consciousness, they had tried to wake her up in the morning but couldn't, and it would soon be 24 hours unconscious meant that we should be preparing ourselves for the inevitable. 24-48 hours, perhaps… that's all I would have my beautiful Poppy in this world with me.

In view of the situation, Poppy's dad and sister had decided to stay one extra night, so that Saturday, they kept me company for a while. Poppy still with us. I felt it provided her sister with some solace, just giving Poppy some water with the syringe and cooling her forehead with the wet cloth: I think it was very comforting for her to be able to do that for Poppy. It is always the little things in life that are the most important and valuable. I learnt that from Poppy. In this case, for her to give some water at that time to her dying sister in bed must have meant the world!

At around 2:00 pm, Poppy had almost opened her eyes and reacted. Just a reflex though. Again, you think, that's it, that's the sign we need, now she'll recover. Realistically thought, you know deep down that it is extremely unlikely she had been unconscious for over 24 hours, and yet, you still hope, blatantly lying to yourself…

That day, at some point, the doctor came and told me that they were going to move Poppy to another room, more private, where we could be on our own. I knew what that meant: if they can help it, they don't want anyone to die in the ward in front of the other patients, the last few hours agonizing and extremely distressing to anyone around. They moved Poppy to the new room, and while Poppy's dad and sister were still there, I quickly went home. I thought, if Poppy leave us now, at least she'll be with her family. I sorted out the cats, had a quick shower and change of clothes, and went back to the hospice. Poppy's dad and sister left around 8:00 pm, and then I talked to my friends and brother. I remember saying to him that I quickly went home and had a tin of minestrone soup, as I wasn't very hungry, but at least that would keep me going. Everybody kept saying to me that I had to eat, and I knew they were absolutely right, but I just didn't have any appetite.

I also remember saying to my brother, "Poppy's family just left. It was great to see them and for them to see Poppy. I don't think they'll see her again alive." I continued, "But now, I won't move again from here. I'll stay by her side. I just want to be with Poppy and spend the rest of the time we have together. We're just gonna talk, holding hands, and that's it, that's what we'll do. Even if she can't hear or feel my touch." My brother said, "I really think she can hear you and knows you are there, but she can't react." "That's what I want to believe," I replied.

As the day was coming to an end and the night was covering everything with its black coat, somehow, the senses were heightened, the hearing sharpened, and the sounds intensified. Particularly now in a room on our own. Also, your brain goes overdrive again. I spent the night just looking at Poppy, holding her hand, talking to her. Every so often, the nurses would come to check on Poppy and also to ask me whether I was ok or if I needed anything. They had been absolutely amazing from day one. I would say I was as ok as one can be in the circumstances, but water, coffee, and juices were truly appreciated at the time. As for food, well, one loses appetite in these situations. Also, there was a foldable bed in the room, so I put it next to Poppy, and I lay down for a couple of hours.

It was now Sunday morning, and around 4:30 am, Poppy woke up with a lot of pain, and she seemed quite lucid. I asked how she was, but she didn't reply. I know, however, she could see me, she could hear me, and she did recognise me. She was awake! I leaned over, gave her a kiss touching her face with my hand, and I said, "Hi Poppy, my love, are you ok? Are you thirsty? Do you want a bit of water?" Again this line won't get me an Oscar. Who cares. The important thing is that she nodded in acknowledgment. I put some water in the plastic cup, got the syringe, and held her head forward so she could drink. And she drank 100ml. I could not believe my eyes, and I was ecstatic. I said, "So good, Poppy, you're doing so well, my love. Do you want a bit more?" She shook her head to say no, she looked at me, and she smiled briefly, just a couple of seconds, and then she took a deep breath and closed her eyes. That was the last time I saw Poppy's eyes, her beautiful blue eyes looking at me. That was also the last time that I saw her beautiful smile, just smiling at me. It hurt so much, but also I will cherish that moment, forever engraved in my mind.

She had closed her eyes and dropped her head to one side, but she was still breathing. I called the nurse, and she came immediately, and I explained. Poppy had woken up, had recognised me, wanted some water and drank a bit. The nurse gave Poppy an injection of morphine, another one, the minimum dose possible, but still so much. Then she told me that this sometimes happens with some people, but it didn't mean much, as it had been very brief and Poppy was unconscious again. In other words, nothing had changed. Poppy was dying. I was talking to Poppy and trying not to cry, but every so often, I couldn't help it. At least we were in our room, so I could cry as much as I wanted, and nobody would see it.

Ours was a beautiful room with a door opening directly to the garden. At some point, on what seemed a very long night, with Poppy making funny and scary noises every so often, it started getting lighter outside. Again the day brightened everything, including my thoughts: I was almost optimistic again. I opened the curtains, and the first rays of sunlight greeted us through the windows. Typical me, I said one of my silly things to Poppy: "Look, Poppy, the sun is coming to see you. It's saying hello to you. It is so beautiful out there, Poppy. Don't you want to see it, my love?" Rhetorical question: of course, Poppy wanted to see it and mostly feel it warmly bathing her skin. She loved the sun! But my beautiful Poppy could no longer see it.

Chapter 68

After Sunday morning, the afternoon followed. I remember talking to my friend in Spain, saying: "It's a gorgeous day. Sunny and 25 degrees. I can't believe that Poppy is going to die today on such a beautiful day." Another silly comment, we don't choose when we die, do we?

In the afternoon, things started getting really bad. To lighten the mood, I was asking my brother what they had had for lunch. My brother is a very good cook and my best friend in Spain is a chef: in fact, I'm probably the useless one in my family at cooking. That Sunday, he hadn't cooked, though: "We just got a roasted chicken with potatoes and peppers. Only ten euros." "Wow! Delicious, and so cheap! Save some for me," I said. Every so often, I just needed to text someone or talk to someone, even for a few seconds, to take my mind off the cruel reality in front of my eyes.

Yes, that was a bad afternoon. Poppy's breathing was now much poorer. I texted my brother around 5:45 pm: "I think I'm losing her. Her breathing is so slow and laborious." "Stay with her," my brother said. "Yes. I'm not moving from here," I replied. "But it's horrible to see Poppy suffering like this. I'm crying so much today." "Yes, I can imagine. It must be awful having that image before your eyes. And all that she's going through, no wonder you're crying. Cry as much as you need. That is good," he said. "In fact, I'm crying so much today, I don't think I'll need to go for a wee!" I said.

It was so difficult to see Poppy like this, suffering so much. I don't know why, I remember I was deeply sad mainly because it was such a beautiful and sunny day. I thought, how unfair Poppy suffering so much on a day like this when she always loved the sun so much. That seemed to me the worse at the time. How your mind plays these funny games is truly unbelievable.

Our friends offered help, food, and anything I needed. I didn't need anything, but it was greatly appreciated. They mentioned about coming to visit Poppy, keeping me company for a while, but I declined: I told them I didn't want anyone to see Poppy like that. I wanted them to have in their minds the image of Poppy as they had last seen her: conscious, awake, interacting with them, chatting, laughing. But mostly, I wanted everybody to have the image of Poppy with her beautiful blue eyes open, looking at them with that amazing smile on her face. I didn't want anyone to see my beautiful Poppy unconscious, her head turned to one side, her face already distorted, her mouth open, gasping for air. That was for me, as her husband, to go through that process of final and terrible physical deterioration together, but nobody else.

At 9:25 pm, my brother texted to check: "How is it going?" "Well, still here. Her breathing stabilised around 7:30 pm. But you can't imagine the couple of hours we had before that. By 6:30 pm, I was kissing her and saying my goodbyes. But now she is more restful." For two hours, it had been agonising to see Poppy struggling to breathe. I truly thought I was losing her then. I continued, "At least now she is very sedated, and I don't think she's in much pain. But her body is so strong. I really don't know where she gets the strength from. She's consumed!"

That Sunday night was very hard. Poppy's breathing was very irregular, her breathing every time more laborious, the pauses longer, the next breath gasping for air louder: I really thought I would lose her a few times. I cried a lot that night, but in between cries, I was talking to Poppy.

Sunday night again gave way to Monday morning: the start of a new week. More movement in the hospital, and everything coming back to life after the weekend, everything except Poppy. She was still unconscious. Soon, it would be 72 hours. The nurses would wash her, clean her sores as gently as they could, her body now so fragile and battered, and try to change her position. It was awful to see Poppy suffer so much.

That Monday was very, very, very long, and Poppy gave us a few scares. She already had sores in her body, that would only get worse. The nurses would come, clean her, and try to change her position. That was already getting very difficult, as when they were trying to mobilise Poppy, it would cause her excruciating pain. Therefore, they had to give her as much pain relief as possible before moving her and more after to try to settle the pain. The nurses were extraordinary, and as careful and gentle as they could possibly be, but still, that afternoon, after they had changed her position and cleaned the sores, Poppy must have been in agony. They had to sedate her after, and my beautiful Poppy was already starting to look more dead than alive, her face now very distorted. I had to leave the room and get some fresh air for a few minutes.

By then, I had already asked God a few times to stop Poppy's suffering, but her body was still fighting. The doctors were saying the end was very near, but her heart was very strong. That Monday was awful, and I cried a lot, but seeing that Poppy wasn't leaving us and could go on for hours, I said one of my stupid things that sometimes would come to my mind. I had just had this image of us spending the night together, the entire night, as we had done many times when we were younger. We would have had dinner in a restaurant by the sea, Poppy's favourite food, enjoying each other's company, savouring the moment. A beautiful summer night, a walk on the beach after dinner, our senses heightened at night: the sound of the waves breaking but unable to see them, the smell of the sea but unable to see in the distance. Then perhaps a little drink somewhere or directly to the hotel or apartment. Then we would make love to each other, lovingly and gently, or any other way that we would feel like it at the time. After, we would lay in bed together silently, words not needed sometimes, feeling each other's presence, and warmth, my arm perhaps around Poppy's shoulders and her head resting on my chest. But while I had all these images in my mind, they were accompanied by that most wonderful Phil Collins' song, 'One more night'. Again, I don't know why, but it just came to me. I held Poppy's hand, and, approaching my face to hers, I said, "Poppy, if you still want, would you give me one more night, just one more night, my love?" Of course, Poppy didn't move. I don't even know whether she heard me or not. She didn't say anything either.

Chapter 69

That night I didn't unfold the bed. I just sat in the chair next to the bed, and we lived in our minds wonderful experiences. We held hands the whole night as we went through the night together. First, we went for dinner. I described the beautiful place we were in, a small restaurant in the harbour by the sea, unpretentious, but with delicious seafood. I was describing to Poppy the table, with white cloth and the comfortable chairs where we sat, on the terrace on the first floor overlooking the sea. It was all open, we could see the little boats moored, and there was a gentle breeze coming from the sea, bringing the fresh and salty sea air of the summer night. The food was the catch of the day, and seafood, fished just a few hours ago, all grilled, so fresh, so delicious. We usually had wine, but being such a special occasion, we decided to get some 'Cava', as we obviously were in Spain, a little restaurant in la Costa Brava. The brut cava from the fridge perfectly accompanied our food. We could drink, we were young, and we weren't driving that night. I could see Poppy's face enjoying the food, looking at me with her beautiful blue eyes, even more beautiful now with the little tan on her face and her wonderful smile, as I had seen so many times in the past when we were sharing a meal. We were talking, relaxed, without worrying about the future, without rushing, just enjoying the moment: we had all the time in the world!

We had our dessert and coffee and left the restaurant: we had a fantastic meal, without a doubt, one of the best in our lives. We thanked the staff for such a wonderful meal, and we walked down the stairs to the wide avenue outside. It was all lit up, with benches between the palm trees with couples sitting and kissing or groups of young people having fun. We just went for a stroll, Poppy's arm wrapped around mine. I always felt so proud when walking with Poppy by my side. I loved having Poppy on my arm, going for a walk with her, without rush, enjoying the contact of our bodies side by side as we leisurely walked, the deliberately lazy steps perfectly synchronised. We sat for a while on one of the benches, my arm around Poppy's shoulders to keep her warm: the temperature was dropping a bit but still pleasant.

After a while, we decided it was time to go back to the hotel. We arrived, went into our room, closed the door behind us, we hugged, and we kissed, and kissed, and kissed a bit more, while the clothes were quickly abandoning our bodies. Without realising we found ourselves on the bed, and then I told Poppy what we were doing, what I was doing to her, and what she was doing to me, but that will remain between Poppy and I.

Our night together in our minds continued: we sat on the bed for a while, resting, content, glad we had enjoyed each other's bodies one more time. We were quiet for a while, feeling the warmth of our bodies next to each other. After a while, we started talking. I was telling Poppy about our cats, about how much I loved her, talking about things we had done, asking her whether she remembered places we had been, moments we had shared imprinted on my mind. Among others, I asked her whether she remembered the time we went to Venice, and she nodded. "Do you remember Poppy when I bought you the white cap with the blue letters, and you were wearing it when we took the Vaporetto?" I said. Of course, she remembered! It had been one of our first holidays abroad, a fantastic deal she had found online. She nodded with her beautiful smile. "And, do you remember what I said to you, my love?" She nodded again, still smiling at me. I continued, "I said that from now on, you were the 'Capitana di Vaporetto,' and you laughed.

Do you remember my love?" It had been over 20 years, and I could still vividly remember that day. Yes, Poppy was that day 'Capitana di Vaporetto', but she was every day since I met her 'Capitana' of my heart and my life. I don't know how to explain it, but I think there is something wonderful about feeling that the person you love so much is 'Capitana' of your heart and vice versa. In any case, I had so many thousands of moments like that, sharing the wonderful journey of our lives together, so we just spent the whole night talking about things, while I held her hand in mine, careful not to disturb the drip administering the medication.

The nurses were phenomenal, coming every so often to check and administering Poppy's medication when required. Of course, they were completely unaware of the wonderful things we were experiencing, Poppy and I together, sharing those precious moments that night, one more night. That was our little secret!

Needless to say, that was a very long night, interrupted every so often by the scares that Poppy gave us. She was deteriorating almost by the hour, and again I thought I would lose her a few times; then I would stop talking to Poppy, and I would tell her to go. She had already given me a few hours, and we had had our dinner, our walk on the beach, and been intimate. I had it all! She had again and, as always, done it for me. She had given me already everything, and I understood if it was time for her to go. But Poppy didn't go, extraordinary, her ailing body still fighting, and she gave me one more night, a whole night, our last night.

Chapter 70

The morning sun broke the spell of our last night together, if there was ever one in the first place. It was Tuesday already. In the morning, the nurses came to wash, clean, and change Poppy's position. There were so many this time, trying to gently move Poppy, but it was almost impossible by now. Also, when they started moving Poppy, we almost lost her: she was hardly breathing, her pauses so long, her breathing so laborious, her inhalations so hard now. I truly thought she was leaving us at that moment, so while the nurses were discussing what to do, I held Poppy's right hand in my left and gently placed my right hand in her face. Then leaning onto her, I looked at my beautiful Poppy, and, trying to contain my tears, I said, "Poppy, my love, you cannot be like this anymore. It's too much Poppy, too much suffering, too much pain." I said it with all the love in the world, but still, it hurt so much when I continued, "You have to go now, my love. I don't want you to go, Poppy, I love you so, so much, but you have to go. It's time to go, my love. Just go." I had to pause, "Now you can be with your mum. I know you've missed her terribly all these years. She loved you so much, and now she's waiting for you, and you can finally be reunited." I had to stop a bit, "I know you don't want to go, and I wish I could go with you, all the journeys we did together, but my love…," this was probably the hardest thing for me to say, "this is a journey that sadly I cannot accompany you on. You'll have to go on your own, I'm so sorry, but I cannot go with you… just please go, Poppy, don't suffer anymore, my love, that's enough. You've given me everything and more, much more than I ever deserved, now just go and wait for me with your mum, and my mum, and my dad. They'll give you a kiss, and they'll look after you. I'm so sorry, Poppy, I couldn't do more for you, I'm really so sorry, but I can't see you like this anymore. Please just go and wait for me, Poppy, my love, just go...."

I couldn't continue. I had almost forgotten that the nurses were there. I looked at them, and I smiled, with a smile of a person resigned to their fate, in my case, the fate of losing the love of my life, my beautiful Poppy. They returned a compassionate smile, the best they could, half of them with watery eyes. I stood up, said that I was going to get a coffee, and let them get on with their jobs, thanking them very much for looking after Poppy so well, so compassionately, so humanely.

That Tuesday was awful. From 11-12 am, Poppy deteriorated more. By 4:00 pm, even worse, and by 6-7:00 pm, it was horrendous. The worse was the pain in the lower abdomen and the cries, the piercing sounds of the agonising pain, and her distorted face. I will never forget that. I had to call the nurses a couple of times: they didn't understand how it was possible with all the morphine already administered. Poppy should not have been in pain, but she was. They had to administer more, and then my beautiful Poppy rested a bit for a while.

My brother texted around 8:30 pm, afraid to hear the inevitable news, but Poppy was still with us. I remember saying to him how much morphine they had to give her that day just to keep her sedated and without pain. I also remember saying: "Her eyes are almost vitreous and she is so deformed already, she's unrecognizable...." "I see. A real fighter, but how sad all this suffering for nothing," he said. "Yes, for nothing. Her hands are so cold already, and her nails are violet! It's very close now. She's suffering so much. The sooner, the better. I just can't see her suffering so much. It's horrible." I continued the best I could, "If one of our cats was suffering half of what Poppy is suffering, I

299

would have taken them already to the vet to put them out of their misery. It's awful…" My brother couldn't really say much, so he just said, "Poor little thing, so much suffering, so unfair." "I wouldn't wish it to my worst enemy. It's horrendous…," I replied.

Apart from when the nurses came in the morning and I had gone out to get a coffee, once I returned, I didn't move from Poppy's side. I just sat there with her, holding her hand, keeping her company until it was time.

At 9:30 pm, the nurse came to check on Poppy and give her medication. I got up and went to the desk to have a drink of the juice they had brought me a while back, which was still untouched. In the meantime, the nurse was checking on Poppy. I was drinking, my eyes lost in the wall in front of me without really seeing, when I heard it. I quickly turned to look at Poppy with the nurse next to her. I didn't need to ask…

What I had heard was Poppy's last breath. I looked at Poppy, and I felt…nothing. At that moment, I couldn't feel anything. I only felt empty inside, lifeless. Finally, after so much pain and suffering for so many years, my beautiful Poppy was resting in peace. I thanked God for having put an end to her suffering and texted closer family and friends. Just a brief text: 'The flame of my beautiful Poppy has extinguished. Please pray for her'.

Chapter 71

Life after Poppy

To say that life after Poppy was difficult is an understatement. It was the worse time of my life. I have no parents, no children, no family here, and Poppy was my world. For 23 wonderful years, she was everything to me, and I really didn't know how I would manage to live without her. Luckily I had wonderful friends, a job to provide me with some routine, and our two little cats to keep me busy and entertained!

When Poppy's flame was extinguished, the nurse gave me some time to spend with Poppy on my own. She said that I could stay for as long as I wanted. I didn't need that long, though. I could no longer do much for Poppy in this life. I looked at Poppy, my beautiful Poppy, lying in bed, her face completely deformed, her body lifeless: there was certainly not much I could do, but there was a lot I could say. I told her how much I loved her, how privileged I felt to have been given the opportunity to meet her in the journey of my life, and how honoured I was she had chosen me to share her life with. Truly honoured.

I did my prayers for Poppy, and I told her that, God willing, I would keep my promise to look after the cats the best I could and then put them all together once gone. Poppy would be cremated as per her wishes, and so would our wonderfully silly little cats. I would also do my best to honour her memory and continue being the person she made me and not the person I was. Finally, I said I would do everything I could so she leaves a legacy and will never be forgotten.

That's because a few weeks before, we were sitting on the sofa, and out of the blue, Poppy said to me in the saddest possible way with a shaky voice and watery eyes: "I'm afraid I will be forgotten. Nobody will remember me as if I never existed." That hurt so much, not because she said it, but because she still thought so little of herself sometimes. Poppy was so special, so incredibly kind and loving and so loved by anyone who met her, and yet she thought she would be forgotten, just like that. But I understand: we didn't have children, and one day, sooner or later, I'll go, and that will be it. I don't mind not being remembered when I go, I'm nothing special, and I'll never be. But Poppy was incredibly special, and I would need to think of a way to keep her memory alive so she'll never be forgotten.

I sat for a while, mostly just holding her hand, as in limbo, my mind a bit empty. With every breath, as deep as possible, I was consciously thinking of accepting the reality of my new life. I would do it one breath at a time, minute by minute, hour by hour, day by day. Then I got up, held her hands between mine, and looking at Poppy I said, "Thank you for being the most wonderful wife and companion all these years." For me, a companion, a true companion in life, is much more than a wife. She's your soul mate. I continued, "You made me the happiest man in the world. Now go and rest in peace, my love. I will see you again one day." With that, I leaned over my beautiful Poppy, awfully deformed by now, put my hand on her face, and gave her a kiss. I couldn't hold my tears anymore, and a few escaped. It hurt so much!

I started packing everything, without rush, folding the clothes and putting them in bags: Poppy's dressing gown, nighties and pyjamas, her socks and slipper, she only needed one, of course, toiletries, towel, biscuits she loved that I had brought with me on Friday but were never eaten, drinks I also brought and still unopened. I was taking my time, doing everything almost in a ritualistic manner, controlling my breath and my thoughts. However, when I started folding the clothes she wore when we came to the hospice, I burst into tears: Poppy would not be wearing those clothes again to go back home now. She was not coming home. Not now, not ever!

I finished packing, took the bags and the crutches, and before I left the room, I kissed my beautiful Poppy goodnight, saying I would see her tomorrow. I said goodbye to the nurses, thanking them from the bottom of my heart for the wonderful and extraordinarily humane way they had looked after Poppy in the last days of her life, and I went home, the cool air of the night most welcomed. The wheelchair was left in the hospice: it was very new, of excellent quality, and hardly used. Someone hopefully could benefit from it.

****

Arriving home that night was not easy. I hadn't been home since Saturday afternoon, our very good friend feeding the cats and cleaning the litter trays. I opened the door thinking that that was it. From now on, I would be opening the door, and Poppy would not be there, not because she was in the hospital, and then she would be back: this time, she would not come back. Poppy would never be there again when I opened the door. I felt extremely sad, completely empty inside, lifeless.

I had to look after the cats now, though: meds, water, food, litter trays, and give them some cuddles and attention. They had been on their own a lot the last few days. When they were more settled, I would have a shower. I hadn't had a shower since Saturday, only washes in the hospital, and I really needed one. I felt better after. I made myself a coffee and sat on the sofa. I was exhausted. I didn't remember when I last slept, yet wide awake: ok, tonight was for mourning, but I would try to get some rest as the day after would be long and difficult.

I slept a little, got up, sorted the cats out, and had another shower. Then I went to the hospice and saw Poppy: she had been taken to a different room, and I was there with her for a short while. She was so cold, and rigor mortis had started setting, the chemical changes in her body stiffening her muscles. She didn't look like Poppy anymore, yet she was still my beautiful Poppy. I told her I would try to do everything the best possible for her and kissed Poppy goodbye. It was time to deal with the cruel reality: I had to arrange everything, and I had never done anything like that before. I put my 'business hat' on and left the hospice to deal with it.

Luckily the hospice recommended a funeral parlour just across the road. I made my way there, and I got all the information I needed; I knew what I wanted, but I didn't make any decisions. Poppy's dad and partner were coming down in the afternoon: I would have all the information ready for them, and then we would go back and decide all the arrangements together. The funeral director was absolutely amazing: I will never forget her, and I can never thank her enough for the kindness they showed Poppy and us in such difficult circumstances. They also took care of Poppy's body, keeping her on their premises until the cremation.

Poppy's family stayed until Sunday and were an invaluable moral support. They also, I felt, greatly benefited from being here, contributing and being part of all the arrangements. They accompanied me to several places to deal with the paperwork and formalities associated with someone's death: there was so much to deal with. I never realised! It started with the death certificate, Poppy's death certificate: that was awful. In addition, Poppy had always taken care of all paperwork and bureaucracy at home, and I didn't even know where she kept half the documents! So we were at home, and they were helping me to look for specific documents that I needed. But, of course, it was never supposed to be like that in the first place, Poppy dying in the hospice now. We had talked about it and said that once Poppy was back from the hospice with her meds sorted and the pain under control, we needed to start checking things, including papers. She had never wanted to do it before. I guess she didn't feel ready and comfortable: I understood that very well, and I wasn't going to push. Probably I would have done the same in her shoes.

I remember talking to my brother that night. He was asking how I was doing and how the day was. I explained what we had done and then said, "I cry a lot, and I miss Poppy so much! So many times, she was in hospital, but she always came home. I would pick her up when she was discharged, and we would make our way home together, always back home together. So many times! But last night, I came back on my own, and she will never be back. I miss her soooooo much!" That was the most difficult thing to get my head round: this time, Poppy was not coming home.

Wednesday, Thursday, and Friday, we dealt with the more pressing paperwork and finalised cremation arrangements, and on Saturday, we chose the flowers. We also booked a function room in a restaurant near the crematorium. Funnily enough, I had already been in that crematorium on two occasions for close friends: I never thought that the third time I went, it would be to cremate my beautiful Poppy. Third time unlucky, one could say.

I explained to my brother, as in Spain things are done differently, that after the cremation, we would go with closest friends and family to 'celebrate' Poppy's passing. I explained that it is not like a 'party', more like a gathering to pay our respects to our loved one gone and to chat a bit while having a drink and a bite together. I said to him, "I will open a bottle of champagne that I was saving for New Year's Eve." Every year I would choose a bottle to open at midnight after the 12 strikes, and as we toasted, I would thank Poppy for having given me another wonderful year and celebrate the start of the New Year together with a big kiss and a huge hug. So incredibly important for me. This year, however, it would not be the case, so I would open it after the cremation and share it with our friends and family. Poppy and I had given up, a long time ago, on the Spanish tradition of 'The 12 Grapes of Luck', where each grape is eaten with each bell strike – the Spanish way to welcome a New Year full of luck and prosperity. Perhaps we should have continued the tradition: my poor little Poppy didn't have much luck in life.

****

Poppy's family left on Sunday and would come back on Wednesday: Poppy's cremation had been arranged for Thursday. During those days, I kept dealing with legal formalities, and also I had to decide what Poppy would be wearing for her 'journey', her final one in this world. Once chosen, I would take it to the funeral parlour for them to dress her up.

On Monday night, I chose a beautiful dress for Poppy to wear, a nice shoe, her favourite lipstick shade, a pair of lovely earrings she liked wearing when we used to go out in the past and her favourite perfume. This was a big occasion, and I wanted Poppy to look very beautiful. I remember saying to my friend that, in reality, I knew very well it didn't make any difference, but for me, it was psychologically important. I also put a bag with some cuddly toys and food for the cats to take with her, so the day they meet again, she can look after them as she always did. How silly of me! When the time came, they would go to her, and Poppy would be reunited with her beloved cats. I only asked God to keep me here long enough so I could fulfil my promise.

Tuesday wasn't a great day. In the morning, I had breakfast, and then I was going to take Poppy's clothes to the parlour. It was around 10:00 am, and suddenly a thought came to my mind for the first time, and I almost panicked: I had not arranged an order of service! I could not believe it. With one thing and the other, I had completely forgotten, and I felt so sorry for Poppy. I had said to her I would do the best possible, and I wanted her to have that at least. I didn't even know where to start: Poppy had always done all these things in the past. I called our best friends in case they knew of someone: they didn't, but they would check and get back to me. In the meantime, I was also checking on the internet, trying to find someone local. I made a few phone calls and finally spoke to an amazing lady from specialized funeral printers. I explained the situation, and she said it could be done and told me exactly what they needed, but it had to be done quickly. There I was, suddenly rummaging through the hundreds of photos we had, kept in different places, as per Poppy's organisation totally unknown to me, looking for a few more meaningful ones to include in the order of service. We had so many!

I included, among others, Gretna Green, dancing in Blackpool, cycling to Spain, some of our holidays, mainly Poppy's birthday celebrations in Paris, Venice, and Luxor, and finally, a couple of Poppy with her beloved cats. I also included my song to Poppy done so many years back, 'Till the end of time'. I rushed everything to the printers and discussed the layout, background, paper, format, and whatever else they asked. I let myself be guided by their knowledge and expertise, and to this day, I still don't know how they managed to do it, but they did. On Wednesday evening, they had produced this incredibly beautiful order of service, and it was ready to be taken to the parlour.

However, now I had to choose the music for the service. The entrance was easy: 'Wake me up before you go go!', I knew Poppy loved it from her teenage years before I met her. That had to be the one. For the reflection music, I chose 'Dancing like lovers', a waltz, as that was Poppy's favourite ballroom dance, and we had danced the particular version I chose on many occasions. The afternoon was already getting quite hard, the lump in my throat getting bigger with every song. But it was when I chose the farewell song 'Save the last dance for me' that I burst into tears, thinking that in less than 48 hours, my beautiful Poppy would be taking the final journey in her modest coffin to the sound and words of that song. At the beginning of being together, we had a CD, and that song was there. I knew Poppy loved it. We had sung along many times on our trips, always laughing, always joking, Poppy saying, "Remember to save the last dance for me," and I would joke back, saying, "But Poppy, my love, now ALL dances are for you!"

I got very down that afternoon, really down. Also, that evening at 9:35 pm, it was already a week since Poppy had left us, and I could not get my head round it. Yes, Tuesday was not a great day, and I still had to write what I was going to say in the special words section. So bloody hard! Thankfully, our friends and families were so supportive that I could go through it all. And I had the little furry monsters to look after.

Tuesday gave way to Wednesday, a tense day, hoping that everything would be ok. I was sitting in the evening, trying not to think too much, as the day after was the big day. Everything was ready for the cremation: the day before, I had taken Poppy's clothes and makeup to the funeral parlour and left it in their capable hands. That morning I went to see Poppy dressed up: she had worn that dress a few times when going out, the earrings, the lipstick, just a bit of make-up, she never wore too much, just right, and I couldn't help thinking of some of those wonderful days together. My heart got very sad. Also, the order of service would now be done. Thank God for making me think of it that Tuesday morning, and thank you to the printers for producing something so magical in so little time. The flowers had been arranged and would be delivered directly to the funeral director in the morning. The music had been chosen and arranged. My little speech was done. I had spoken to everybody to arrange the time to meet up, and taxi arrangements had been done. The menu in the restaurant had been decided. All was ready for the big day, or was it?

Suddenly I thought, 'what am I wearing tomorrow?'. I hadn't even thought of it until now, almost 11:00 pm. I honestly couldn't decide, so I ironed 3 shirts, prepared 2 trousers and polished the shoes. I thought, when I get up in the morning I'll think about it, I just couldn't decide. However, someone made a decision for me, and up to this day, I still don't know how. I was lying in bed, unable to sleep, my mind a roller-coaster of thoughts and emotions. It was around 1:00 am, and there she was, my beloved grandmother from up there, telling me what to wear. They, my loved ones, when 'talking' to me, are always high up, at the corner of the room to my left, since the first time with my mum all those years back. That took me by surprise as I was not expecting it. If it had been my mum, my dad, or

309

even Poppy, it would have been more expected. But my grandma, who had been dead for over twenty years, and I didn't think of her that often, definitely took me by surprise. Then again, my grandparents loved me very much, and we always had an amazing relationship. I've said it before, and I will say it again: I truly believe that our loved ones never leave us. We may not think of them too much or often, but they are always there when we need them. At least in my case, they have always been there for me in my hardest, most difficult, and darkest times, and God knows there have been many, providing help, support, and guidance. So that's how I came to wear the black trousers, white shirt, black waistcoat, and red tie that I had worn on a few competitions with Poppy at the beginning of our dancing career together. I had hardly worn those clothes since. But that's what my grandma said I should wear, and that is what I did. Thankfully, they still fitted!

****

Thursday came, and in all honesty, I just wanted it out of the way. All went according to plan though, and as hard as it was, we had a beautiful service. The contributions from Poppy's dad, his partner, and Poppy's sister were very emotional. I cried a lot with the reflection music interval, and then it was my turn. I got out the piece of paper with the little speech I had prepared, and off I went. I have a terrible memory, and without the piece of paper, I would have forgotten half the things. I said everything I had to say, and it was done now. I always got extremely nervous when talking in front of people. I never had the confidence, but today it was different. No matter how nervous I was, I was going to do it, and I did it. Now, there was only one last thing left: as they started playing the farewell music, we got up, and before exiting, we gave Poppy's coffin a kiss. Our last kiss, our last dance. That was it: the next time I saw

Poppy, it would be in a little box I had chosen containing her ashes.

After the service, we went to the function room we had arranged and had our little drinks and snacks, our little chats, and our bottle of champagne. We toasted to Poppy, and it was done. Funnily enough, as sad as the circumstances were, I have very fond memories of that day, with our friends and her family, talking about Poppy. None of my family could come, but that didn't matter as I knew they were all with me that day, including my parents and grandparents, no doubt about that.

In life, everything has a beginning, and everything has an end, good and bad, and the end of the day came. I remember sitting at home thinking that it had been a long and difficult day, but it hadn't been a terrible day. On the contrary, all went well, and now I could sit with a coffee, thinking that at least I had done my best for Poppy on her cremation day. Now, wait for the funeral parlour to call me when Poppy's ashes were ready for collection.

On Saturday, I bought thank-you cards and boxes of chocolates, and I felt like Father Christmas: I took some to the hospice, the funeral parlour, the printers, and the local pharmacy that for years had been amazing with Poppy, and then I would also do the surgery and Poppy's doctor the week after. I can never thank her GP enough for the professionalism, kindness, and support for Poppy all those years. He truly is a wonderful man. In the afternoon, I visited our best friends, had a coffee with them, chatted for a while, and then went home. I was invited to my friend's birthday party: the whole family was going to a nice restaurant, but I just didn't feel in the mood. I went home to our cats. They knew something was different and were a bit unsettled. The day after, I would go to church after mass as customary to do my prayers, light a candle, and mostly thank God because Poppy was no longer suffering. Also, to thank Poppy again and always for the wonderful 23 years she gave me.

On Monday, I got a phone call saying that Poppy's ashes were ready for collection. I picked them up, and I remember thinking that, indeed, those were Poppy's ashes, but what is really Poppy? Of course not! My beautiful Poppy would never be a pile of ashes. That was only her cremated body, so emaciated, ravaged by the disease, and deformed as not to be of use to her anymore. Why she had to suffer so much in this life, I will never understand. I feel it was utterly unfair and undeserved. However, I believe also that in life, everything happens for a reason, although many times we may leave this world without finding out. For a long time now, I've thought that my mum's death was the beginning of a period of my life that would ultimately result in meeting Poppy. Out of the bad, something good came out: I met Poppy and had the best time of my life. It is extremely unlikely I would have ever met Poppy without my mum's death in those circumstances. Destiny gave me Poppy, but destiny also took her away. Now, Poppy was gone, and I didn't know why: again, like my mum, she was worth a thousand of me. Would I ever find out why? I didn't know, but I truly hoped so, and that something good comes out of her sad passing.

The day after, I went for lunch with Poppy! It may be difficult to understand, but I booked a table in the restaurant where we had celebrated Poppy's passing. I did it because when we went all together, Poppy was on her journey to be cremated; now, the cycle had been completed, and she was with us. I wanted to have that last meal together with Poppy, just the two of us. The staff at the restaurant obviously knew of the situation: I said I had Poppy's ashes with me in a bag, but they would sit next to me so nobody would see them. I asked for a quiet table away from the main area, and I sat there with the photo of Poppy and I in Gretna Green all those years back and the order of service opposite me and two glasses. Kind of our beginning together and our end. I went late, so there was hardly anyone in the restaurant at the time. We had our lunch, and as I raised our glasses to Poppy, I thanked her for what she did for me all those years and gave her a kiss. When I asked the waitress to take a photo, they were all quite moved, saying it was the first time anyone had done anything like it. Well, I'm sure other people have done it, but it probably is not that common. I know I'm quite odd, and in any case, I stopped a long time ago worrying about what other people may think and how it looks: to me, it is more important how it feels.

****

Life continued day by day. I remember saying to people that I felt very sad and empty, which was normal, I guess. What was a bit less normal is like a part of me was missing, truly missing, physically missing. The best way I could explain it was by saying that I had a totally empty, void space on my left side, extending from under the armpit to the hip in a half-moon shape, pitch black like a black hole. That's how I would see myself if I closed my eyes, and that's how it felt with my eyes open. Interestingly though, if looking at the mirror, I would see myself with the void on my left side, and the reflection in the mirror I would also have it on the left side. That is not physically possible with a mirror image, so I didn't understand. That lasted many months, the void slowly filling up from light haziness to progressively denser matter until one day, it felt kind of normal, and I would no longer have that image in my mind. Almost a year, I would say, and to this day, I can't explain it.

As days went by, I was cancelling Poppy's documents: passport, driving licence, pension, electoral role, and bank accounts. Every document cancelled was like a stab in my heart, getting to the point that it was like she never existed. That reminded me painfully of her words a few weeks back: I definitely had to think of a way, so she's not forgotten. However, the hardest was to cancel Poppy's contract for the new car. When we got it two years back, we were full of hope for a future together, but sadly, things had turned out very differently. I was given the option to buy the car at a very good price, but I didn't want to: that was Poppy's car, and we got it for Poppy to give her more independence. It was a beautiful car, just two years old, with very low mileage, and in excellent condition: it was a great deal, no doubt about it, but everything in life is not about money. I just didn't want Poppy's car without Poppy, and I certainly didn't need it: I would keep driving my old Ford.

As I could no longer drive the car, they had to come home to pick it up. That was one of the saddest days, giving back the keys and car documents of the car that had meant so much to Poppy. The driver was checking the car and commented, almost surprised, that it was in such good condition. It certainly was: Poppy was a very good driver, prudent, courteous and careful.

I also had to change the cats' insurance policies and many other contracts and policies to my name: although all direct debits were from my account, most of the things were in Poppy's name, as it was easier if there was a problem or a claim to make, she being the main policy holder. In any case, she was much better than me at all those things. However, that posed a few issues, as I didn't know many of the passwords. Some I could find, others I couldn't, so there would always be lengthy conversations to sort things out.

One of my cats also needed an operation in October, so all that had to be arranged. By now, they were getting quite old, and S also had a big lump in his ear that became ulcerated and needed to be treated topically daily and required antibiotics. It was surgically removed, but it came back. Unbeknown to us at the time, we later found out it was cancer.

At the same time, I had decided that all donations in memory of Poppy would go to the hospice. I approached it with my usual obsessive nature: that was my project, and it would keep me motivated. We know it was not supposed to be like this, but sadly, that is how it happened. Poppy spent her last few days in the hospice, looked after by a very dedicated team of doctors, nurses and volunteers. They were absolutely amazing, and the truth is that such organizations employ exceptional people and are almost always underfunded. Clearly, although Poppy would not benefit from it, someone else would, and in that way, it was like her last will on earth, as she was a truly kind and generous person. Therefore, organising those donations, gave me great comfort in being Poppy's agent to do that, and that's why I decided to do it. I was doing that in her memory so she wasn't forgotten.

I started contacting people and sending messages and emails to anyone I could think of. Some of them I had not seen for years, but I had always had a fantastic relationship with them. Everyone was so kind and generous, 90% of the people donating didn't even know Poppy. They only knew of Poppy through me. I was truly humbled by everybody's generosity, and we managed to raise thousands of pounds for the hospice, one of the biggest donations from an individual. I was so proud to do that for Poppy. That was the first thing I did in memory of Poppy to raise funds for the hospice, and it felt really good. I would think of what else to do in the future.

****

I was back at work, it provided me with stability and routine, and I would see colleagues and friends. Tuesdays in the evening were difficult, and I got used to go for a drive so that I was not at home at the exact time Poppy passed away. Just half an hour driving up and down the motorway, quiet and dark at that time, driving at 60 mph in the slow lane, gently thinking about things. I would talk to Poppy, discussing things about the future, a future that was clearly now my future, not our future anymore, that was gone. I really didn't know what to do. So hard, it was so difficult and painful to live without Poppy. I missed her enormously, and I felt completely lost.

As life continued, I had to confront the first of many things without Poppy: the first month without her, the first visit somewhere, the first silly little things like the first kebab takeaway, and of course, the first celebrations. The first Christmas was particularly hard, and although a few people had invited me to celebrate with them, I preferred to be on my own. I got in the car, and I drove to a place that meant something to us: then I went home, and in the evening, I cooked a paella. The tradition of the paella for Christmas had started our first year together when I was working in the hotel: I kept eating turkey from 2 weeks before Christmas, and I said to Poppy that I was starting to get a turkey face and perhaps we should do something completely different for a change. She loved paella, and so did I, and that's how it all started: every Christmas, we had our amazing paella and everything else she fancied, usually a selection of Spanish cold meats and seafood. Also, it was

316

quick to cook and easy to clean up after, which did appeal to us.

Then it was the first New Year's Eve. No kiss this year, no France, and no chasing the cats: I just gave them a kiss mixed with tears and one from Poppy. I just stayed at home, and on New Year's day, I went out for a while. However, in the evening, I went for dinner with my friends: Poppy didn't want me to be sad, crying, and on my own all the time, I was sure of that, and we went to a restaurant and celebrated the beginning of the New Year together. It was lovely.

The first Valentine came, which always meant a lot to us. For every celebration, I would always buy the relevant card and write something meaningful. Poppy would keep them and look at them when she pleased. That day I wrote:

'My beautiful Poppy,

Today is Friday, 14th February 2020. As I am writing this, I can't help but cry. It is almost 5 months since you went with the little angels. There is no day that goes by that I don't think of you; I miss you sooooooo much!!! I am continuing with my life the best I can, my love, and I'm trying to do well for the 'gatitos'. I am so sad you are not here. Nothing is the same without you, and I really don't know how to live without you by my side. It didn't go according to plan, my love. So many words left unspoken, so many things still to be done. Today I can only say how much I love you. I am so sorry I couldn't do better for you, my love. I love you so much! Happy Valentine's Day, my love'.

Yes, Valentine's Day always meant a lot to us, although it was very clear in our minds that it was just one more day, and it is what we did every day that made the difference in our relationship and our lives. Valentine's Day, we just did that little bit extra: how different this year, though.

I got out the beautiful card Poppy bought me our last Valentine: a deep blue card with two white swans together, their long necks extending away from their bodies and then their heads coming back together at the top, drawing a figure of a heart under the moonlight. Just beautiful. More beautiful though were the words in the card: 'We belong together. With you, my heart found its home, my love found its forever, and I found my everything'. The back of the card read: 'I'm so grateful for each and every moment we share. Happy Valentine's Day'. Poppy always chose wonderful cards, that one just being an example. Yes, we did belong together, but destiny had other plans. That was a very sad day…

After Valentine's Day, the others first of everything without Poppy followed: Poppy's birthday, Easter, bank holidays in May, my birthday. My first birthday without Poppy was very hard, she had always made my birthdays truly special and memorable, regardless of what we were doing or where we were. I had so many fond memories of my wonderful birthdays with Poppy. Even the year before, we had still 'celebrated' together with my brother. This birthday there was no Poppy for the first time in 24 years in my life. I still missed Poppy an awful lot. The last few months, I hadn't felt like much going out with people and socializing, so I was at home a lot with my cats or going out on my own, and when the pandemic hit us, I became a bit of a recluse. That day, however, I got in the car and went out to Canterbury for the day. Don't ask me why. I just like Canterbury.

Then, without realising, it was already a year since Poppy passed away. Time had flown, but every day had been so painfully slow and depressing.

****

I have always said that I feel I have been very fortunate in life. I had a fantastic childhood, teenage years, and early adulthood. Tragic events would happen at times, but they could have been much worse. Somehow, I was given another chance. I have met fantastic people in the journey of my life, and of course, I met Poppy. She changed my life in ways that many people couldn't comprehend. She saved me, and the way she made me feel cannot be described with words. It can only be experienced. I have always favoured quality over quantity, and for 23 years, I was blessed to have Poppy in my life. Those years were amazing, and to me, it was much more than what many people will have in their entire lives. For that, and much more, of course, I will be eternally grateful to my parents for bringing me to this world, to God for giving me a second chance, and to Poppy for making me feel the way I did. I could go now and be happy with what I had, truly happy. But I still have a few promises to fulfil, so I'm not ready to go yet, not yet.

To say that a woman can make or break a man is an understatement. A woman can destroy you, and your confidence, make you feel utterly useless, a waste of space and time. I have seen it many times with other people, extremely toxic and destructive relationships, and it almost happened to me once. On the other hand, if you have the right woman at your side, she won't break you but make you, as my beautiful Poppy did to me. Poppy made me feel as if I could conquer the world, that I could do anything if I put my mind to it. Poppy made me feel truly unique, one in a million man. And Poppy gave me an internal confidence

319

in myself I had never had, and it is fair to say that when she went, I lost that confidence, which I have not regained. Going places with her, I felt special; sitting at a table in a restaurant with her, I felt special; to the many parties we used to attend when she was well or having her in my arms when dancing, I felt special; just simply walking together holding hands, I felt special. Poppy definitely knew how to make me feel unique, and truly special anywhere we were.

It was not supposed to be that way, my beautiful Poppy leaving us so early. It was not part of our master plan, but that is what happened, and it cannot be changed. Poppy and I will not grow old together, and we will not go out for walks on the beach holding hands as we always dreamt we would. The life I had made no sense once Poppy left, but it is the life I have now, and I have to make the most of it. Not doing so, I feel it would be disrespectful to Poppy, and I would be doing her a disservice. Wasting my life is the worst I could do.

One day, Poppy said to me just before she passed away, looking at me with her always and still beautiful blue eyes: "Now my love, you can do all the things you wanted to do but couldn't because of me. Go and live your life as we always did, with true love and to the full. I don't want you to be sad, I don't want you to be unhappy and, most of all, I don't want you to be on your own."

I know she meant well. Poppy always did, but hearing those words was so painful, words I never thought I would hear. I just lowered my head, looking at the floor, fighting the tears. Then, as she was caressing my face with her hand, gently said, "Please, look at me, my love. I know it's not what you want to hear, and it's not what I would like to say, but there is someone out there waiting for you, someone who will make you happy and who you will make as happy as you've made me all these years. I know you will because I know you. One day you will find someone and live as we did. Someone will knock at your door, or perhaps, it will be you knocking on someone else's door, but I know you will find that person. I want you to find that person one day. I need you to find that person. You have to do it for yourself, but, mostly, you must do it for me." To that, I had no reply, I couldn't say a word, just crying, as I understood very well what she meant: I must do it for her, I must live for her. Poppy was dying: she wouldn't be able to do it herself. She would live through me.

What Poppy didn't realize is that I didn't need anything else, I didn't need anyone else, and I didn't need to do anything that I hadn't done. I only needed Poppy. Yet, to my despair, she was slowly, clearly, hopelessly being taking away from me right in front of my very eyes.

****

Over a year had passed and destiny, again by serendipity, put someone in my way. It would be fair to say it took me completely by surprise, but from the moment I met this person, that very first time, I saw something special in her, not outside, but inside. I could not understand what was happening, but it felt like if I was attracted to her. Surely, that couldn't possibly be, it was not probable that another woman could exist in my life after Poppy. Was destiny mocking me? I discarded the idea and fought for weeks about what I was feeling inside, finding it very difficult to accept it.

At the same time, Christmas was approaching. One of our cats had been deteriorating over the previous months, the ulcerated lump in his ear, now a proper tumour, so vascular, enlarged and perforated, constantly bleeding. The biopsies taken a few months back had confirmed the diagnosis: it was cancer. I could not believe my ears when the vet got the results from the biopsies and told me the type of cancer he had: the same as Poppy! I was speechless. Truly unbelievable. In any case, as I had promised, I would do my very best for him until the time came.

Christmas was hard, the second one already without Poppy: again, I preferred to be on my own, with my memories, cooking a paella and eating it without much gusto. I was mainly enjoying the company of my cats, as I could see that S didn't have long. New Year came and passed, all the excitement and enjoyment of all the years shared with Poppy now vanished.

After the festivities, I would return to work. That weekend though, S had been very poorly, so I phoned the vet on Monday to make an appointment: my regular vet was off that day so I made an appointment for the day after. After dinner I sat on the sofa, put S on my lap, but he made a funny noise when I lifted him up: it reminded me of the crying pain from Poppy when trying to be moved by the nurses in the hospice her last couple of days. It suddenly brought back all those painful memories. I placed him gently on the rug at my feet, I closed my eyes for a few minutes and when I opened them again and checked on him he was gone. I looked at the little body, quite consumed by now, lying at my feet, lifeless. It hurt so much, but again I thanked God for stopping the suffering of our beautiful little cat. He had done so much for Poppy for so many years, and for me, once Poppy was gone, I will be eternally grateful for what he gave us all those years and will always have a place of honour in my heart.

I have hundreds of anecdotes I could tell with S: he was silly, a clown, loving and always giving those wonderful cuddles. As soon as you touched him he would start purring and had this amazing de-stressing and healing effect on one. He was a Houdini, totally fearless until he got badly hit by a bus and we almost lost him, not even 2 years old. He certainly gave us quite a few scares over the years and some sleepless nights. He was determined and persistent, and more stubborn than Poppy and me together, which says something about his personality. The truth is that we loved him to bits. I was deeply sad to see him go but at the same time happy he was no longer suffering and would be reunited with Poppy, who loved him so much.

I phoned the vet, took S and left him there with the wonderful Ros for her to arrange the cremation. I chose the little box and I would be contacted when his ashes were ready for collection. One down, one to go. I went back home, I lit a candle and together with Poppy we did our prayers, but mainly I thanked God He was keeping me here so I can fulfil my promises.

****

Weeks went by and destiny played its hand again. I coincided a few times just by luck with that person that to me seemed quite special and then, after pondering what to do for ages I made what to me was a momentous decision: I invited this special person for dinner on Valentine's Day! What a day I chose, I was so nervous and scared! Valentine's day had always been very special for Poppy and me: if I was sharing Valentine's Day with that person it was because she was extremely precious to me. I had spoken to Poppy though and I had her blessing. However, it was all completely new to me: I didn't do it very well at the beginning, probably quite badly in all honesty. Not only we were coming from opposite ends of the spectrum in our relationships, I also hadn't dated for 25 years! We lost touch for a while, then somehow destiny crossed our paths again. I felt so indebted to her for what she had done for me: she got me out of the automated pilot life I was living and made me realise that I could have a life after Poppy. She gave me hope for the future and that to me was priceless. Yes, I felt very indebted to her.

Covid time was hard on everybody, many people losing their jobs including her, so I tried to be around and help when I could. I saw her once in a while and eventually, I could be of assistance in her getting a job followed by a much better one, with good salary and great working conditions. I was so pleased for her. Somehow, I felt at least I had repaid her, albeit minimally, for what she did for me. I knew she hadn't been very fortunate in life overall and perhaps now things would start getting better and she would have a chance of true happiness. I kept saying to her, not to worry about anything, everything would be ok. Every time she needed me, I tried to be there for her.

Slowly but surely, again the days had been passing, already many seconds of everything: Poppy's birthday, Easter, my birthday. Suddenly, it was two years since Poppy went away. That day I decided to spread a handful of Poppy's ashes in the sea with a red rose. I didn't spread all the ashes, as that would be done in the Mediterranean in due course. It was symbolic though. I was almost in the same spot where we had last been to the beach together. As I was looking at the horizon with tears in my eyes, I reminisced on the day that we stood there, now over two years back. That was a seminal moment for me: with the ashes and the rose I was telling Poppy how much I loved her, without a doubt she will always have a hugely special place in my heart. That will never change. How could it? True love never dies. However, in a way and maybe most importantly I was telling her that perhaps I was ready to try to redo my life. I knew she wanted me to, she had told me so many times lately. In any case, I let her go, now my beautiful Poppy would roam free in the seas taking the rose of my love to accompany her forever, but I would stay here and try to live my life again, a life without Poppy. Among all the women I had met, there was only one I wanted to be with but it hadn't worked out: I was asking Poppy, and even my parents, to help me and guide me to try to do it better next time, if that was on the cards.

To me a relationship is like a train on two tracks. Sometimes the train goes uphill: life is difficult, challenging and we have to push hard. Sometimes it goes downhill: easy going, enjoyable, almost effortless. Sometimes there will be obstacles on the way and we must change direction: the train can go to the right or to the left, and although both rail tracks will move in the same direction, the degree of curvature would be different. Therefore, one will always have to bend more than the other, sometimes the right, sometimes the left: adapt more, compromise more, accept more, but with both tracks moving in the same direction the train will overcome any obstacles in its way and will arrive at its destination.

Poppy and I understood that very well and we were very fortunate that we had pretty much the same values and principles, shared the same main interests and worked together to achieve our goals. Our tracks moved in the same direction, quite naturally, without forcing.

However, if both tracks move in different directions, one pulling to the right and one pulling to the left, the train will stop and will never reach its destination. And if you try to push forward the train, it will derail! My philosophy had always been that when that happens, perhaps it is better not to waste too much time in that train: if the tracks don't get back together, no matter how much you would like to, that train is not going anywhere. Get off and jump on another one that takes you somewhere and perhaps that way you can reach your dreamed destination. If you want to get somewhere, sitting in a train that doesn't move, will only create frustration, disappointment and unhappiness.

****

I had also been thinking for a long time what I could do to raise funds for the hospice again. It was my way to keep Poppy's memory alive so she would not be forgotten, but also help the hospice: perhaps it would not happen to someone else what happened to Poppy and there would always be a bed available when needed. Only 40% is funded by the NHS, the rest depends on donations and I was just trying to do my bit.

I thought I would run one of the organised races, 5 or 10 km perhaps. When I mentioned that to my best friend in Spain he said, "forget 10 km. Let's run the London marathon for Poppy!" Of course, why didn't I think of it? Clearly a piece of cake, for him: he was a semi-pro triathlete, super-fit and had done a few marathons. I, on the other hand, hadn't run properly for over 30 years and I had a painful hip, result of the accident we had on our first weekend away with Poppy where I fractured my hip all those years back. I had already started paying the price a while back.

In any case, he convinced me and I spoke to the event organiser at the hospice. She told me that the 5 places for the marathon that year in October were taken but she put my name down for April 2022. Perfect, thank you very much. I had plenty of time, around a year, so I started my training gently in April and by June I could run 9-10 km without a problem. Still far from the 42 km or 26 mi but I had time. However, at the end of June I received an email from the hospice and all changed: someone had pulled out of the marathon in October and they were offering me the place. Wow, only 3 months away! I asked them to give me 24 hours to decide: I spoke to my friend and asked him what to do. He said "You can do it, it's going to be hard and it's going to hurt, but I know you very well and I know you can do it: say yes." And that's how it came about that I was on the starting line on the 3rd October to run the London marathon 2021 to raise funds for the hospice in memory of Poppy.

My friend was right: the training was hard and it was painful and my hip 'complained' a lot. Luckily I had an exceptional sports injuries therapist and he worked miracles to keep me going those three months as I had to visit him regularly. Furthermore, the Tuesday before the race on Sunday I had the worse cramp in my calf and I couldn't even walk, let alone run. I saw him the day after and said to him, "Do whatever you have to do but get me on the starting line on Sunday!" That was the most painful session ever, as he was trying to dissolve the enormous knot in my calf. But he did it and I'll be eternally grateful to him: we both know without him it is unlikely I would have been on the starting line that Sunday. Neither without my best friend in Spain, whose advice and support was invaluable. He couldn't come though so I had to run on my own.

Interestingly, my sports therapist is a very spiritual person who has done amazing charity work for deprived and displaced communities in many countries around the world. I've known him for many years and he has always been an inspiration to me. He knew my circumstances very well and when Poppy passed away he wrote to me one of the most beautiful letters I ever read, very emotional. Among others, a clear message was 'I see you', meaning as I also believe, that true love never dies. You'll see the sun in the sky, the leaves rustling in the trees, the little bird flying and suddenly you'll see the big eye, 'I see you', meaning that person, your loved one, will always be with you, in your heart and your mind.

In any case, the day of the race came. I hadn't been well on Thursday and Friday, with temperature and shivers. The stress I guessed. I rested the best I could on Saturday, and on Sunday I got up early, had a shower, light breakfast, got the bag I had prepared the night before and made my way to the starting point, where I joined the almost forty thousand crazy and masochistic people like me pushing themselves to the limit for a wonderful cause!

To say that it was a struggle is an understatement: 2 km into the race I realised I couldn't get air into my lungs very well and I thought, 'Oh dear, this is gonna be a long day. Please God give me the strength to do it'. Again, strength was given to me, from somewhere, so my legs kept going, breathing the best I could. From km 16 my hip hurt, from 23 it hurt more and from km 26 every step was sending sharp pain up my hip, now running unbalanced. From km 32 every single step was agony. But something kept me going, the memory of my loved ones in my heart pumping the blood around my body so my legs wouldn't stop and, also, mainly the reason why I was doing it. In any case, somehow I crossed the line, just out of my expected time of 4:30 hours: not bad considering I could hardly breathe, neither run very well the last 10km. But time was unimportant, what really mattered is that I did it: I had run the London Marathon to raise funds for the hospice in memory of my beautiful Poppy! It was done now.

Again, people had been so generous and we managed to raise a phenomenal amount of money for the hospice, the highest donation from an individual that year as I later found out. I even received a beautifully framed certificate from the hospice as 'Fundraiser of the Year'. However, although I ran the race, we all did it together, we all put our hands in our pockets for a wonderful cause.

When a few months after I was asked to write a note explaining why I had run the marathon and my experience of it, this is what I had to say: "Poppy was an amazing person that gave me 23 wonderful years. Her last few days in the hospice made me realise what extraordinary human beings the staff there are. Running the marathon in Poppy's memory to raise funds for them was one of the most incredible experiences of my life.

Physically challenging to the extreme due to my hip condition, I am certain that is was Poppy and the supporters that so kindly contributed to the cause that gave me the strength to do it. However, it was the crowd that made all the difference on the day. When every step is agony, the unknown faces lining the streets cheering you up as you go by, become a beacon of hope that you will make it to the finishing line. I could have never done it without them and I will cherish the experience for the rest of my life."

****

I had run the marathon, but it's true I don't think I would have managed without the crowd. It is also true that the event organiser had been absolutely amazing from day one and I couldn't have done it without her either. She supported us and guided us form the beginning until the starting line. She replied to my quote by saying: "Thanks for this really lovely message. You are a true inspiration and these words will inspire others to follow in your footsteps and do something incredible for the hospice. Truly thank you."

Those words were really appreciated but after what I saw in the hospice, they were the truly inspiring ones. Therefore, I replied, "Thank you very much for such kind words, but believe you me, I'm nothing special and I doubt I can inspire anyone to do much. However, I am special due to the wonderful people I meet in the journey of my life. Poppy was exceptional, and also people like you at the hospice are the truly special ones, as you make a difference in people's lives every single day. You and people like you are the true inspiration! I am just the tool to accomplish that."

I will certainly cherish the experience for the rest of my life. But it is also true I will cherish marathon day for the rest of my life for another reason. Surely I had run the race for the hospice and in memory of Poppy, but the race was over, time to go back to reality. My beautiful Poppy had given me a wonderful past, but as amazing and incredible as it was, it could never be my present, nor my future. It had been a very emotional experience and that day, after the race, there was only one person I wanted to see, only one person I wanted in my present and my future. That special person came to meet me at the end of the race with a bunch of flowers and I have some of the fondest memories of my life. Since that day those flowers took a place of honour at home and they're still there. She will never know how much that meant to me, how important she was in my life and how I will cherish forever the time spent with her that sunny Sunday afternoon after the race in Trafalgar Square.

On Monday I took the day off to recover and on Tuesday I went to work. I didn't feel too good, I did a Covid test and then I knew why I had struggled to breathe on

Sunday: I tested positive for Covid. I went home and self-isolated for the required period, as life went on.

****

Time doesn't stand still for anyone. Before I knew it, the third Christmas was upon me. That Christmas Eve was different though. In one of my travels I had met someone: a wonderful lady, mid-forties, classy, well-educated and in good financial position. She was very attractive, a lawyer but she was not working now, she didn't need to. Sadly, she had lost her husband, a doctor, a couple of years back and he had left them financially secure. She had a son and a daughter both doing her university studies, a lovely family. They lived a couple of hours away by car so I went to meet them after lunch.

They're a Christian family, not too religious either but a bit more than me and they would always attend the Midnight Mass: it was a family tradition. I understood that very well as it was done in my family when I was little. When I was visiting her town I saw announced this wonderful display of Christmas carols outside the Cathedral in the evening and then the Mass at midnight so I was quite interested. She had invited me to go with her and the kids and I had promised I would go. Also, it had been many years that I hadn't been to one, since I was little in Spain in fact, almost 50 years I would say. I remembered going with my parents, my grandparents and my uncles and being very cold. It brought very fond memories of me quite little with my blue navy coat and red scarf, hat and gloves walking up the hill towards the Church with my family in the cold winter night. So I said yes, very much looking forward to it.

In the afternoon she was going to the cemetery to visit her late husband and put some flowers. She said, quite

331

A couple of months went by and somehow destiny brought us together again. When the person you want to be with is the same person that wants to be with you, wonderful things may happen, as I have been fortunate enough to experience in my life. I had one good relationship and two very good ones in Spain but I messed it up. Badly! However, somehow destiny gave me another opportunity and then I met Poppy. I was truly blessed by having Poppy in my life. I think that my relationship with Poppy was exceptional not only because of how extra special she was, indeed exceptional, but also perhaps because I was at a stage of my life where I could really appreciate what Poppy had to offer. Sadly, Poppy had left us and I had to continue with my life.

****

Days again went by, the third of everything: Poppy's birthday, Easter, May bank holidays. By now my other cat had deteriorated a lot: he was getting very old, the renal failure now very advanced and unable to control it with the medication he had been under for many years already. His kidneys were not retaining the protein as they should have done and therefore he was losing weight, a lot. Every year we would always take our little monsters for a full check-up, full MOT as I used to say to Poppy: bloods, urine, blood pressure, examination and anything else the vets advised. For many years Poppy had dealt with everything, but as she got less capable of doing it we would do it together. Once Poppy left, of course, I continued doing it. The full MOT was usually done in July, as then we would be travelling at some point in the summer: if there were any issues we had time to deal with them.

However, from March-April H was getting weaker, losing muscle mass and it was getting more difficult for him to jump. Not having all the power in his back legs, sometimes I would hear a suspicious sound: his jump wasn't successful and he had fallen, again, on the floor. Big bang! I would rush to pick him up and give him a little cuddle. He couldn't understand why he couldn't jump so he kept trying.

He was still doing well in terms of eating, drinking and bodily functions though, just getting old. At the end of May he was getting quite small and weaker so in June I took him for his MOT. H had always been a big cat, lean, muscular and incredibly powerful: from a 6.4 kg cat at his peak 10 years back, last year in July he weighed 3.9 kg and this year when I took him in June 2.9 kg.

Our vets had always been absolutely amazing and our last vet was in the practice for many years: she was super professional and also knew the cats very well. However, now there was someone new, which is always a concern when you go with an elderly cat like H. At least the wonderful Ros was still there, just in case. I should not have been worried: the new vet was extraordinary. She was very gentle with H and very professional: she did all the tests required, adjusted the medication and made a follow-up appointment.

My life also continued the best I could. I was going out a bit more, meeting more people. Sometimes out with friends, mostly however on my own. It's been very difficult the last few months, extremely difficult at times, writing all this, all what happened, painfully going back to the conversations with friends and family, but mostly with Poppy. Just listening to her voice messages, a voice that I hadn't heard for over two and a half years, the voice of my beautiful Poppy. Extremely hard, sad and distressing at times, so I would just have a shower and go somewhere to grab a quick bite or a drink, depending on the mood. That doesn't give people much notice, does it? If I was really down I would take the car, so I knew I wouldn't drink too much as I had to drive back home. In any case, although I don't like being on my own, I don't mind being on my own either: in fact, nowadays I prefer to be on my own unless it is with people I really like. I was never the most social person to start with, now even less, and I can't stand all the bullshitting anymore: it just seems to me so artificial and hypocritical. It brings bad memories of my shitty life thirty odd years ago, a very empty and hedonistic life. Luckily I have many wonderful friends and many, many more people who I appreciate enormously and I very much enjoy their company. But people have their lives as well.

Furthermore, I've never been one of the 'lads', never fitted in that culture, not even when I was much younger. I have been going to restaurants and other places a lot on my own and sometimes there is a group of men, some younger than me, some my age, some even older than me: I hear their conversations about 'this girl in the office this, the other one in the gym that'. I hate it. I guess they're mostly divorced or separated, otherwise they would be with their wives or partners. I also come across groups of women, and after a couple of drinks their conversations get louder and acquired a different tone as well. I'm sure it's very funny and they're having a very good time, but they are not my type either. I finish my meal and go home, to an empty home, that's true, but that is what I have now. It won't be like this forever, I know, it's just a matter of time.

I think that perhaps I'm moving in the wrong circles and I should change that. I seem to attract business women/PA type, most divorced or separated, no offence to anyone. All lovely at the beginning but as soon as I see they are more interested in themselves, their make-up and selfies on their own, their expensive designer handbags and in going out for cocktails with her friends, also mostly divorced or separated, I lose interest very quickly: I thank them very much for the opportunity and their time, I wish them all the best and I'm gone. I don't judge nor criticize, but it doesn't work for me. Not all of them are like that of course and I've met some lovely ones.

However, what puzzles me the most is the other demographic, under thirties, under twenty-five in particular. I don't get it, I really, really don't understand: where are the guys their age that should be taking care of these ladies? And what do they see in me? The world is going mad! In any case, as lovely as they are, I have no interest whatsoever in engaging in a serious long-term relationship with someone 30-35 years younger than me. That I lost my confidence when Poppy went is undeniable and I haven't got it back, practically in the slightest. However, I certainly don't need to wear a beautiful young woman on my arm to prove something: I don't have anything to prove. What I had to prove that was really important to me and to people that truly mattered to me I already did it. Now I only have to prove things to myself, and if, or rather when, such time comes one day in the future, to my loved one.

****

Time to me is very precious. My dream would be to find someone and to spend at least 24 years with that person. I already had 23 wonderful years: I want to surpass that! Our human nature, never satisfied, always wanting more. Time, however, is not on my side, so I will settle for whatever I can get, provided it has a minimum standard. If you drive everyday a Ferrari for 23 years, it's difficult to suddenly get into a FIAT Panda!

Time equals interest equals feeling. When someone has time for you, it's because they are interested in you, and perhaps have some feelings for you. On the other hand, when someone doesn't have much time for you, coming up with different excuses all the time, but it seems to have time for everybody else and everything else, it's clearly saying they're not that interested in you. That is absolutely fine if you want that type of relationship: everybody is different and I've also had that many times in the past. That's ok. However, if you are used to something different, much better, and expect also something much better, then it probably is a good advice, as I always say, to jump off that train and get on another one.

Time never has a break, it never stops, and every second gone, every minute gone, every hour and day gone, you never get it back. That is also something that Poppy and I understood very well, that's why I guess it was so precious to us and we tried to spend so much time together when we could.

As time continued his never ending progression it was now July. H was not doing well at all, losing weight, now light as a feather, and more lethargic so I took him to the vet again. A few days went by, I couldn't get him to eat hardly anything: back to the vet and again she was wonderful. She weighed H: now 2.35 kg, he was a little sack of bones, so thin and fragile now and very dehydrated. The vet administered some fluids and an injection to stimulate his appetite and we went home hoping for the best: we had given him every possible chance to recover.

It was Friday and when we got back from the vet, I tried to get him to eat something again, but he didn't. He mostly was in his bed, hardly moving. That night was very long, I didn't go to bed, I just sat on the sofa looking at H on his favourite bed: he was tiny in that big cat bed now. Again, I missed my beautiful Poppy so much in these situations, so as always I talked to her. I said, "He is going, isn't he? Oh Poppy my love, I wish so much you were here! You always knew what to do."

It was now around 5:00 am, the darkness of the night gently pushed away by the first rays of the new day. I said to Poppy: "Oh Poppy, I feel so much frustration and anger inside and I would just want to hit something. Of course, I'm not doing it but is that feeling of impotence that I've had already so many times, there is nothing you can do and you see that life slowly going away in front of your eyes, like water in your hand when you make a fist, it slips through your fingers, despite your attempts to hold on to it, no matter how hard you try, desperately, hopelessly, that little life is taken away...."

I had made my decision: at 9:00 am I would call the vet and take H. Unfortunately, that day on Saturday morning there was nobody I knew at the practice. Neither the receptionist nor the vet, therefore I had to explain everything. Also, all the appointments were taken, but I couldn't wait until Monday. There was no way in the world I would keep H suffering like this the whole weekend. I would have taken him anywhere. However, they were very gracious and kindly gave me a time to be there and I would be seen at some point when they could. I really appreciated that.

You cannot imagine how hard it was to put H in the carrier that day. Poor H was none the wiser but I was taking my wonderful little cat to his death. It hurt like crazy, but I had to do it for him. I just missed Poppy so much that day...

When I got to the vet, I didn't actually have to wait too long. The receptionist was very kind and the vet I saw was fantastic. She went through all the notes, mainly the ones from the previous day, and examined H: she was gentle and compassionate, and we agreed that given the fact that H had not improved overnight and he was so poorly, the kind thing to do was to administer a lethal injection. She took her time and explained was she was going to do and how, and then took H to the back of the surgery to insert the cannula into the vein. When H was ready they took him to another room and she called me. The time had come…

She said that it would be very quick and totally painless: my beautiful little cat wouldn't feel anything. She asked me to hold him and gave me a couple of minutes to say goodbye. I held H's little and fragile body gently in my hands: he was tiny, now only 2.25 kg. I looked at him, I said sorry H, thank you for everything and gave him a kiss. It was time. I said to the vet I was ready and before I knew my wonderful little cat was gone, my last link to Poppy. And that's how it came to be that from the amazing life I had all those years back with Poppy and our cats, I was now on my own. They were all gone, my little family as it were, but at least my consolation was that the three of them would now be reunited and my beautiful Poppy would have again her two little cats, that she so much loved. Now I had to fulfil my promise and put the three of them together.

Again, like with S, it hurt so much, but I thanked God for giving me the strength to stop the suffering of our beautiful little cat. Again, H had done so much for Poppy for so many years and for me once Poppy was gone. I will be eternally grateful for what he gave us all those years and, like S, will always have a place of honour in my heart. No doubt about that.

340

Also, as with S, I have hundreds of anecdotes I could tell: he was a very serious cat, extremely independent and didn't give cuddles like S. But he was incredibly loyal, always by Poppy's side. He was the most patient cat when he wanted to catch a mouse and could sit motionless for ages. He oozed confidence and was the terror of the neighbourhood for years. He never started a fight but never backed down of one either, so we had visits to the vet every so often. For many years H ruled undefeated, until he got older, and much younger cats stole the crown. He also gave us many sleepless nights when he would disappear for hours at night and some people reported to have seen him by the canal or the railway tracks, quite a few blocks away. Also, apparently he was vicious with the nurses in the practice: it was hard to believe, the almost angelic nature with us, Jekyll and Hyde!

He would jump on the bed, come between us and always put his beautiful pinky nose in Poppy's face but the other end to my face. What a lovely 'gatito'! I would say to Poppy, "Can you please tell your cat off?" and she would say laughing, "No, no, it is your cat", to what I would reply, "No, no, no, no, no, Poppy my love, after midnight it is certainly YOUR cat", and we would keep going like this laughing. The truth is that we also loved H to bits and I think he had an extraordinary connexion with Poppy. Again, I was deeply sad to see him go, even more in the circumstances, as he was the last link and I had to put him down. At least, he was no longer suffering and would be reunited with Poppy, who loved him so much. Now the three of them were all together.

After the vet administered the injection, she left me there with H on my own. I was there for a while, and gosh, how I missed Poppy. But I talked to her and we thanked H together for being such a wonderful pet. He gave me almost

20 years of happiness. I left him there to be cremated, chose the little box and went home. From now on, every time I opened the door, there wouldn't be anyone to say hello, no Poppy, no S, no H. I lit a candle and again, together with Poppy, we did our prayers. Mostly, I thanked God very much he was still keeping me here so one day I can fulfil my promise.

****

There are lots of things I don't understand in life. That day, I was quite sad, I almost felt like the last Samurai or the last Mohican! I sat in the sofa, with my 'Perfect-ted' matcha based energy drink which I favoured of late, a pear-ginger flavour I seem to recall. I was just thinking 'You are all gone: grandparents, parents, you my love, and our two cats. That's it. All gone now'.

When Poppy was here she was my reason to live. When she left, I had the two cats to look after and now there were both gone. I would put them together with Poppy and then I would fulfil my promise. I said to Poppy: "Poppy, my love, I will take you where you have to be, in the waters of the Mediterranean, as you always loved it so much. I'll go to the beach where we would have been going for walks in our old age and I'll let you free forever, with your beloved cats. One day perhaps, when my time comes, and my ashes are also spread in the Mediterranean the currents will bring us together and we will be reunited again. Until then my love, roam free, independent, brave and strong as you always were, knowing that my love, the true love that I learnt from you, will accompany you to the confines of the sea." That I said to Poppy a long time ago I would do, now I just had to do it. I only need God to keep me here a bit longer and I pray that's the case.

I was sitting on the sofa on my own and suddenly I remembered a song from 'The Beauty and the Beast,' one of my favourite Disney films. Funnily enough I used to say to Poppy jokingly, that we were a bit like the Lady and the Tramp or the Beauty and the Beast. Mind you, I said that to all my girlfriends, as they were all very beautiful and I was the beastly and hairy one. The song that came to my mind is when Belle sings 'there must be more than this provincial life'. There I was that night, sitting on the sofa and thinking that there must be more in my life, something else, some purpose that I still haven't found. Was it the purpose of my life to look after Poppy, as my neighbour in France had said to me all those years back with her funny comment 'an angel put on earth to look after Poppy?' If so, what now, with Poppy gone?

As I said, I believe things happen for a reason but we may not always know. I have thought now for a long time that the reason for my mum to go was for me to meet Poppy. My beautiful Poppy changed my life beyond words and gave me so much love that could last me ten lifetimes! I believe now that the reason that Poppy left is so I can pass all the love she gave me onto someone else, someone that perhaps hasn't been that fortunate in her life. That's maybe the purpose I haven't found. If so, I hope to be able to do that before I go.

I thought I had perhaps found my purpose when I met that special person and I could help to better and enrich her life, but it was not to be. Since Poppy left she had been the only one that really had a very special place in my heart, and her family as well. I did many things that were enormously meaningful to me, always with Poppy's blessing. She was the one I invited many times to a restaurant and some days out, I spent Valentine's Day with and I bought perfumes and presents for her and her family at Christmas. The one I arranged something special and also bought presents for her birthday and name day. The one whom I bought flowers, cooked for and invited home. Most importantly, the one that being with I didn't think of Poppy, I felt special when I was with her, and had moments of internal happiness. That was almost unprecedented for me, as it had ever so rarely happened to me in the past apart from with Poppy. I even wrote poetry to her, only the third woman in my life, as my poetry comes deep from the heart and that person must be in my mind.

In fact, she was so special to me that my electric guitar went to her son. I bought that electric guitar just before my dad died, so it was very important and unique to me. It's difficult to explain but it is like my dad passed it to me, and I wanted to pass it to my son, which I never had. For 17 years I had it at home waiting for the special person I wanted it to go. I found that special person in her son: I took it to the shop, new strings, full service and it was like new. Now it was ready to go and I gave it to him last year, in September, after Poppy's second anniversary of her passing, when I spread her ashes and a rose in the sea and I said to Poppy that, with her blessing, I would try to start a new life. I thought that if everything was going well, I could perhaps in time have my new life with her and her family: I would have treated her sons like mine, like the ones I never had, and her family also like mine. I would have given her everything really. Sadly, it was not to be. No regrets though: I did my best but it wasn't enough.

We are all different, have our priorities and need to be realistic: we can choose who to be with, but we cannot choose who wants to be with us. For that person, I just didn't tick all the boxes, one could say probably I ticked very few boxes. I don't blame her though: I'm late fifties, not very attractive any more, going bald, with an expanding waste line, living in one-bedroom flat and driving a 15-year old car. On top of that, I have lost all my confidence, which I guess it showed and didn't help. No, I don't blame her, who would?

Furthermore, I could never give her the lifestyle she wanted. However, for the first time in my life I tried to stay on the train with the tracks going in separate directions: I had never done it before but I felt I owed her that much for what she had done for me. I thought it was worth it, so I stayed in the train for as long as I could. I don't regret it, I tried, it didn't work. Nobody's fault.

I also think when you reach certain age you have very clear in your mind what you want, what you would like and what you need. I could say: I want a car, I'd like a Bugatti, but do I need a Bugatti? Well, not really. I have an old Ford: it is a car, which is what I want, and it's reliable, cheap to run and takes me from A to B, which is what I need. It works for me. But perhaps most importantly, with age you definitely know what you don't want and what you don't need. I don't want a poor relationship and I don't need the headache, frustration, disappointment and unhappiness that it brings. That is very clear in my mind, but we are all different, it might not work for everyone.

However, the most important thing for me is that when you really care about someone, you don't want them to be unhappy with you. If you cannot make them happy, hopefully someone else will. I don't know why destiny kept crossing our paths before but it's been many months now and probably I'll never see her again. I'm sure she's forgotten me by now, but I will never forget her, because I never forget people that have been truly special in my life. Therefore, she and her family will always have a place of honour in my heart and they're in my prayers every day. I'm sure she's met someone else by now, that won't be difficult. I only hope the person she finds can give her what she wants and makes her happy, but mostly I wish her to find someone kind and that looks after her, helps her, supports her, respects her and loves her with real and true love. I know she hasn't been very lucky in that area, so I wish her all the best. It was a privilege to meet her in the journey of my life and I'll always be grateful to her for what she did for me. I loved her and her family much more she can ever imagine.

****

I remember what Phileas Fogg said, 'when you have found love, real love, life without it has no purpose'. How true that is, but you only know that when you have loved and been loved so much. I truly believe now that life without love has no purpose. I learnt love, true love from my beautiful Poppy and she enlarged my heart far beyond what I could ever imagine. I cannot believe how much love she gave me and I still have to give in my heart. That's what Poppy did for me. Poppy occupies a huge part of my heart, of course, and I have also my parents, grandparents, my cats, beloved uncles, all now gone. And all my loving family and friends and so many people who I appreciate enormously, they are all there in my heart. Yet, that seems to occupy very little and there still seems to be so much more for other people. I don't fully understand…

Indeed, life without real love has no purpose. I remember what Poppy said to me once: "At the end of the day to feel loved, cherished and wanted is life itself." How right she was: without true love there is no real life. But also a life without sharing is a life half lived. Since Poppy left I have been fortunate enough to be in a position to help some members of my family and friends when they've gone through some vicissitudes. I will continue trying to help people where I can and I hope one day to be able to share my life again with someone. It is something I really miss: the comfort, companionship, laughing at the silly jokes together, words, expressions, behaviours only known to the two of us. And travelling: I really miss having someone with me in the car and going places together. But mostly I miss going for a walk holding hands or with that person's arm around mine making me feel truly special. Nobody can ever substitute Poppy, but I have always said I don't want another Poppy, no matter how much I loved my beautiful Poppy, how extraordinary she was and how special she made me feel: I don't want another Poppy as that would be destined to failure.

However, I would be extremely sad if I was to abandon this life taking with me all that love. Poppy gave it to me and I couldn't repay her as she left us too soon. However, if that love can go to someone else, at least I'll feel it's not wasted. That would be a tragedy.

I remember what Poppy said to me that time and I will never forget: "there is someone out there waiting for you, someone who will make you happy and who you will make as happy as you've made me all these years. I know you will because I know you. One day you will find someone and live as we did. Someone will knock at your door, or perhaps, it will be you knocking on someone else's door, but I know you will find that person." How much that hurt at the time is beyond words, but I know she meant well and she was right. That's what Poppy said to me and I believe her.

Therefore, I'll continue the journey of my life until I find another special person and, hopefully, the next one will see past my age, my lack of attractiveness and my 15-year old car, and the lifestyle I can offer her will be enough. Perhaps this time that special person will see something a bit more than meets the eye. Then, if we share the same basic values and principles, we can have a solid foundation on which to start building a relationship with the pillars of communication, trust and intimacy, but mostly respect and love. Love is so important!

Furthermore, I vividly recall one morning when Poppy was already quite poorly and what she also said to me that I will never forget. She'd had all the treatments, and nothing had worked. They had tried everything possible: amputation, chemo, radio, immunotherapy, the intrusive and traumatic operation that had a devastating effect and the more aggressive chemo by then. Absolutely nothing had worked and there was nothing else they could do.

I was looking at Poppy, resting in bed half-up, dozing on and off, already looking so poorly. I was by her side, looking at her, in disbelief and started shedding a few tears. She turned her head towards me and looked at me with a smile. Although the cancer had taken all her beauty away, she still had the most beautiful blue eyes and the most divine smile. She looked at me in the eyes and said, "Don't cry, everything will be ok, you'll see." As soon as she said that, I burst into tears, crying desperately, disconsolately and said to her, "How can you say that Poppy, it's not gonna be all right, it's never gonna be all right: you're dying, you're actually dying, can't you see? What am I gonna do without you...," and looking at me with that peaceful, serene, beautiful smile she said, "Everything will be all right because I love you SOOO much!"

I sank in desperation, lying down next to her, and couldn't stop crying, neither could I say any words. There we remained lying down next to one another for a while, holding hands, savouring that precious time we still had left.

348

It wasn't much though: a few weeks after, the flame of my beautiful Poppy extinguished.

****

Our loved ones never leave us, my best friend reminds me of every so often, and I know very well that to be the case, through my own experience after losing all my loved ones. Someone once said, 'Gone from our sight but never our memories; Gone from our touch but never our hearts'. I couldn't agree more: my beautiful Poppy will always be in my memories and my heart. But also my parents, and grandparents, and anyone else that I have loved and have truly loved me: our loved ones will always be with us. Fortunately, I still have left many friends and family I really love.

However, I wonder sometimes how it can hurt so much, how you can miss someone so much, that nothing seems to be right or makes any sense any more. My friend told me that's what happens when you have lived half of your life so intensely, in all aspects, with one person. That is true I suppose and to be honest I wouldn't have it any other way. All the pain I went through, and I am now going through again writing all this, it was and it is worth it because of what I had. I was truly fortunate and privileged to have Poppy for 23 years in my life. My pain is the price of love.

I always had difficulty accepting the inevitable and I kept pushing Poppy. I kept saying to myself the statistics are only estimates. I know sometimes she kept going for me and I apologise to her. I was just so afraid of the outcome. Hope, sometimes, perhaps is not the best thing, I don't know, but I personally cannot live without it, so I keep pushing and fighting until the very end. In any case, I had almost started to believe Poppy was immortal, but she wasn't…

I would be writing and sometimes start laughing remembering a funny situation we encountered or start crying and it would become impossible to write. I knew Poppy was worried so I would say: "It's ok Poppy my love, don't worry about me, I know we're doing it together, it's fine. It's just a bit difficult at times, that's all, don't worry, I'm ok." When it was impossible to write, I would take a deep breath, close my eyes briefly and remind myself why I was doing this: in memory of Poppy and hopefully to help others. It would be Poppy's legacy and the proceedings would help other people: people in the hospice, people in the hospitals, other cancer patients, all thanks to Poppy. More selfishly perhaps, if one person read the story of Poppy, she would be remembered, she would not be forgotten. That's all I could do. So I would take a break and then say: "It's ok Poppy, just a bit hard, let's try again, let's try to do the best we can." That's what I did.

When Poppy passed away three years ago, I vowed God's willing to keep my promise to look after the cats the best I could and then put them all together once gone. Our furry little monsters are now gone and will accompany Poppy in her voyages in the Mediterranean. I said I would also do my best to honour her memory, and continue being the person she made me and not the person I was. I had endeavoured to do so every day and tried consciously to help people and not to hurt anyone. Finally, I said I would do everything I can so she leaves a legacy and will never be forgotten. This book, the story of Poppy, will hopefully accomplish that.

Those are the three things I had to do for Poppy. I have one more thing though to do for my dad and one for my mum which were not done at the time. Therefore, I ask God to give me a bit more time so I can fulfil all my promises. After, I will leave it in the hands of the Almighty. If then is my time to go, I'll be happy with what I had in my life, much more than I ever deserved. However, I won't be happy taking Poppy's love with me, and I hope I am given the opportunity so it can go to someone else.

The truth is that we never know what life has in store for us. My friends keep saying that good people like me we'll get the reward sooner or later, and something good we'll happen to me. Well, of course, they're my friends, what else would they say? What they mean by that is that one day I will meet someone, and I will have the opportunity to restart my life and be happy again. We're sure there are still a few little dinosaurs like me roaming around on planet Earth. Time will tell.

For the time being, what Poppy said to me that day, keeps me going. I know how much she loved me and I have no doubt she looks after me from wherever she is, together with my parents and loved ones. She will make sure that one day 'everything will be all right', I have not the slightest doubt about that, because of how much she loved me, one day. How, however, of course I don't know, neither when nor where for that matter, only the ones up there know. I, as a mere mortal, I haven't got the faintest idea, therefore I can only keep going through the journey of my life, day by day, one step at a time, a journey now sadly without my beautiful Poppy.

****

FINAL TWIST

All was ready for Poppy's journey to the Mediterranean to roam free forever with her beloved cats. I had their ashes in three little wooden caskets in a bag. Small suitcase ready with the few things I was taking. Car ready: washed outside, cleaned inside, levels and pressures checked, and brakes replaced. On the last MOT, the mechanic had advised me to replace them in a few thousand miles, and I was going to do a few thousand miles now, so I didn't want to take any risks.

Yes, I was ready to leave and take Poppy's ashes to the Mediterranean. However, something happened the night before. I was a bit restless. I couldn't sleep. I knew that something was going on, and I knew it had to do with Poppy. I was trying to think what it could be, but after a while she said it, I heard it inside me: "Please don't take me there, I don't want to go."

That took me a bit by surprise as I had said to Poppy that once the cats were gone, I would put them together and spread hers and the cats' ashes in the sea. Poppy loved the sea. I had spread a handful the year before in the place we last went to the sea, but the rest I thought would be spread in the Mediterranean. I didn't understand. I said, "But Poppy, my love, what's happening? That was our dream, so I thought that by taking you there, you could still do it." As always, with her patience and wonderful smile, my beautiful Poppy took the time to explain so I could understand: "Yes, my love, that was our dream, but it never materialised. It was wonderful being on holiday there and all the many places we went, but it was a dream you had of doing something with me that sadly you will never be able to do." I was starting to understand what Poppy was saying. My dream all those years back of growing old together and going for walks on the beach holding hands will never happen now. She continued, "I am also very tired, I have helped you a lot these three years, and I don't feel like making this long journey for nothing." That was true: Poppy had given me so much help, the days I didn't know how to get out of bed or why for that matter, let alone how I would reach the end of the day. With that special person, she had guided me to do my best for her, to be more patient, and to give her more time. I kept asking Poppy to help her and her family in the difficult times, and she did. Yes, Poppy was always there for me in the difficult and dark times these three years.

I didn't really know what to say, so I just said, "Ok, Poppy, my love, I don't mind. I'll put you together with the 'gatitos' and take you wherever you want to go. Just tell me where and I'll take you there." She said, "Take me home. I just want you to take me where we last were together by the sea, where it was real, and I want to be with my mum. I don't want to be in the Mediterranean on my own because you won't be there."

And so I did. As I didn't know where Poppy's mum was buried, I drove the three hours to Poppy's dad. I explained and asked them for their permission. I was delighted when they agreed and even accompanied me to the cemetery. There, we spread most of Poppy's ashes and the cats. Then, we went to the sea where we last were, late in the evening, the reflection of the rays of the sun, hues of orange coming through the grey clouds on the horizon under the blue skies. I lit a candle and did my prayers for Poppy to the roaring sound of the waves crushing into each other and foaming when breaking, then receding: it felt like they were calling Poppy to go with them to roam the seas free, strong and brave forever. It was truly magical. Again, Poppy took a red rose, so my love will always be with her wherever she goes.

Now my beautiful Poppy will roam free the seas with her cats and will also be with her mum forever. I have fulfilled my promise.

****

THE END

Writing this has been one of the most painful experiences in my life but also one of the most rewarding. The hours and hours timidly, and possibly not very successfully, trying to find the right words to articulate what happened and how it felt. The painful memories purposely resurfaced for this exercise, some still as raw as ever, thankfully mixed with the myriad of wonderful times spent together. Those amazing experiences that Poppy and I shared left an indelible print in my heart and mind. Wherever I go, they will accompany me for the rest of my life.

However, all of this would not have been possible without Poppy's help and support, as was always the case. Because we always did everything together, everything that was important or meaningful to us, that is, and this has been just one more of many, but our last one together. The many times that I was in tears and, frankly, it was too painful to continue, I would take a deep breath and think of my beautiful Poppy. She would then smile at me, like saying, "I understand it's painful, but you can do it. Remember, we're doing it together as we always did. I'm by your side. Most of all, remember why you're doing it."

People sometimes ask the typical question of how I knew she was the one. How does anyone ever know? The thing is that you just know because you feel it. You feel it inside yourself. You feel it in your heart. It's how you feel when you are with that person, or rather, how that person makes you feel, and even more, how you feel when that person is not with you. Like a part of you is missing. Some things in life cannot be explained with words. I think this is one of them and unless someone has experienced it, surely

I'm not alone, words cannot do justice. It just is, and to me, it is the most wonderful thing to have that feeling inside you.

If this ever benefits anyone, it will be Poppy's legacy, as it's been written in her memory. In that way, perhaps I will be able to atone, albeit minimally, for my shortcomings with Poppy. I truly loved her with all my heart, but I didn't say it as often as I should have. I should have treated her better and done more and earlier for her, but that cannot be changed now. I will never have now the opportunity to repay all the love, kindness, patience and support that she unconditionally gave to me over the years, and it's the price I will have to pay for the rest of my life.

Without ever preaching, Poppy was the greatest teacher. I have learnt my lesson, and if the stars line up and one day someone else appears in my life, as undeserving as I may be, I hope to be able to do better next time. I still have so much love to give thanks to Poppy! That way, out of the terrible tragedy of Poppy's passing, something positive may come out of it. And I know that is what Poppy would want.

The question is, how will I know? I will know because of how that person will make me feel. To anyone just experiencing even a fraction of it, I would say, don't think twice, embrace the opportunity, as it may turn out to be the best thing in your life, as it did happen to me. And do it today if you can, as we don't know what tomorrow will bring. Run to that special person, tell them how much you love them, and enjoy a wonderful life together. I, for one, know if I am ever given a chance again, I certainly will. It's wonderful. It's priceless. It's magic! That I learnt from my beautiful Poppy.

****

AUTHOR'S NOTE

Poppy was this extraordinary and amazing person: she was truly special and unique. However, her story, the story of Poppy, is sadly not unique. Poppy had her friends and family, but there are many people like Poppy with friends and family as well.

For this exercise, I felt that names were not important, the experience was. Anyone that has remotely gone through what Poppy went through will know what I'm talking about, but also their husbands, wives and partners, sons and daughters, mums and dads, dear friends, all with different names but all sadly sharing the same pain.

That is why I consciously chose not to use names, apart from our pets and a couple of short names, which are not how those people are called, and neither did I mention the specific type of cancer Poppy had. There will be many other 'Poppies', with different cancers and different names, and so will be the names of their friends and family.

They say together we will beat cancer: I truly hope one day we can eradicate this most horrible disease that, one way or another, affects us all. In the meantime, if this can help to provide cancer treatment and end-of-life care to at least one person, all the effort and pain will have been worth it. That will be Poppy's legacy, and on her behalf, I thank you from the bottom of my heart.

50% of all proceedings from the sales of this book will go to charity organisations and hospitals that were directly involved in the treatment of Poppy's cancer.

'TILL THE END OF TIME'

A Song For My Beautiful Poppy

The moment I saw you for the first time,
I fell in love with you so much that I wanted to cry.

Tears in my eyes, my heart running wild,
I never knew such happiness a man could have.

Seeing you so beautiful made me just realise,
What life is all about, to love you, till the end of time.

I hold your hands. I kiss your lips, the moonlight's so bright,
The stars are dancing in the sky till the end of time.

We get so close. It feels so good, makes me feel so alive,
I look at you, you look at me, and we know we're just one.

Seeing you so beautiful made me just realise,
What life is all about, to love you, till the end of time.

Seeing you so beautiful, loving you so much,
Life has a new meaning to me, till the end of time

****

Printed in Great Britain
by Amazon